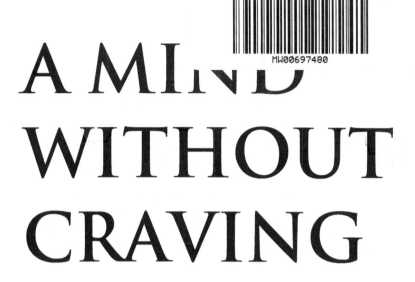

A MIND WITHOUT CRAVING

A ten-day program on developing the Noble Eightfold Path by Delson Armstrong

Suttaváda Foundation

Hilversum, the Netherlands

To request permissions, please contact the publisher at
info@suttavada.foundation

Library of Congress Control Number: 2021909666

ISBN: 978-0-9840497-4-5 (Hardcover) and
978-0-9840497-5-2 (Paperback)

First Edition, November 2021, Revised Sept 2022

Printed in the United States of America

Edited by Syl Zuhorn

Book Design by Clark Kenyon

Cover Art from Adobe Stock

Published by Suttavāda Foundation

www.suttavada.foundation

Table of Contents

Acknowledgments

This book would not be possible without the wisdom and practice that one has received through the efforts and introduction of the path by the Most Venerable Bhante Vimalaraṁsi. As a monk for many decades, his dedication to the teachings of the Buddha and goal to get to the heartwood of the practice have benefited numerous beings.

Bhante's insight has helped clarify many of the deepest elements of the Dhamma, including Dependent origination – a vast, profound, and complex subject that is the root of understanding how the practice works -, and how one uses the 6R process to continually gravitate toward total mental and emotional freedom, and the knowledge of that freedom.

Bhante's humor and candor, as well as his generosity and compassion have been a mainstay example of conduct, meditation, and insight. It was through his introduction of TWIM, Tranquil Wisdom Insight Meditation, and the repackaging of the process of Right Effort into the 6R's, that many have achieved various degrees of awakening to the true nature of reality. I am immensely grateful for his teachings and guidance.

My initiation into the TWIM practice was made possible by the patient and harmonious guidance of David Johnson, the author of **The Path to Nibbana**. David's wisdom, suggestions, encouragement, and lucidity during my online retreat in 2016 brought about profound transformation of one's mind, and revelational insights into the meaning behind many of the Buddha's teachings on the various meditative states of awareness, perception, relaxation and awakening.

The editorial development of the book as it has been presented to you is thanks to the tireless efforts of Syl Zuhorn. Her dedication to the Dhamma, meticulous attention to detail, diligent transcribing of the talks and Q&A sessions, as well as the careful organization of the content in this book, has brought to fruition one's effort to provide beings an opportunity to deepen their own practice and wisdom.

The online and physical retreats organized by the Suttavāda Foundation, with Koen Biggelaar at the helm, and with the immense support of Syl as well as Khin Maw during those retreats, have provided much of the backbone of content and for that I am ever grateful. Koen has also aided in the critique of the initial drafts of the book. My sincere thanks to Bhante Ananda, Venerable Obhasa, Wut Win, Mark and Antra Berger, Scott Jordan and Indu Shakya in participating in the first round of critiques and providing invaluable recommendations, which have helped this book evolve into what it is now. I also want to thank Els Ryokan Knappen for providing her careful attention to the text and proofreading it, so that it is presented to you in a clean and crisp manner, and also David Johnson for additional editing in this lightly revised edition. A deep bow of gratitude for the translations of the suttas featured in this book that have been provided by Bhikkhu Bodhi, Bhante Sujato, and Bhante Ananda.

Finally, I want to offer my heartfelt thanks for the vital contribution by the meditators who have progressed using the teachings and suggestions in this book. They have provided a wonderful dimension to the content, offering up to you readers a personal and relatable glimpse into the practice, levels of meditation, and attainments, with concrete and real-world descriptions of their own profound experiences.

Preface

The title of the book, as well as the retreat format it is based on, came from an email exchange between David Johnson and oneself. David is the author of **The Path to Nibbana** and the most senior student of the Most Venerable Bhante Vimalaraṁsi. We stay in contact as best as possible every now and then, since David is understandably quite a busy person, conducting various retreats, answering emails from students all around the world, teaching online and offline, and looking to the upkeep and welfare of the Dhammasukha Meditation Center in Annapolis, Missouri.

After my online retreat with David in 2016, and at his suggestion, I began to further deepen the practice and read the Suttas to gain greater clarity on many of the challenging concepts of the Dhamma. One realized that the heart of the Dhamma is always the Four Noble Truths. It is from the Four Noble Truths that everything else in the Suttas is discussed and elaborated.

Four years later, after the practice deepened and one's understanding began to bring to fruition a profound moment of clarity and insight, there were numerous communications with David which brought about a discussion on the mind of an Arahant – the one who has completed the practice of the Noble Eightfold Path and seen reality as it is without any distortions whatsoever.

In that exchange was a discussion of a special state of mind that the Arahant experiences and there were many references to the late Venerable Nanananda's books, in which he talked of the Arahant's mental state. As the email conversation progressed, David came to the conclusion, "So what we are talking about is the natural state of the Arahant. A mind with no craving." Hence, came the title in one's mind upon recollecting that conversation – A Mind Without Craving.

Months later, after spending time in self-retreat, one decided upon offering to those who wanted it, the opportunity to discuss and clarify various points on the Dhamma. From that came the inception of the idea to bring all of these concepts into a structured manner to be presented as material for daily reflections, used in online and physical retreats attended by advanced practitioners. One offered a series of Dhamma talks for those attending the online retreats and to that were also added question and answer sessions for each day of the initial online retreat. A compilation of transcriptions of those talks and sessions, as well as the reflections and descriptions of personal experiences by those practitioners resulted in the book as you see it now.

This book is intended to be a small contribution to the oceanic community of Dhamma practitioners and one's sincerest wish is that as many beings as possible benefit from its content.

-The Author

Introduction

Having evolved from the initial Daily Reflections booklet for online and physical retreat participants, with the aim to shed greater light on the importance of the Noble Eightfold Path, as well as deeper concepts such as Rebirth, Kamma (Karma), Consciousness, and Awakening, this book became a compendium of talks and sessions conducted by oneself in those retreats. With the added clarity of personal reflections and descriptions of various experiences by meditators attending these, it is the wish of all who contributed their stories that the content herein will be of value to the reader.

The structure of this book, therefore, is based on those retreats, meaning each section is centered around one particular day, making up in total nine days of discourses, reflections, question and answer sessions, and experiences. In that sense, for someone who wants to follow a self-guided retreat program, they can do so by going through each section dedicated for a particular day, as is laid out in the table of contents. It is then recommended that one on such a retreat, whether or not facilitated by the Suttavāda Foundation, should go through the entire book as intended with the purpose of getting acquainted with and deepening one's understanding of the ideas presented. Of course, the author's foremost recommendation would be to allocate more time for practice sessions than anything else. It is the meditation that brings about intense changes as one continues along the path, and so it can be expected that when one revisits the same material in this book one will have a different perspective, guided by, and based on the experiences of one's practice, on the topics discussed.

As a companion to one attending an online or physical retreat guided by a teacher, using the format of this book, the material will prove beneficial and supportive, not only for the practice, but as a way to bring up questions one may have that may not have been answered in here. With that in mind one is urged to reflect deeply while on such a retreat, on the topics discussed with the intention of clarifying doubts as well as cementing the deeper ideas of the Dhamma. It would be best if one were to investigate not for the sake of investigation alone but to confirm what is being read with what is being experienced in one's practice. Let the ideas discussed in this book be confirmatory steppingstones for the mind to understand through observation and practice. Again, practice is the bedrock of transformation. This book is like the finger pointing to the moon, not the moon itself. It is the description of the taste of sugar, not the sugar itself.

After retreat, whether guided or self-guided, it is recommended to revisit this book from time to time. Not necessarily in order, but as a reference guide that one can peruse whenever one wants and in any order that is deemed fit and relevant to one's journey to awakening. With that stated, remember - the Suttas will always be the authority for informing and guiding one's practice, as well as confirming where one is on the practice. Ultimately, at a certain point, intuition and the mind, and how they respond to the world and situations, will be the best tools to verify where one actually is on the path to Enlightenment.

Day 0:
Introduction and Instructions

The Teacher

Dhamma greetings.

Welcome to the 10-day guided or self-directed retreat program.

My name is Delson Armstrong, and I am very happy that you decided to embark on this journey of understanding and utilizing the eightfold path. This program is primarily centered around the fourth noble truth of the Buddha's rediscovery of the dhamma, as it is understood.

My meditation experience began when I was 13 years old, where I was introduced to *hatha yoga* by a family friend. My very first time into the spiritual practices began with understanding the *asanas* [steady and comfortable body postures, used in yoga], and practicing them. That deepened my desire to learn more about meditation and concentration exercises.

When I was 16 years old, I had a chance to go to the Himalayas, where I learned from a lot of different masters about different philosophies, including Vedanta, Samkhya and deeper yoga philosophies that are rooted in the *Yoga Sūtra of Patañjali.*

In that process of studying and practicing these different meditation techniques, I got acquainted with other techniques within yoga, known as *Kriya yoga.* And their version of insight practices, in terms of understanding the mechanics of cognition from their philosophies, related to the connection with the *divine spark* as they would call it. The brahman, the cosmic entity, joining and immersing with that divine spark, which is considered to be the soul.

However, as I started to experience the different states of meditation on higher practices, I noticed that there was not as much of a personality shift as I would have wanted, or as I would have expected. Having said that, I definitely acknowledge the benefits of having understood and seen through these various philosophies. It helped me to understand where I should be focusing on, putting my mind toward, and where I should not be.

3

Then, a few years ago, I was introduced to what is known as the TWIM practice, when I was watching a video by Bhante Vimalaraṁsi. I signed up for an online retreat with his center – Dhamma Sukha Meditation Center. My teacher David Johnson at the time, was the one who guided me through that online retreat practice for the ten days. And I am most grateful and appreciate everything that David Johnson has done for me, in clarifying a lot of points when I began my practice.

Since then, I have done a lot of self-retreats, and a lot of self-studies of the suttas, understanding them better through the clarity of my own experiences in the practice. Since the beginning of 2020, I have decided to start teaching and guiding more people. Whether it is over the phone, Skype calls, Zoom calls, weekly Dhamma talks, or guided 10-day online retreat programs like this one.

I had begun my teaching experience as an online guide with Dhammasukha, and I continue to do that when I have the time.

The Program

Throughout the next ten days, you will understand one or more of the components of each of the factors of the eightfold path. You will learn how to practically apply them in your daily life, as well as in your meditation practice.

This program can be adapted according to your needs. This is an online program, since you do not have the ability to really stay within the confines of a monastery or a secluded area, where you could fully absorb your mind into the studies and understanding of the dhamma.

I would encourage you to spend at least one to two hours for meditation. You can begin with thirty minutes, if you are completely new to the practice. As the days go on, you will see that your effort is simple, easy, and comfortable in the meditation practice. This practice encompasses sitting, walking, and maintaining the foundations of mindfulness in whatever other activities you do. These are so beautiful, so easy to manage, that they become quite pleasant. Indeed, the desire to sit longer naturally flowers into your being.

This program consists of watching the pre-recorded dhamma talks for each day, as well as reading the material that is in the reference page on the website. Along with that are question & answer videos that you can access whenever you would like.

Take this program according to your own pace. Meditate as long as comfortably possible. If you feel there is a lot of information, I will always encourage you to make more effort toward your *practice*, rather than the study of this program.

Once you start to practice, the experience of the practice will inform you. It will verify many things that will be discussed throughout the days of this 10-day program.

As your practice deepens, you will start to recognize many of the different concepts, ideas and tools that are being discussed.

Of course, things are starting to get busier, as more and more people sign up for the online retreat programs. So, there are now two options, where people can do a self-directed program, at any point of time that they wish to do so. And there are also guided meditation retreat programs, in which they do one-on-one interviews with me for about ten to fifteen minutes each day, along with some sort of a question & answer session. This is either every day, or once in between the retreat, and once at the end of the retreat.

There are various versions of the program, but the backbone is the collection of pre-recorded dhamma talks, and the pre-recorded questions and answers that are available on the Suttavāda Foundation YouTube channel.

You will find that there are a lot of terms in this booklet that are different interpretations from my experience of the eightfold path, in relation to translation choices. However, after some reflection I decided to let go of my original desire to change the wording of the eightfold path to something other than "Right" this or that.

- Right View
- Right Intention
- Right Speech
- Right Action
- Right Livelihood
- Right Effort
- Right Mindfulness
- Right Collectedness

Then there are two factors that are the final **fruition** of the path:

- Right Knowledge
- Right Liberation

After more research, I found that the word Right is not entirely as black and white as I thought. It has survived at least the last hundred years of discussion since the English translations were done by Rhys Davids, founder of the Pāli text Society of London, in the late 1800s.

Right is not necessarily Right vs. Wrong, which could be this view or that view – but it is defined as what works and is correct. But it has an even deeper meaning. When you look up Right in the dictionary, you see that it is defined in the first selection as "1. Conforming with or conformable to justice, law, or **morality.**" So, we have what is right in terms of morality and what is righteous here. So, not only correct, but what is *wholesome*. The eightfold path is that path that leads to the wholesome. Additionally, the origin of the word "right" is from the Sanskrit word "*rta,*" which means wholesome!

Thus, I will leave this as it is.

The Practice

I would like to divide the meditation instructions into two components.

There is the component of the brahmavihāras, and there is the component of right effort.

Let me get into what the brahmavihāras are and why, for this meditation retreat, the choice has been made to use them as the object of meditation, the vehicle of your awareness or attention upon which it rests.

There are different meditation objects that the Buddha has clarified in the suttas. A few of them are:

- The Ānāpānasati meditation: using the breath as a reminder to stay with your awareness of the present.
- The meditation object of understanding the impermanence of this body; by seeing each component of the body, also known as the *asubha* meditation. Here, you see the extent of the impermanent aspects of the body.
- The understanding of the impermanence of this body as a corpse.

Depending on the inclination and mindsets of an individual, the Buddha suggested different practices and techniques. He was the first and foremost expert within the dhamma, able to understand what techniques were most useful for a person, depending upon their evolution in the dhamma.

The whole purpose of this practice is to understand the mindfulness aspect, which is rooted in right mindfulness. This naturally progresses into right collectedness, which is the mind being in the jhānas. The mind bathed in the light and power of the jhānas.

The first jhāna, for example, begins with what is known as thinking and examining thought, and imagination. This particular meditation object is the first brahmavihārā, which is loving-kindness or *mettā*. It is a friendly attitude, an attitude of benevolence. An attitude of happiness and joy is most conducive to bringing up the first jhāna. Here, the jhāna factors present are:

- thinking and examining thought, and imagination
- joy and bliss, which is called *pīti*
- comfortable happiness, comfort, and ease, which is called *sukha*

When you start to practice in this way with loving-kindness, it is quite natural for the mind to incline toward joy and ease.

What's important to understand is that jhāna is one thing and the brahmavihāra is another – that is, we are not looking to make the factors of the jhānas our object of meditation. They arise naturally as a result of a collected mind, one that is observing and unified around loving-kindness, or the other brahmavihāras. So, if you notice the mind starts to become attentive to a factor of a jhāna, then treat it as a distraction and return to your object of meditation – the brahmavihāra – using the following instructions.

The Instructions

How do you begin the practice?

First, you take a comfortable sitting position. That could be cross-legged, in a chair, on a mat, or whatever you find is most comfortable.

Keep your back relatively straight, but you do not need to stiffen it. You need to be in a sitting position that provides natural comfort to your body. This translates to natural comfort and ease of the mind, so take whatever position you are most comfortable with. Make sure that your head does not droop down, or you bend down or forward. Try to keep your back relatively straight.

Secondly, when you close your eyes, put a little smile on your face. It does not have to be a Joker smile, or a very wide smile. Just a very subtle smile, like you would see in the iconography and statues of the Buddha. Indeed, in the suttas you will read that the Buddha, the arahants, and all the monastics on the path, were quite happy. They always dwelled in pleasant abidings of mind. And though they may not have been smiling *all* the time, they were naturally in a happy state of mind, free of suffering and mental discomfort. So, the smile is very important, as you will see as I continue with the instructions.

So, you close your eyes, put a little Buddha smile on your face and you can maintain a smile in your heart, your mind, and in your eyes.

If you wish, you can take in a deep breath and deeply exhale and feel the tension dissipating. Melting away from your body, as your mind and your body naturally incline toward comfort and ease.

Once you see this, allow the thoughts to be there, whatever they may be. But do not let your attention drift to one thought or another. Just let them pass on like clouds in the sky, or like watching traffic, like cars, going by on the road.

Maintain your awareness of the body, maintain awareness of the sensory experiences, which are coming in through the ears, through the nose if certain fragrances and odors come, or on your skin if you are outside and there is a light breeze.

What you are doing is slowly, gradually, coming to the four foundations of mindfulness and you get rooted in the body, in the mind, in the sensory feelings, and in the mental contents of the mind, without any sort of involvement.

Come up with an image, feelings of gratitude, or a wholesome memory that makes you most happy. It could be:

- The image of an infant, of a puppy or kittens, or any sort of baby animal
- seeing the things that you are grateful for in this life
- The recollection of the Buddha, the recollection of the Dhamma, and the recollection of the Sangha. In other words, the recollection of the Triple Gem, the three Jewels
- a happy memory that you might have from your childhood. This is what the Buddha started with, when he mentions that he went back in his mind and remembered a time when he was sitting under the rose apple tree. There was quite naturally a pleasantness in his feeling, which was not born from, or originated from the five physical senses, but it was a mental clarity, a mental happiness and joy.

Along with that image, memory, recollection, or feeling of gratitude, mentally verbalize a wish to ignite that feeling of joy. Whatever works for you: "*May I be happy; may I be at ease; may I be comfortable; may I be free of suffering.*" This is loving-kindness; friendliness and benevolence to yourself. The combination of the smile and that feeling of gratitude, wholesome image, or memory, along with the mental verbalization and wish for yourself, will surely ignite this feeling of loving-kindness.

You effectively use thinking and examining thought – v*itakka* and *vicāra* - and imagination, which is within that.

This is the beginning of the first jhāna and quite naturally, as you begin this way, your mind will incline toward paying attention to the feeling of loving-kindness.

Once you start to feel that little inkling of joy, that little feeling of loving-kindness, of friendliness toward yourself, rest your awareness on that. Let go of the mental images, let go of the wholesome memories, let go of the feelings of gratitude, and let go of the verbalization. Allow your mind to stay in the awareness of the feeling of loving-kindness and joy, which has been naturally ignited because of those things. You do this because, as your mind naturally progresses to higher peaks of joy, bliss and comfort and ease, the mind will let go of the thinking and examining thought, through your intention, along with the imagination, which are the verbalizations you started with, the wholesome images, memories, or the feelings of gratitude. This naturally progresses into the second jhāna, in which there is this comfort, ease, joy and bliss.

As you maintain your awareness, you will find quite naturally that the mind becomes distracted. This is because of certain hindrances - five in particular -, which we will discuss later. Just understand the mechanics of what must be done to understand and let go of these hindrances. This is the second component of the practice. You essentially use the four right efforts.

The Spiritual Friend

Now, you have been with your feeling of loving-kindness toward yourself, resting the awareness in this loving-kindness. Perhaps, when you are content with that, you naturally incline it toward a spiritual friend. This spiritual friend is someone you respect and admire. Somebody who naturally brings a smile to your face when you think about them. Somebody who is alive and preferably of the same gender. You then allow the flow of this feeling to go out to your spiritual friend. If you are visually oriented, you can imagine that feeling flowing out from your heart and connecting with the heart of your spiritual friend. It can also help, if it feels like there is too much tension, too much activity to imagine and visualize these things, to have the *intention* that you are sending it out. Let your mind rest in the awareness and the feeling flowing out. Thirdly, you could also just feel like the friend is in your spiritual heart, and you are sending it out. Bathing them in your loving-kindness and they are basking in your feelings of good wishes and feelings of benevolence toward them.

Distractions

As you are doing this, the mind will naturally become distracted as you start your practice. But it is important to understand that the hindrances and distractions should be welcomed, to the extent that you know where your attachments lie. The hindrances are your teachers; they provide you with an understanding of where the mind is inclined toward, in terms of attachments. Whether it is sensual craving; ill will; restlessness; doubt; or sloth & torpor. Do not worry about what sort of hindrance it might be. This is not a meditation in which you are noting what sort of hindrances are rising. You know when a hindrance or a distraction has arisen if your attention is no longer on the feeling of loving-kindness.

You may experience certain thoughts in the *background* of your mind. But so long as your awareness resides with loving-kindness, those thoughts behind will dissipate on their own. Without any of the fuel of your attention, providing them nutriment to grow, and then distracting you.

The four Right Efforts and the 6R's

If the mind has already become distracted and your attention is no longer on the feeling of loving-kindness, what you will do next is within the context of right effort. I will go over it very briefly. This is where we use the *6R* process. The 6R's are a simplistic understanding of the four right efforts. The 6Rs is a way for the mind to easily understand and practically apply them so that you can return to your meditation and continue to stay in the jhānas.

The first right effort is to **recognize** any unwholesome states - the hindrances - arising.

13

The second right effort is to **abandon** the already arisen unwholesome states of mind.

The third right effort is to **bring up** a wholesome state once you have abandoned the unwholesome state.

And the fourth right effort is to **maintain** that wholesome state. That wholesome state, in the context of this meditation, is one of the brahmavihārās. At the start, this would be loving-kindness.

When you get distracted, how do you come back to your object of meditation - the brahmavihārās? You notice that the mind is no longer aware of the feeling of loving-kindness, it has drifted away. Whether that takes you a few moments or a few minutes to realize, does not matter. What is important is you *have* realized it, you have **Recognized**, which is the first R. You recognized that you became distracted, that the mind is no longer aware of its object of meditation. This is the first right effort – becoming aware of the arising of the distraction.

The second R is where you **Release** your attention to those distractions. This is where you put your attention back on the mind and the body. In releasing, you have effectively stopped the flow of those distractions from further moving forward.

Next, you **Relax** the mind and the body. When you relax, you are effectively tranquilizing the formations. Tranquilizing the tension that may have arisen in the mind and body. Even if you do not feel tension in the mind and body, there is a very subtle sense of that in the way of craving and of being distracted. To let go of that craving and let go of the tension from that distraction, you effectively relax the mind and the body.

When you have released your attention from the distraction and come back to the awareness of mind and body, and then relax it, you are releasing your tension and relaxing. These two are interwoven in the second right effort, which is to abandon unwholesome states that have arisen. When you take your attention away, you are abandoning that distraction. When you relax the tension, you are abandoning the craving that might have arisen from that.

Which is understood on a physical level as tension in the brain; tension in the body; tension in the mind. Releasing and Relaxing are the second right effort.

Once you have relaxed, you **Re-smile**, which means you come back to the awareness of the smile. And you allow that smile to be an anchor point for you to come back to the feeling in your heart, the feeling of loving-kindness, which is then generated as you smile. Allow the smile to be a memory point if you will, which lets you know that you can come back to the feeling. And quite effectively, you will have again started the awareness of the feeling.

When you re-smile and **Return** to the feeling, you are effectively doing the third right effort, which is to bring up a wholesome state of mind. In the context of this meditation practice this is loving-kindness - the first of the brahmavihāras.

Finally, the fourth right effort is to maintain that wholesome state, so when you return and continue to stay with the awareness of the loving-kindness, you are effectively practicing the fourth right effort.

And then you **Repeat** whenever necessary. That is to say; you repeat whenever the mind is distracted again, and you continue doing that.

It might be that the distraction is particularly strong in the sense that, after you have let it go, it comes back again. But because you use the four right efforts, through this process of the 6R's, you weaken that distraction or that hindrances' hold on the mind. As you continue to let go of it through the 6R process, it becomes weaker and weaker and weaker, until it finally disappears.

The whole purpose of doing this is to recondition the mind from the unwholesome to the wholesome. We will talk about that more throughout the series of this program.

So, that is basically the technique; understanding the brahmavihāras, and understanding the four right efforts to continue to maintain an easy, comfortable awareness, without *suppressing* the hindrances.

You see, the moment you suppress the hindrances, it will cause those hindrances to arise with full force when you stop the meditation. You are not actually dealing with them and letting them go, but just for those few minutes, or maybe an hour or more of that meditation practice, you are not allowing them to arise. However, they will arise unless you effectively and intentionally let them go.

So, this is the reason why you do the right efforts. It is not to suppress, but to acknowledge, understand and let go, and to transform the mind by reconditioning it in this manner.

I wish you a wonderful retreat, and I look forward to seeing you all, whenever we have our question & answer sessions, or our individual interview appointments.

May you all be happy and may you all share in the wealth of the dhamma and attain nibbāna.

Daily Reflection Day 0

A Note on Translation

GENERALLY, THE EIGHTFOLD PATH is translated in English as:

Right View (*Samma Diṭṭhi*)

Right Intention (*Samma Saṅkappa*)

Right Speech (*Samma Vācā*)

Right Action (*Samma Kammanta*)

Right Livelihood (*Samma Ajiva*)

Right Effort (*Samma Vāyāma*)

Right Mindfulness (*Samma Sati*)

Right Concentration (*Samma Samadhi*)

We will keep this original wording and meanings as explained previously.

Āsavas

The **āsavas**, which are translated as the defilements or taints, which include sensual craving; being or craving for existence/non-existence; and ignorance, have been translated to **projections**. Generally, *āsavas* can mean inflows/outflows of the mind, or fermentations. This can be seen as the result of a mind that "leaks" and is not collected.

Therefore, it seems the word **"projections"** as mental "leaks" or outflows that arise and push forward the factors for conditioned existence, due to non-mindfulness, would be a good fit for the purposes of this material.

The Seven Awakening Factors

In the case of the awakening factors, there are certain word selections made –

Mindfulness becomes **Observation**

Investigation remains **Investigation**

Energy becomes **Application**

Rapture becomes **Joy**

Tranquility becomes **Relaxation**

Collectedness remains **Collectedness**

Equanimity remains **Equanimity**

The Four Foundations of Mindfulness (or Observation of the Four Aspects of Conditioned Existence)

Body remains **Body**

Feeling remains **Feeling**

Mind becomes **Mindset & Moods**

Dhamma becomes **Phenomena**

The Four Bases for Psychic Development

Chanda (wholesome desire) becomes **Cultivated Intention**

Energy becomes **Application**

Mind (or Consciousness) becomes **Mindset**

Analysis becomes **Reflection**

Five Faculties and Energies

Faith becomes **Conviction**

Energy becomes **Application**

Mindfulness becomes **Observation**

Concentration becomes **Collectedness**

Wisdom becomes **Intelligence**

Other Word Choices

Samatha is now **Restfulness**

The Three Marks (or Characteristics) of Existence becomes **The Three Symptoms of Reality**

A few abbreviations that are used:

DO is short for Dependent Origination

NPNNP is short for the eighth jhāna of Neither-perception-nor-non-perception

Retreat Outline

This retreat is centered on the 6R's, using the brahmavihārās as your object of meditation, with a sutta-based reflection on the fundamentals of the dhamma that guide you to nibbāna, namely –

- The Four Foundations of Mindfulness (or Observation of the Four Aspects of Conditioned Existence)
- The Five Aggregates
- The Three Characteristics
- The Four Noble Truths
- The Seven Factors of Awakening
- The Eightfold Path of the Noble Ones
- The Twelve Links of Dependent origination
- Kamma, Consciousness, and Rebirth

The suttas and themes that will be explored for each dhamma talk are as follows:

Day 1 – Right Intention (Samma Saṅkappa) and Right Effort (Samma Vāyāma)

Right intention is the choice to be in a wholesome state, while Right effort is the process in which mind roots out unwholesome states, brings to fruition wholesome states, and maintains them. This will be shown through the process of what is known as the 6R's, while using the brahmavihārās as the object of the meditation.

Sutta References:

> *And what, bhikkhus, is right intention? Choosing renunciation, choosing non-ill will, choosing harmlessness: this is called right intention.*
> > SN 45.8 – Vibhanga Sutta (section on right intention)

> *The Ganges River slants, slopes, and inclines to the east.*

> *In the same way, a bhikkhu who develops and cultivates the four right efforts slants, slopes, and inclines to nibbāna.*
> > SN 49.1-12 – Pācīnādi Sutta (four right efforts)

Objective: Understand what right intention means in relation to making an intention for this retreat, and learn how to apply the four right efforts to keep your observation unified with the object of meditation.

Day 2 – Right Mindfulness (Samma Sati)

Right Mindfulness is seeing how mind's attention moves when observing the four aspects of conditioned existence, namely the body, feeling, mindset, and the phenomena, to liberate the mind. This, as you will see, is done through proper attention, with an emphasis on replacing the five hindrances with the seven factors of awakening. You will also see how applying the 6R process is also utilizing the seven factors of awakening.

Sutta References:

It is when a bhikkhu meditates by observing an aspect of the body—keen, aware, and mindful, rid of desire and aversion for the world.

They meditate observing an aspect of feeling—keen, aware, and attentive, rid of desire and aversion for the world.

They meditate observing an aspect of mindset —keen, aware, and attentive, rid of desire and aversion for the world.

They meditate observing an aspect of phenomena —keen, aware, and attentive, rid of desire and aversion for the world.
> MN 10 – The Satipaṭṭhāna Sutta (right observation of the four aspects of conditioned existence)

Bhikkhus, when you attend improperly, sensual desire, ill will, dullness and drowsiness, restlessness and remorse, and doubt arise, and once arisen they increase and grow.

Bhikkhus, when you attend properly, the awakening factors of mindfulness, investigation of principles, energy, joy, tranquility, collectedness, and equanimity arise, and once they've arisen, they're fully developed.
> SN 46.35 - Yonisomanasikāra Sutta (how proper attention brings about the awakening factors and destroys the hindrances)

On an occasion, bhikkhus, when the mind becomes sluggish, it is timely to develop the enlightenment factor of investigation, the enlightenment factor of energy, and the enlightenment factor of joy.

On an occasion, bhikkhus, when the mind becomes excited, it is timely to develop the enlightenment factor of tranquility, the enlightenment factor of collectedness, and the enlightenment factor of equanimity.
> SN 46.53 – Aggi Sutta (balancing mind with the seven factors)

Objective: Understand how to pay attention in an effective manner to know reality as it is and as it unfolds, while developing the seven factors of awakening.

23

Day 3 – Right Collectedness (Samma Samadhi)

Right collectedness is the maintaining of your attention on an object of meditation. In right collectedness, you utilize right mindfulness and right effort to continue staying with that object.

Sutta References:

> *And he meditated without attraction or repulsion for those phenomena; independent, untied, liberated, detached, his mind free of limits.*
> MN 111 – Anupada Sutta (levels of mental collectedness)

> *Bhikkhus, the liberation of mind by lovingkindness has the beautiful (the fourth jhāna) as its culmination*

> *Bhikkhus, the liberation of mind by compassion has the base of the infinity of space as its culmination*

> *Bhikkhus, the liberation of mind by altruistic joy has the base of the infinity of consciousness as its culmination*

> *Bhikkhus, the liberation of mind by equanimity has the base of nothingness as its culmination*
> SN 46.54 – Mettāsahagata Sutta
> (brahmavihāras and the four spheres)

Objective: See and understand that effectively observing your object of meditation and keeping that observation collected, leads the mind to release.

Day 4 – Right View (Samma Diṭṭhi)

Right View is the complete and thorough knowledge of the four noble truths – that is:

There is suffering in life (not: life is suffering)
The cause of suffering – The projections of craving, being and ignorance
The cessation of suffering – The destruction of the projections

The path leading to cessation – The eightfold path of the noble ones

With correct understanding and experience of this wisdom, you have rooted out the causes and conditions for rebirth and attain the unshakeable release of mind.

Sutta References:

> *When, friends, a noble disciple understands suffering, the origin of suffering, the cessation of suffering, and the way leading to the cessation of suffering, in that way he is one of Right View…and has arrived at this true Dhamma.*
>
> MN 9 – Sammādiṭṭhi (Right View)

Objective: Understand what right view is in regard to the four noble truths, the experiential insight of which takes you off the wheel of saṃsāra.

Day 5 – The Five aggregates

The projections are what cause rebirth over and over, but when you see the five aggregates with wisdom, destroy the craving attached to them, and then non-identify with them, destroying the fetters of conceit and ignorance as well, you thus invariably destroy the projections. This leads to Right Knowledge (*sammā nana*) and Right Liberation (*sammā vimmuti*).

Sutta References:

> *Seeing this, a learned noble disciple grows disillusioned with form, feeling, perception, formations, and consciousness.*
>
> *Being disillusioned, desire fades away. When desire fades away they're freed. When they're freed, they know they're freed.*
>
> *They understand: 'Rebirth is ended, the spiritual journey has been completed, what had to be done has been done, there is no return to any state of existence.'*
>
> MN 109 – Mahāpuṇṇamasutta (discussion of the five aggregates)

Objective: Understand that the five aggregates are to be penetrated with insight to destroy the projections of craving, being, and ignorance.

Day 6 – Consciousness and Rebirth

Consciousness is purely cognition, and only measured by the six sense receptors through the faculties for mentality-materiality. However, when this cognition becomes fueled by intention that you take personal, rebirth occurs. This process can be stopped with correct understanding in meditation and daily life.

Sutta References:

> *They don't approve, welcome, or keep clinging to that equanimity (or compassion, joy, or tranquility). So, their consciousness doesn't rely on that and grasp it. A bhikkhu free of grasping becomes extinguished.*
> MN 106 – Āneñjasappāya Sutta (detaching consciousness)

> *But bhikkhus, when one does not intend, and one does not plan, and one does not have a tendency toward anything, no basis exists for the maintenance of consciousness. When there is no basis, there is no support for the establishing of consciousness. When consciousness is unestablished and does not come to growth, there is no descent of name-and-form.*
> SN 12.39 – Dutiyacetanasutta (intention and rebirth)

> *"So, Ānanda, deeds are the field, consciousness is the seed, and craving is the moisture. The **consciousness** of sentient beings—hindered by ignorance and fettered by craving—is established in a higher (or lower, middle) realm. That's how there is rebirth into a new state of existence in the future.*

> *"So, Ānanda, deeds are the field, consciousness is the seed, and craving is the moisture. The **intention and aim** of sentient beings— hindered by ignorance and fettered by craving—is established in a higher (or lower, middle) realm. That's how there is rebirth into a new state of existence in the future.*
> AN 3.76 and AN 3.77 – Pathambhava Sutta and Dutiyabhava Sutta
> (fuel for existence)

Objective: Understand the mechanics of consciousness and intention to apply in the meditation and daily life, to stop the process of rebirth.

Day 7 – Kamma and Cessation

Kamma is not just the inherited effects of our actions but also the present actions we commit. The key is to understand the process in such a way that you only experience inherited effects, without producing new causes to experience in another rebirth.

Sutta References:

> *And what is the cessation of kamma? From the cessation of contact is the cessation of kamma; and just this eightfold path of the noble ones—right view, right intention, right speech, right action, right livelihood, right effort, right mindfulness, and right collectedness—is the path of practice leading to the cessation of kamma.*
>
> AN 6.63 – Nibbhedika Sutta (penetrating the four noble truths)

> *And what, bhikkhus, is old kamma? The eye is old kamma, to be seen as generated and fashioned by volition, as something to be felt. The ear is old kamma, to be seen as generated and fashioned by volition, as something to be felt. The nose is old kamma, to be seen as generated and fashioned by volition, as something to be felt. The tongue is old kamma, to be seen as generated and fashioned by volition, as something to be felt. The body is old kamma, to be seen as generated and fashioned by volition, as something to be felt. The mind is old kamma, to be seen as generated and fashioned by volition, as something to be felt. This is called old kamma.*

> *And what, bhikkhus is new kamma? Whatever action one does now by body, speech, or mind. This is called new kamma.*

> *And what, bhikkhus, is the cessation of kamma? When one reaches liberation through the cessation of bodily action, verbal action, and mental action, this is called the cessation of kamma.*

> *And what, bhikkhus, is the way leading to the cessation of kamma? It is this eightfold path of the noble ones— right view, right intention, right speech, right action, right livelihood, right effort, right mindfulness, and right collectedness.*
>
> SN 35.146 – Kammanirodha Sutta (cessation of Kamma)

Then a bhikkhu accomplished in collectedness realizes the undefiled freedom of heart and freedom by wisdom in this very life. And they live having realized it with their own insight due to the ending of defilements.

They don't perform any new actions, and old actions are eliminated by experiencing their results little by little.

This wearing away is visible in this very life, immediately effective, inviting inspection, relevant, so that sensible people can know it for themselves.

AN 3.74 – Nigantha Sutta (cessation of kamma)

"But sir, when a bhikkhu has emerged from the attainment of the cessation of perception and feeling, how many kinds of contact do they experience?"

"They experience three kinds of contact: emptiness, signless, and undirected contacts."

SN 41.6 – Kamabhu Sutta (formations and cessation)

Objective: Understand that kamma is not deterministic and that choices in the present moment are given to us by the effects of our past choices, and that the choices we make now - which are fettered by craving, conceit, and ignorance -, lead to choices in the future that will continue to lead to suffering. Ultimately, you see how this process applies to cessation and contact with the nibbāna element during each of the Path and Fruition levels.

Day 8 – Eightfold Path of the Noble Ones

The eightfold path is the way leading to release. It leads to the cessation of kamma, to the cessation of craving, and the cessation of suffering. There is the eightfold path you practice, and then there is the elevated path which is perfected and the automatic functioning of an arahant.

Sutta References:

"And what things should be fully understood by direct knowledge? The answer to that is: the five aggregates affected by clinging, that is, the

material form aggregate affected by clinging, the feeling aggregate affected by clinging, the perception aggregate affected by clinging, the formations aggregate affected by clinging, the consciousness aggregate affected by clinging. These are the things that should be fully understood by direct knowledge.

"And what things should be abandoned by direct knowledge? Ignorance and craving for being. These are the things that should be abandoned by direct knowledge.

"And what things should be developed by direct knowledge? Serenity and insight. These are the things that should be developed by direct knowledge.

"And what things should be realized by direct knowledge? True knowledge and deliverance. These are the things that should be realized by direct knowledge."

MN 149 – Mahāsaḷāyatanika Sutta (The path and fruition)

Objective: Knowing and understanding the practical application of the eightfold path to come to the elevated factors of fruition –

The Path

Right View,
Right Intention,
Right Speech,
Right Action,
Right Livelihood,
Right Effort,
Right Mindfulness,
Right Collectedness,

The Fruition

Right Knowledge
Right Liberation

29

Day 9 – The Arahant

The arahant is one who understands reality as it is, with wisdom rooted in Right View. They interact and function in the world by automatically living the elevated fruition of the eightfold path, without having to think about doing so – to them, it is hardwired into their thoughts, speech, and actions.

Sutta References:

When my mind had immersed in collectedness like this—purified, bright, flawless, rid of corruptions, pliable, workable, collected, and imperturbable—I extended it toward knowledge of the ending of defilements.

I truly understood: "This is suffering" ... "This is the origin of suffering" ... "This is the cessation of suffering" ... "This is the practice that leads to the cessation of suffering".

I truly understood: "These are the projections" ... "This is the origin of the projections" ... "This is the cessation of the projections" ... "This is the practice that leads to the cessation of the projections".

Knowing and seeing like this, my mind was freed from the projections of sensuality, desire to be reborn, and ignorance.
    MN 112 – Chabbisodhana Sutta (the perspective of the arahant)

And since for you, Bāhiya, in what is seen there will be only what is seen, in what is heard there will be only what is heard, in what is sensed there will be only what is sensed, in what is cognized there will be only what is cognized, therefore, Bāhiya, you will not be with that; and since, Bāhiya, you will not be with that, therefore, Bāhiya, you will not be in that; and since, Bāhiya, you will not be in that, therefore, Bāhiya, you will not be here or hereafter or in between the two—just this is the end of suffering.
    Udana 1.10 – Bāhiya Sutta (destroying conceit)

Reverend, going totally beyond the dimension of neither-perception-nor-non-perception, I entered and remained in the cessation of perception and feeling.

But it didn't occur to me:

'I am entering the cessation of perception and feeling' or 'I have entered the cessation of perception and feeling' or 'I am emerging from the cessation of perception and feeling'."

SN 28.1 – 9 – Sāriputta Vagga (How an arahant meditates)

Objective: Understand the way in which the arahant sees the world and how to apply that understanding to recondition your mind, to see the world in the same way, through daily activities and practice.

Day 1:
Right Intention and
Right Effort

Suttas

Saṃyutta Nikāya 45.8 Vibhaṅga Sutta - Breaking Down the Path
Translation by Bhante Ananda.

Once in Sāvatthi,

[The Buddha]

"Righteous is this Eight-spoked path monks,

That I will explain and break down to you.

Listen carefully and apply your mind to what I will say."

"Yes Bhante" replied the monks.

The Awakened One spoke thus:

What is this Righteous Eight-Spoked Path?

It is here as follows:

Wise Understanding

Wise Attitude

Wise Speech

Wise Behavior

Wise Living

Wise Practice

Wise Awareness

Wise Meditation

Wise Understanding

What is this wise understanding?

That is:

Knowing what is unwholesome;

Knowing the increase of the unwholesome;

Knowing the release from the unwholesome;

Knowing the way to release the unwholesome.

This is called wise understanding.

Wise Attitude

What is wise attitude?

That is,

The attitude of contentment.

The attitude of non-anger.

The attitude of harmlessness.

This is called wise attitude.

Wise Speech

And what is wise speech?

That is,

Abstaining from false speech,

Abstaining from spiteful speech,

Abstaining from unkind speech,

Abstaining from senseless talk.

This is called wise speech.

Wise Behavior

And what is wise behavior?

That is,

Abstaining from mistreating living beings,

Abstaining from taking what is not given

Abstaining from sexual misconduct.

This is called wise behavior.

Wise Living

What is wise living?

That is,

A righteous meditator abandons wrong modes of living

And shapes a life by right modes of living.

This is called wise living.

Wise Practice

What is wise practice?

1. One generates the intention for the non-emergence of inexistent,
   unfavorable, unwholesome states of mind.
   One endeavors with determination,
   strives and supports this with one's mind.

2. One generates the intention for the abandonment of existent,
   Unfavorable, unwholesome states of mind.
   One endeavors with determination,
   strives and supports this with one's mind.

3. One generates the intention for the emergence of inexistent,
   Wholesome states of mind.
   One endeavors with determination,
   Strives and supports this with one's mind.

4. One generates the intention for the persistence of already emerged
   wholesome states,
   For their non-confusion, growth, maturation, development and
   culmination.
   One endeavors with determination,
   strives and supports this with one's mind.

This is called wise practice.

Wise Awareness

What is wise awareness?

1. One meditates, observing body as body,
   Intent, fully aware and present,
   Abandoning worldly desire and regret.

2. One meditates, observing feeling as feeling,
   Intent, fully aware and present,
   Abandoning worldly desire and regret.

3. One meditates, observing mind as mind,
   Intent, fully aware and present,
   Abandoning worldly desire and regret.

4. One meditates, observing Dhamma as Dhamma,
   Intent, fully aware, present,
   Abandoning worldly desire and regret.

This is called wise awareness

Wise Meditation

What is wise meditation?

1. Disengaging oneself from the outward desire
    and detaching oneself from unwholesome mental states,
    Attended by thinking and imagination
    With the joy and happiness born of mental detachment
    One understands and abides in the first level of meditation.

2. With the calming of thinking and imagining,
    With inner tranquilization,
    With the mind becoming unified,
    Unattended by thinking and imagination
    With joy and happiness born of samādhi,
    One understands and dwells in the second level of meditation.

3. One abides in bliss, unclenching, balanced,
    Present and fully comprehending,
    Experiencing happiness within one's body
    That which the awakened ones describe as:
    "Steady presence of mind."
    "This is a pleasant abiding"
    One understands and abides in the third level of meditation.

4. Leaving behind the notions of happiness and unhappiness.
    With the earlier settling of mental gladness and affliction,
    With neither distress nor excitement,
    Purified by unmoving presence,
    One understands and abides in the fourth level of meditation.

This is called wise meditation.

Samyutta Nikāya 49.1-12 The River Ganges. Sloping East
Translation by Bhante Sujato.

At Sāvatthī.
There the Buddha said:
"Bhikkhus, there are these four right efforts. What four?

39

It is when a bhikkhu generates enthusiasm, tries, makes an effort, exerts the mind, and strives so that bad, unskillful qualities don't arise.

They generate enthusiasm, try, make an effort, exert the mind, and strive so that bad, unskillful qualities that have arisen are given up.

They generate enthusiasm, try, make an effort, exert the mind, and strive so that skillful qualities arise.

They generate enthusiasm, try, make an effort, exert the mind, and strive so that skillful qualities that have arisen remain, are not lost, but increase, mature, and are completed by development.

These are the four right efforts.

The Ganges River slants, slopes, and inclines to the east. In the same way, a bhikkhu who develops and cultivates the four right efforts slants, slopes, and inclines to Nibbana.

And how does a bhikkhu who develops the four right efforts slant, slope, and incline to Nibbana?

They generate enthusiasm, try, make an effort, exert the mind, and strive so that bad, unskillful qualities don't arise.

They generate enthusiasm, try, make an effort, exert the mind, and strive so that bad, unskillful qualities that have arisen are given up.

They generate enthusiasm, try, make an effort, exert the mind, and strive so that skillful qualities arise.

They generate enthusiasm, try, make an effort, exert the mind, and strive so that skillful qualities that have arisen remain, are not lost, but increase, mature, and are completed by development.

That's how a bhikkhu who develops and cultivates the four right efforts slants, slopes, and inclines to Nibbana."

Dhamma talk – Meditation Practice

Today's theme is Right intention and, traditionally what is known as right effort. Right Intention is the choice to be in a wholesome state of mind. It is the choice to let go of unwholesome states of mind, and the choice to apply your mind toward nibbāna.

Right Effort

The unwholesome and the wholesome states of mind that arise, are to be divided into two: by first recognizing the unwholesome, then abandoning and releasing whatever has arisen in the way of the unwholesome. And then generating, bringing up, the wholesome, and maintaining that. These four make up what is right effort.

This is done within the meditation, for example if you are doing a particular process like the 6R's. You first stay with your object of meditation. In this case it might be one of the four brahmavihārās; *mettā, karuṇā, muditā,* or up*ekkhā*. In other words, loving-kindness, compassion, empathetic joy, or equanimity. Or it might even be the tranquil mind itself once you attain it at a higher state of meditation.

The meditation is essentially two things:

Observe the wholesome state of mind, in other words the brahmavihāra that you have generated. You just observe it within your mind. How it flows to your spiritual friend. Or you observe how it flows out from you if you are radiating it in all directions, if you choose to do it that way. That is the first aspect of the meditation.

The second is the process to make sure that your mind is not distracted. And that is the use of what is known as mindfulness.

Mindfulness

The word mindfulness is being used a lot nowadays, and it means a lot of things to different people. But if you go back to the root word of mindfulness from the Pali, which is *sati*, and you also look at the Sanskrit version, which is *smriti*, it means essentially memory. Or to recollect, or to remember.

You use mindfulness in this way; you make sure that the attention that you have on your object, or on the brahmavihārā, is just being there. It is not being distracted. In other words, mindfulness is the ability to keep your observation, the attention - rooted in reality -, on the brahmavihārā, on the wholesome feeling that you have generated.

The exercise of using mindfulness is to use the four right efforts. You notice that you have become distracted. Once Recognizing you were distracted, you become aware of the arising of a distraction by noticing you are no longer on your object of meditation. You then *abandon* or release your attention from the unwholesome state, from the distraction that takes you away from the meditation. Once you take your attention away from the distraction, you Relax any tension that might be there in the body. You relax the craving, let go of the craving. By letting go you are practicing right effort, which means that you practice, in that moment, letting go of craving and of the unwholesome states that have arisen. By relaxing any kind of subtle tension that arises in the mind and body as a reaction to having this distracted mind, you then come to a wholesome object, or a wholesome state of mind. And you generate that through the help of a smile. You already started your meditation by having a little Buddha smile on your mouth or, as well, having a smile in the eyes and in the mind, essentially having a relaxed mind. Just allow that smile to carry forward the wholesome quality of mind. Next, you Return to your meditation, you come back to the wholesome quality of mind. By doing this you first *brought up* the wholesome quality through your smile, if that helps, and then come into the wholesome quality of feeling that you use as your vehicle of meditation. By doing so, you *maintain* your attention on that vehicle, that wholesome quality of mind. Then you

Repeat any time you become distracted. You repeat the entire process every time other unwholesome qualities of mind start to arise.

Right Intention

Within right effort you can see that you practice right intention as well. Doing this in the meditation creates a feedback loop; the more you abandon and let go of unwholesome states of mind, and the more you bring up wholesome states of mind, the more you can do this in choices that are given to you in every moment of your daily living. And by doing that while meditating, you recondition the mind to be more present. It becomes more aware of what is happening and what choices are presented to it. So, it is a *response* versus a *reaction*. A reaction is almost reflexive; the mind, if it's used to reacting in a certain way which might be unwholesome, will immediately go toward the unwholesome choice in every given moment. But as you continue with the practice in meditation, it will become more apparent to you to take a pause in the choices that come, and you will be able to respond with wisdom. You can respond from one of the brahmavihārās, according to the situation. If the situation requires to come at it with loving-kindness or compassion, joy, or equanimity, you can do that because you have trained, conditioned your mind within the meditation.

Feedback loop

As I said, this is a feedback loop. When you can do this in your sit, you can do this in daily life too. And the more you are wholesome in daily life, the more it has an immediate effect on the mind, because mind becomes more clarified, more purified by these wholesome actions that you take. That comes from the right choice of letting go of the unwholesome and cultivating the wholesome. Cultivating an attitude of harmlessness and an attitude of sloping, slanting toward seclusion, toward nibbāna. Having a wholesome state of mind in your daily life by making right intentions creates a stable, clear foundation for your next meditation session.

Doing this every time creates a mind that is ready for the meditation. It allows the mind to go even deeper in the meditation. Therefore, after you come out from that sit, you can act according to the wholesome choices, according to the right effort.

Right Effort comes into play not only in meditation, but also when you are presented with choices. You come into a situation with either a wholesome or an unwholesome mindset. When you find that a situation is inherently unwholesome and tries to bring out an unwholesome quality of mind through that choice, you become aware, take a pause, and use the four right efforts to come at it from a wholesome standpoint.

Suppose somebody tries to bring out anger from you, and you realize and recognize an ignition of anger coming out; you recognize in that moment that anger is arising, you let go of it and replace it with a loving and kind attitude.

So, when you see anger arising, you can prevent it from *further* arising. Because it is in the unawareness, in the lack of mindfulness, that you are unable to have that anger be under control, and therefore you cannot let go of it. Because of that lack of mindfulness, anger will just flow out. But if you are mindful, if you do have the awareness, you will be able to know through your attention that anger is arising. Then you let go of that hint of anger. By doing that, you *release* the anger and *abandon* it. Then you *bring up* a warm, friendly attitude by understanding that the situation may require a loving and kind attitude, a patient attitude. You bring that up and *maintain* it, and therefore you make the right choice of being in a state of wholesomeness, an attitude of harmlessness. Consequently, you cultivate a mind that is ripe for nibbāna.

So, it is essential to see that feedback loop. Understanding it, motivates the mind to not only have this right effort and right intention process within the meditation but also in daily life.

Daily Reflection Day 1

Right Intention

What is Choice?

Every thought, word and action begin with a choice, rooted in intention. Think and reflect on the following and see for yourself how your choices, thoughts and intentions arose –

Why did you join this retreat? Is it to find more peace in your life? Is it to attain nibbāna? Is it something else?

Reflecting on the intentions behind your choices, now clarify whether they arose from a craving mindset or a wholesome mindset, born from letting go for the need to control and accepting reality as it is.

Once you understand the intentions behind your choice, you begin to see how choices come to be.

Reflect on how your intentions come to be. Do they arise as a reaction or as a response?

Reaction vs. Response

A reaction is immediate and filled with taking everything personal and the need to control a situation, and therefore it doesn't provide a space for thoughtful reflection.

In choosing to react, you are choosing to act out of craving and when craving blinds you, you do not act with wisdom or understanding, and may choose to cause harm through thoughts, words, or actions.

A response is reflective, arising out of wisdom. A response provides you a pause between what you have received in the way of your senses, and the output you provide to the world.

In this way, you act from a choice rooted in wisdom and as such you are attentive to each situation as it occurs, always being understanding and always thinking, speaking, or acting out of loving-kindness, compassion, joy, equanimity, or tranquility, in this case you do not harm another through thoughts, words, or actions.

This choice is therefore rooted in right view, in that you understand, first on an intellectual level, then on an experiential level, the four noble truths, and therefore strive, using right effort to know when craving has arisen, which causes you suffering, then let go of it and experience peace by applying the eightfold path.

What is Right Effort

The 6R's

Say that your object is mettā. You suddenly think back to a time with nostalgia, or you consider the future or think about anything other than the mettā.

You RECOGNIZE, seeing the distraction.

RELEASE is immediately letting go of the distraction - not attending to it, turning mind's attention now to -

The RELAX step - the stilling of formations. Having relaxed the craving in the form of tension in the mind and body, the mind is now clear and free of tension and craving. It is the step through which you experience a mundane preview of nibbāna, and now you are ready to attend to -

RE-SMILE, or checking if you are still smiling,

then RETURN to the object of meditation,

then REPEAT, every time you see mind has been distracted.

All of this happens in less than 5 seconds. It is a flow, a rolling of the R's.

Relax – the cornerstone of the practice

Many people seem to glaze over the relax step, not really taking time to understand what it is. It is the relaxing of the mind, body, and tightness in both.

Relaxing the bodily, mental, and verbal formations leads the mind into a clear space, a pristine, thoughtless space with no craving. Body is relaxed but not slouching. Mind is clear, like a cloudless sky, and thoughts are gone, barely wisps if they are present at all.

When you learn to pinpoint the relaxing of the formations in this manner, you can immediately understand the relax step.

The suggestion here is to just let mind be and then intend the relaxation. Relax, relax, relax - then, you can see what it means to cease craving and have that open spacious mind, so you can quickly go to it, as you let go of the distraction, and then see that open mind.

Some people seem to associate the relax step with a sharp intake of air and a letting go of breath. This is a reactionary aspect of the relax step, but not the relax step of stilling formations in and of itself.

Just Observe, Don't Force It

The other thing to consider is that mind may have the tendency to attach itself to the *mettā* (loving-kindness), *karuna* (compassion), *muditā* (empathetic joy), or *upekkhā* (equanimity).

Here, it is important to pay attention to mind **observing** - just watching, *not becoming* the object. It is an object; therefore, you are **watching** it, *not becoming* it.

The feeling that comes up from the object should be observed, and 6R'd if it distracts you from your object.

Likewise, you observe that you were distracted – *not becoming* the distraction by fighting or ignoring it. Any such effort will only cause more craving and clinging.

Allow the mind to do its work. **It will unravel itself.**

You let mind observe (*I* do not observe) and let it (not *my* mindfulness) develop its mindfulness with right intention and right effort.

Observation is not focus – it is the mere watching and seeing what occurs, not becoming involved or identifying with the feeling or the object. This then becomes absorption concentration; too much focus, pushing down insights that should naturally arise.

Focus is something *I* am doing for an extended period, *I* identify with the action, with the sensation and with the object and hence, mind is not developing mindfulness.

This is why relaxing is important - it provides the mind space required for insights to naturally arise.

Of course, one caveat - you should not just relax during the actual meditation. Once you understand what it feels like, you use it as part of the 6R effort. Then, there is development and progress as it is intended. Besides, you should not just relax, relax, relax in the beginning, because mind will become dull without an object.

It is only after the mind reaches stability through the jhānas, that it can then watch its own clarity, luminosity, and radiance - the bright, quiet, clear mind, where at this point all crude formations have been relaxed, and now you let go of the subtler formations.

The Four Right Efforts and the 6R's

The four right efforts are fundamental to root out unwholesome notions, concepts, and conditions in mind and replace them with wholesome conditions.

In doing so, you effectively purify the formations to create the circumstances for mind to experience release.

Clear Comprehension

It is when a bhikkhu generates enthusiasm, tries, makes an effort, exerts the mind, and strives so that bad, unskillful qualities don't arise.

When you RECOGNIZE that mind has strayed due to a hindrance, you effectively see and then stop that hindrance from further distracting the mind.

Releasing

They generate enthusiasm, try, make an effort, exert the mind, and strive so that bad, unskillful qualities that have arisen are given up.

When you RELEASE your attention from the hindrance, you effectively give up that hindrance, and when you RELAX the tension in mind and body, you let go of the craving that arose due to that hindrance.

Bring Up Wholesome Qualities of Mind

They generate enthusiasm, try, make an effort, exert the mind, and strive so that skillful qualities arise.

When you SMILE (or RE-SMILE), you are immediately and effectively bringing mind back into a wholesome state.

Smiling reconditions the mind to be light and relaxed, to see reality without taking it personally or imposing demands upon it.

When you smile, you understand reality as it is and are not fighting it. If that reality is unwholesome for that present moment, smiling shifts that perception and brings mind back to a state of balance, replacing the previously unwholesome quality of mind.

Maintaining

They generate enthusiasm, try, make an effort, exert the mind, and strive so that skillful qualities that have arisen remain, are not lost, but increase, mature, and are completed by development.

When you RETURN to your object (one of the brahmavihāras), which is itself a wholesome quality, you effectively allow that quality to grow and come to fruition to the next level of a wholesome quality.

When you REPEAT the process, if required, you fundamentally tranquilize the formations and recondition those formations to be able to bring about a wholesome level of thought, word, and action.

In doing so, you practice in meditation the deepening of right mindfulness and right collectedness, and in daily life you apply right intention, right speech and right action.

Questions

Does one need to start up with Right Intention?

"Sometimes, when I start a sit, I literally just sit and see what is arising, rather than bringing up the wholesome qualities of mind, because my mind is quite tranquil already. I see things arising, I relax them and quickly, my mind becomes collected.

However, when I consciously bring up a wholesome quality of mind – mettā for example –, it moves to the first jhāna almost instantly.

Is it dependent on the situation or the context, or is it best to start up with right intention, bringing up the brahmavihāra – the mettā – and then move to the quiet mind?"

Answer:

From what you are describing, in the first case, you have right mindfulness. Which means that you are aware of body as body, sensations as sensations, mind as mind, and phenomena as phenomena. So, you are just watching where the mind is in that moment. That too is right intention, since it is in line with right mindfulness. It is in accordance with the noble eightfold path because of that right mindfulness. You are aware what that present situation is.

In other words, you are aware if the mind is tranquil or not. If it is agitated or at ease. If it is upset or at peace. This is practicing one aspect of the four foundations of mindfulness. So, you can start that way and once you are aware of where your mind is presently, say, it is already tranquil, you then still bring up a wholesome quality so that you can get into the first jhāna.

But once you are in the first jhāna, let go of any of the jhāna factors that come into play. Do not allow the mind to be distracted by the occurrence of the first jhāna. Stay with the feeling. As you stay with the feeling, it will evolve and transform on its own, without you pushing or interfering. If you keep observing, you will see that it keeps changing.

As I mentioned, the steps you do in the meditation are 1. you bring up the feeling and are aware of what mind is doing at the beginning of the meditation. Then, if you need to 6R, you let go of any unwholesome states that may be there. Then you bring up the mettā and continue with the jhāna; mindful of what is happening in the first, second, third jhāna, and so on. But keep observing, keep your attention – mindfulness -, stay with that feeling. Do not get distracted by the factors of the jhāna. If you are, just use the 6rs to come back.

Intention and bringing up the brahmavihārā

"When you move to the second jhāna, where verbal formations disappear, can you relax the intention to bring up the brahmavihārā?

Because then it has started, if you do not get distracted. And you just continue to observe this feeling. And if you get distracted, you 6R and you come back to the object of meditation."

Answer:

That is correct. In the second jhāna, the thinking aspect, the verbalizing and examining aspect of the mind, gets abandoned. So, the intention is to bring up, for example, mettā. Once that has been generated, with whatever way you do it, the intention is let go of. Because now that the mettā is free flowing, you are effectively in the second jhāna. Now you have let go of the verbalization or let go of the imagining, if you use that, to bring up the wholesome state of mettā. You let go of it and allow that feeling to just freely flow. I always liken it to watching a movie; just sit back, enjoy, have your popcorn, and watch the loving-kindness continue.

Bodily distractions and meditation pain.

"Sometimes, when you start to meditate, you might feel an itch, some pain, or you want to move your hand. Do all these things arise in the mind, and is it the *intention* that is going to move your body? So, you should sit as still as possible, no movement at all?"

Answer:

That is also the understanding that I have. If you feel an itch or discomfort in the body, it arose out of your control. You did not cause the itch; it was just caused by a series of causes and conditions. You use mindfulness to be aware that there is itchiness in the body now. Let go of it, let go of your attention to it. If you continue to be aware of the itchiness and allow your attention to rest on it, you are not only distracted and therefore no longer on the object or on the vehicle of your meditation – mettā –, but you are also feeding the itch with that attention. It becomes worse. What you need to do then is 6R, or the four right efforts. It might require a few times of using that, but every time you do it, the attention will fade away more from the itch and come back to its object.

The itch might appear again, so you do the same thing and then return to the mettā. Even when it happens a few more times, don't fight it. Instead of allowing your mind to become so affected through that attention to the itch, allow it to be there, let go of it and come back. Eventually, the itch will no longer be noticeable, and you will be with your vehicle of meditation.

There can also be some tension in the body after sitting for quite some time, which can be described as *meditation pain*. This is pain that disappears as soon as you get up, not an actual physical pain (in which case you should not sit that way anymore). You handle this the same way as you do with the itch.

There is yet another kind of discomfort of tension in the body and tension in the mind. You might be trying too hard by striving to push the mind to stay with mettā, to stay with the feeling, rather than sitting back and observing. If you notice there is tension, first see whether you are pushing too much. See whether you are trying to make something happen, which is a form of craving. You are trying to change the present situation by forcing something upon it, which is not there, instead of accepting the reality of the situation and letting go of the need to control it. If there is such a tension arising, you use the 6R's and let go of it, and then return to the mettā.

Craving for a previous relationship.

"In the past I had quite some craving for a former relationship. It has taken me time to let the formations and the craving go, and in my daily living it does not come up. But it can still come up in my dreams or during the night. I am not completely mindful in my dream, so I can't let it go. I find it a bit confusing that it still comes up in my dreams. Is there any way I can release it in my sleep?"

Answer:

You can try to be a little more lucid in dreaming. It might be difficult at first, but it is a process in which you use right effort within the dreaming process. If you can become mindful enough to become aware of dreams that are rooted in some form of craving, you can let that go as well.

Another way to do it is, if you remember that you had that dream, upon waking up in the morning or later; have the intention to let go, through using the 6rs.

Or after remembering that dream, use your retrospective view and you can then let go of it. It is the same process as when you are in the eighth jhāna of neither-perception-nor-non-perception, where you are not fully aware of the contents or state of the mind. When you come out of it, you spend a few minutes to retrospectively look back at what was occurring. Then you 6R to let go of those thoughts or ideas, concepts, or formations.

Dreaming and Mindfulness

"In my dream I am aware that I am dreaming. I know this is coming up and I should be letting it go. However, my mindfulness is not strong enough to let go."

Answer:

Yes, it is just a matter of being able to take that one step. If you are not able to, you will still recollect it upon waking up. And then, it will be easier for you to let go of it.

Meditator's Reflections

The 6R's

"Because I want to get rid of the conditioning that causes craving, my practice is very simple. My conditioning is causing me to be unhappy. Conditioning causes me to feel mental pressures, so I want to reduce these pressures in mind. So, my entire practice is about releasing mental pressure (or tension). Whenever my conditioning is causing me to suffer, I let it go using the 6R's.

I use the 6R's to relax mind. As I relax more, both physically and mentally, mind becomes collected. This relaxation causes mind to become still and then enter jhanic states. And at various points of the journey, I change the object of meditation.

But it's all about letting go, physically, then mentally, watching for pressure (RECOGNIZE).

RELEASE: Every time I feel any pressure, I release it by releasing or expanding the space between my eyes, kind of like an opening or like depressurizing a liquid so it turns to a gas.

RELAX: Relaxing my body by opening my chest.

RESMILING: Allowing joy to fill that opening that ends in a smile.

RELISHING IT AS I RETURN: Relishing that feeling of equanimity and openness as I return to the object of meditation, whereafter I refocus on the Object of Meditation until I feel pressure again and REPEAT the whole process.

In this way, I am retraining my conditioning not to bother or pressure me with experiences that cause undue stress and unpleasantness."

- Meditator from California, USA

"For me, "Recognize" is one of the most critical and prominent steps now. The moment that I recognize any distraction (Recognize), releasing it (Release), the steps of Relax, Re-Smile, and Return to the object of meditation becomes a natural process.

However, there was a time that I had to work on the "Release" step. I remembered asking one of my teachers to tell me how to "let go." She said, "Just like when you watch a scary movie. The part becomes too scary, what do you do? You close your eyes. You do not watch it anymore, just like that. You do not try to drop it but just drop it. That's all." Along with that advice I adopted the following ways to help myself.

1. Pay more attention to recognize the arisings: If I am mindful, I will notice my attention moves away from the object and goes toward the distraction.
2. Or, somehow, if I lost my mindfulness momentarily and caught myself in the middle of a distraction, I smile (sometimes remind myself "just a thought!") and relax into it. And then come back to the object. And I will know if I did it right or not by noticing some spaciousness or openness in my mind.
3. Pay attention to where the muscle tightness is: For me, when I get distracted, especially my legs or shoulders tend to tense up. So, I had to l pay attention to the body signals at that time. By "Relaxing" whatever that tensed up, it improves my letting go of distractions.

As I mentioned above, when I relax, I relax the body and mind. And always follow with a big smile. The smile (Re-Smile) part of the process is the most fun part for me. This step never fails to improve my mindfulness. In the earlier days, there are too many distractions, and it was easy to lose mindfulness. Some of the excellent meditation sessions of my earlier days were when I put my attention on the smiles.

Another vital part of the process is "Return" to the object. Again, I found it essential to make sure there is no tension or tightness in mind. In the beginning, I always worried that I might lose the object, and I rushed all the other "Rs." It just does not work. It created more restlessness. So, being patient with each process is key to success.

I practice 6R's daily every time I remember. I found it one of the most helpful tools for everyday activities, especially in the work environment dealing with complex individuals or at home dealing with teenagers :-)"

- Meditator from Toronto, Canada

Day 2:
Right Mindfulness

Suttas

Majjhima Nikāya 10 Satipaṭṭhāna Sutta - The four Foundations of Mindfulness
Translation by Bhikkhu Bodhi.

1. Thus have I heard. On one occasion the Blessed One was living in the Kuru country where there was a town of the Kurus named Kammāsadhamma. There he addressed the bhikkhus thus: "Bhikkhus." - "Venerable sir," they replied. The Blessed One said this:

2. "Bhikkhus, this is the direct path for the purification of beings, for the surmounting of sorrow and lamentation, for the disappearance of pain and grief, for the attainment of the true way, for the realization of nibbāna - namely, the four foundations of mindfulness.

3. What are the four?

Here, bhikkhus, a bhikkhu abides contemplating the body as a body, ardent, fully aware, and mindful, having put away covetousness and grief for the world.

He abides contemplating feelings as feelings, ardent, fully aware, and mindful, having put away covetousness and grief for the world.

He abides contemplating mind as mind, ardent, fully aware, and mindful, having put away covetousness and grief for the world.

He abides contemplating mind-objects as mind-objects, ardent, fully aware, and mindful, having put away covetousness and grief for the world.

(CONTEMPLATION OF THE BODY)

1. (Mindfulness of Breathing)

4. And how, bhikkhus, does a bhikkhu abide contemplating the body as a body?

Here a bhikkhu, gone to the forest or to the root of a tree or to an empty hut, sits down; having folded his legs crosswise, set his body erect, and established mindfulness in front of him, ever mindful he breathes in, mindful he breathes out.

Breathing in long, he understands: *I breathe in long*; or breathing out long, he understands: *I breathe out long.*

Breathing in short, he understands: *I breathe in short*; or breathing out short, he understands: *I breathe out short.*

He trains thus: *I shall breathe in experiencing the whole body*; he trains thus: *I shall breathe out experiencing the whole body.*

He trains thus: *I shall breathe in tranquilizing the bodily formation*; he trains thus: *I shall breathe out tranquilizing the bodily formation.*

Just as a skilled lathe-operator or his apprentice, when making a long turn, understands: *I make a long turn*; or, when making a short turn, understands: *I make a short turn*; so too, breathing in long, a bhikkhu understands: *I breathe in long*; or breathing out long, he understands: *I breathe out long.*

Breathing in short, he understands: *I breathe in short*; or breathing out short, he understands: *I breathe out short.*

He trains thus: *I shall breathe in experiencing the whole body*; he trains thus: *I shall breathe out experiencing the whole body.*

He trains thus: *I shall breathe in tranquilizing the bodily formation*; he trains thus: *I shall breathe out tranquilizing the bodily formation.*

(INSIGHT)

5. In this way he abides contemplating the body as a body internally, or he abides contemplating the body as a body externally, or he abides contemplating the body as a body both internally and externally. Or else he abides contemplating in the body its nature of arising, or he abides contemplating in the body its nature of vanishing, or he abides contemplating in the body its nature of both arising and vanishing. Or else mindfulness that 'there is a body' is simply established in him to the extent

necessary for bare knowledge and mindfulness. And he abides independent, not clinging to anything in the world. That is how a bhikkhu abides contemplating the body as a body.

2. (The Four Postures)

6. Again, bhikkhus, when walking, a bhikkhu understands: *I am walking*; when standing, he understands: *I am standing*; when sitting, he understands: *I am sitting*; when lying down, he understands: *I am lying down*; or he understands accordingly however his body is disposed.

7. In this way he abides contemplating the body as a body internally, or he abides contemplating the body as a body externally, or he abides contemplating the body as a body both internally and externally. Or else he abides contemplating in the body its nature of arising, or he abides contemplating in the body its nature of vanishing, or he abides contemplating in the body its nature of both arising and vanishing. Or else mindfulness that 'there is a body' is simply established in him to the extent necessary for bare knowledge and mindfulness. And he abides independent, not clinging to anything in the world. That too is how a bhikkhu abides contemplating the body as a body.

3. (Full Awareness)

8. Again, bhikkhus, a bhikkhu is one who acts in full awareness when going forward and returning; who acts in full awareness when looking ahead and looking away; who acts in full awareness when flexing and extending his limbs; who acts in full awareness when wearing his robes and carrying his outer robe and bowl; who acts in full awareness when eating, drinking, consuming food, and tasting; who acts in full awareness when defecating and urinating; who acts in full awareness when walking, standing, sitting, falling asleep, waking up, talking, and keeping silent.

9. In this way he abides contemplating the body as a body internally, or he abides contemplating the body as a body externally, or he abides contemplating the body as a body both internally and externally. Or else he abides contemplating in the body its nature of arising, or he abides contemplating in the body its nature of vanishing, or he abides contemplating

in the body its nature of both arising and vanishing. Or else mindfulness that *there is a body* is simply established in him to the extent necessary for bare knowledge and mindfulness. And he abides independent, not clinging to anything in the world. That too is how a bhikkhu abides contemplating the body as a body.

4. (Foulness – The Bodily Parts)

10. Again, bhikkhus, a bhikkhu reviews this same body up from the soles of the feet and down from the top of the hair, bounded by skin, as full of many kinds of impurity thus: *In this body there are head-hairs, body-hairs, nails, teeth, skin, flesh, sinews, bones, bone-marrow, kidneys, heart, liver, diaphragm, spleen, lungs, intestines, mesentery, contents of the stomach, feces, bile, phlegm, pus, blood, sweat, fat, tears, grease, spittle, snot, oil of the joints, and urine.* Just as though there were a bag with an opening at both ends full of many sorts of grain, such as hill rice, red rice, beans, peas, millet, and white rice, and a man with good eyes were to open it and review it thus: *This is hill rice, this is red rice, these are beans, these are peas, this is millet, this is white rice*; so too, a bhikkhu reviews this same body up from the soles of the feet and down from the top of the hair, bounded by skin, as full of many kinds of impurity thus: *In this body there are head-hairs, body-hairs, nails, teeth, skin, flesh, sinews, bones, bone-marrow, kidneys, heart, liver, diaphragm, spleen, lungs, intestines, mesentery, contents of the stomach, feces, bile, phlegm, pus, blood, sweat, fat, tears, grease, spittle, snot, oil of the joints, and urine.*

11. In this way he abides contemplating the body as a body internally, or he abides contemplating the body as a body externally, or he abides contemplating the body as a body both internally and externally. Or else he abides contemplating in the body its nature of arising, or he abides contemplating in the body its nature of vanishing, or he abides contemplating in the body its nature of both arising and vanishing. Or else mindfulness that *there is a body* is simply established in him to the extent necessary for bare knowledge and mindfulness. And he abides independent, not clinging to anything in the world. That too is how a bhikkhu abides contemplating the body as a body.

5. (Elements)

12. Again, bhikkhus, a bhikkhu reviews this same body, however it is placed, however disposed, by way of elements thus: *In this body there are the earth element, the water element, the fire element, and the air element.* Just as though a skilled butcher or his apprentice had killed a cow and was seated at the crossroads with it cut up into pieces; so too, a bhikkhu reviews this same body, however it is placed, however disposed, by way of elements thus: *In this body there are the earth element, the water element, the fire element, and the air element.*

13. In this way he abides contemplating the body as a body internally, or he abides contemplating the body as a body externally, or he abides contemplating the body as a body both internally and externally. Or else he abides contemplating in the body its nature of arising, or he abides contemplating in the body its nature of vanishing, or he abides contemplating in the body its nature of both arising and vanishing. Or else mindfulness that *there is a body* is simply established in him to the extent necessary for bare knowledge and mindfulness. And he abides independent, not clinging to anything in the world. That too is how a bhikkhu abides contemplating the body as a body.

6. (6-14. The Nine Charnel Ground Contemplations)

14. Again, bhikkhus, as though he were to see a corpse thrown aside in a charnel ground, one, two, or three days dead, bloated, livid, and oozing matter, a bhikkhu compares this same body with it thus: *This body too is of the same nature, it will be like that, it is not exempt from that fate.*

15. In this way he abides contemplating the body as a body internally, or he abides contemplating the body as a body externally, or he abides contemplating the body as a body both internally and externally. Or else he abides contemplating in the body its nature of arising, or he abides contemplating in the body its nature of vanishing, or he abides contemplating in the body its nature of both arising and vanishing. Or else mindfulness that *there is a body* is simply established in him to the extent necessary for bare knowledge and mindfulness. And he abides independent, not clinging to

anything in the world. That too is how a bhikkhu abides contemplating the body as a body.

16. Again, as though he were to see a corpse thrown aside in a charnel ground, being devoured by crows, hawks, vultures, dogs, jackals, or various kinds of worms, a bhikkhu compares this same body with it thus: *This body too is of the same nature, it will be like that, it is not exempt from that fate.*

17. In this way he abides contemplating the body as a body internally, or he abides contemplating the body as a body externally, or he abides contemplating the body as a body both internally and externally. Or else he abides contemplating in the body its nature of arising, or he abides contemplating in the body its nature of vanishing, or he abides contemplating in the body its nature of both arising and vanishing. Or else mindfulness that *there is a body* is simply established in him to the extent necessary for bare knowledge and mindfulness. And he abides independent, not clinging to anything in the world. That too is how a bhikkhu abides contemplating the body as a body.

18. Again, as though he were to see a corpse thrown aside in a charnel ground, a skeleton with flesh and blood, held together with sinews - a bhikkhu compares this same body with it thus: *This body too is of the same nature, it will be like that, it is not exempt from that fate.*

19. In this way he abides contemplating the body as a body internally, or he abides contemplating the body as a body externally, or he abides contemplating the body as a body both internally and externally. Or else he abides contemplating in the body its nature of arising, or he abides contemplating in the body its nature of vanishing, or he abides contemplating in the body its nature of both arising and vanishing. Or else mindfulness that *there is a body* is simply established in him to the extent necessary for bare knowledge and mindfulness. And he abides independent, not clinging to anything in the world. That is how a bhikkhu abides contemplating the body as a body.

20. Again, as though he were to see a corpse thrown aside in a charnel ground, a fleshless skeleton smeared with blood, held together with

sinews - a bhikkhu compares this same body with it thus: *This body too is of the same nature, it will be like that, it is not exempt from that fate.*

21. In this way he abides contemplating the body as a body internally, or he abides contemplating the body as a body externally, or he abides contemplating the body as a body both internally and externally. Or else he abides contemplating in the body its nature of arising, or he abides contemplating in the body its nature of vanishing, or he abides contemplating in the body its nature of both arising and vanishing. Or else mindfulness that *there is a body* is simply established in him to the extent necessary for bare knowledge and mindfulness. And he abides independent, not clinging to anything in the world. That is how a bhikkhu abides contemplating the body as a body.

22. Again, as though he were to see a corpse thrown aside in a charnel ground, a skeleton without flesh and blood, held together with sinews - a bhikkhu compares this same body with it thus: *This body too is of the same nature, it will be like that, it is not exempt from that fate.*

23. In this way he abides contemplating the body as a body internally, or he abides contemplating the body as a body externally, or he abides contemplating the body as a body both internally and externally. Or else he abides contemplating in the body its nature of arising, or he abides contemplating in the body its nature of vanishing, or he abides contemplating in the body its nature of both arising and vanishing. Or else mindfulness that *there is a body* is simply established in him to the extent necessary for bare knowledge and mindfulness. And he abides independent, not clinging to anything in the world. That is how a bhikkhu abides contemplating the body as a body.

24. Again, as though he were to see a corpse thrown aside in a charnel ground, disconnected bones scattered in all directions - here a hand-bone, there a foot-bone, here a shin-bone, there a thigh-bone, here a hip-bone, there a back-bone, here a rib-bone, there a breast-bone, here an arm-bone, there a shoulder-bone, here a neck-bone, there a jaw-bone, here a tooth, there the skull - a bhikkhu compares this same body with it thus: *This*

body too is of the same nature, it will be like that, it is not exempt from that fate.

25. In this way he abides contemplating the body as a body internally, or he abides contemplating the body as a body externally, or he abides contemplating the body as a body both internally and externally. Or else he abides contemplating in the body its nature of arising, or he abides contemplating in the body its nature of vanishing, or he abides contemplating in the body its nature of both arising and vanishing. Or else mindfulness *that there is a body* is simply established in him to the extent necessary for bare knowledge and mindfulness. And he abides independent, not clinging to anything in the world. That too is how a bhikkhu abides contemplating the body as a body.

26. Again, as though he were to see a corpse thrown aside in a charnel ground, bones bleached white, the colour of shells - a bhikkhu compares this same body with it thus: *This body too is of the same nature, it will be like that, it is not exempt from that fate.*

27. In this way he abides contemplating the body as a body internally, or he abides contemplating the body as a body externally, or he abides contemplating the body as a body both internally and externally. Or else he abides contemplating in the body its nature of arising, or he abides contemplating in the body its nature of vanishing, or he abides contemplating in the body its nature of both arising and vanishing. Or else mindfulness that *there is a body* is simply established in him to the extent necessary for bare knowledge and mindfulness. And he abides independent, not clinging to anything in the world. That is how a bhikkhu abides contemplating the body as a body.

28. Again, as though he were to see a corpse thrown aside in a charnel ground, bones heaped up, more than a year old - a bhikkhu compares this same body with it thus: *This body too is of the same nature, it will be like that, it is not exempt from that fate.*

29. In this way he abides contemplating the body as a body internally, or he abides contemplating the body as a body externally, or he abides contemplating the body as a body both internally and externally. Or else he

abides contemplating in the body its nature of arising, or he abides contemplating in the body its nature of vanishing, or he abides contemplating in the body its nature of both arising and vanishing. Or else mindfulness that *there is a body* is simply established in him to the extent necessary for bare knowledge and mindfulness. And he abides independent, not clinging to anything in the world. That is how a bhikkhu abides contemplating the body as a body.

30. Again, as though he were to see a corpse thrown aside in a charnel ground, bones rotted and crumbled to dust, a bhikkhu compares this same body with it thus: *This body too is of the same nature, it will be like that, it is not exempt from that fate.*

(INSIGHT)

31. In this way he abides contemplating the body as a body internally, or he abides contemplating the body as a body externally, or he abides contemplating the body as a body both internally and externally. Or else he abides contemplating in the body its nature of arising, or he abides contemplating in the body its nature of vanishing, or he abides contemplating in the body its nature of both arising and vanishing. Or else mindfulness that *there is a body* is simply established in him to the extent necessary for bare knowledge and mindfulness. And he abides independent, not clinging to anything in the world. That too is how a bhikkhu abides contemplating the body as a body.

(CONTEMPLATION OF FEELING)

32. And how, bhikkhus, does a bhikkhu abide contemplating feelings as feelings? Here, when feeling a pleasant feeling, a bhikkhu understands: *I feel a pleasant feeling*; when feeling a painful feeling, he understands: *I feel a painful feeling*; when feeling a neither-painful-nor-pleasant feeling, he understands: *I feel a neither-painful-nor-pleasant feeling*. When feeling a worldly pleasant feeling, he understands: *I feel a worldly pleasant feeling*; when feeling an unworldly pleasant feeling, he understands: *I feel an unworldly pleasant feeling*; when feeling a worldly painful feeling, he understands: *I feel a worldly painful feeling*; when feeling an unworldly painful feeling, he understands: *I feel an unworldly painful feeling*; when

feeling a worldly neither-painful-nor-pleasant feeling, he understands: *I feel a worldly neither-painful-nor-pleasant feeling*; when feeling an unworldly neither-painful-nor-pleasant feeling, he understands: *I feel an unworldly neither-painful-nor-pleasant feeling.*

(INSIGHT)

33. In this way he abides contemplating feelings as feelings internally, or he abides contemplating feelings as feelings externally, or he abides contemplating feelings as feelings both internally and externally. Or else he abides contemplating in feelings their nature of arising, or he abides contemplating in feelings their nature of vanishing, or he abides contemplating in feelings their nature of both arising and vanishing. Or else mindfulness that *there is feeling* is simply established in him to the extent necessary for bare knowledge and mindfulness. And he abides independent, not clinging to anything in the world. That is how a bhikkhu abides contemplating feelings as feelings.

(CONTEMPLATION OF MIND)

34. And how, bhikkhus, does a bhikkhu abide contemplating mind as mind? Here a bhikkhu understands mind affected by lust as mind affected by lust, and mind unaffected by lust as mind unaffected by lust. He understands mind affected by hate as mind affected by hate, and mind unaffected by hate as mind unaffected by hate. He understands mind affected by delusion as mind affected by delusion, and mind unaffected by delusion as mind unaffected by delusion. He understands contracted mind as contracted mind, and distracted mind as distracted mind. He understands exalted mind as exalted mind, and unexalted mind as unexalted mind. He understands surpassed mind as surpassed mind, and unsurpassed mind as unsurpassed mind. He understands collected mind as collected mind, and uncollected mind as uncollected mind. He understands liberated mind as liberated mind, and unliberated mind as unliberated mind.

(INSIGHT)

35. In this way he abides contemplating mind as mind internally, or he abides contemplating mind as mind externally, or he abides contemplating mind as

mind both internally and externally. Or else he abides contemplating in mind its nature of arising, or he abides contemplating in mind its nature of vanishing, or he abides contemplating in mind its nature of both arising and vanishing. Or else mindfulness that *there is mind* is simply established in him to the extent necessary for bare knowledge and mindfulness. And he abides independent, not clinging to anything in the world. That is how a bhikkhu abides contemplating mind as mind.

(CONTEMPLATION OF MIND-OBJECTS)

1. (The five Hindrances)

36. And how, bhikkhus, does a bhikkhu abide contemplating mind-objects as mind-objects? Here a bhikkhu abides contemplating mind-objects as mind-objects in terms of the five hindrances. And how does a bhikkhu abide contemplating mind-objects as mind-objects in terms of the five hindrances? Here, there being sensual desire in him a bhikkhu understands: *There is sensual desire in me*; or there being no sensual desire in him, he understands: *There is no sensual desire in me*; and he also understands how there comes to be the arising of unarisen sensual desire, and how there comes to be the abandoning of arisen sensual desire, and how there comes to be the future non-arising of abandoned sensual desire.'

There being ill will in him, a bhikkhu understands: *There is ill-will in me*; or there being no ill-will in him, he understands: *There is no ill-will in me*; and he understands how there comes to be the arising of unarisen ill-will, and how there comes to be the abandoning of arisen ill-will, and how there comes to be the future non-arising of abandoned ill-will.

There being sloth and torpor in him, a bhikkhu understands: *There is sloth and torpor in me*; or there being no sloth and torpor in him, he understands: *There is no sloth and torpor in me*; and he understands how there comes to be the arising of unarisen sloth and torpor, and how there comes to be the abandoning of arisen sloth and torpor, and how there comes to be the future non-arising of abandoned sloth and torpor.

There being restlessness and remorse in him, a bhikkhu understands: *There is restlessness and remorse in me*; or there being no restlessness and remorse in him, he understands: *There is no restlessness and remorse in me*; and he understands how there comes to be the arising of unarisen restlessness and remorse, and how there comes to be the abandoning of arisen restlessness and remorse, and how there comes to be the future non-arising of abandoned restlessness and remorse.

There being doubt in him, a bhikkhu understands: *There is doubt in me*; or there being no doubt in him, he understands: *There is no doubt in me*; and he understands how there comes to be the arising of unarisen doubt, and how there comes to be the abandoning of arisen doubt, and how there comes to be the future non-arising of abandoned doubt.

(INSIGHT)

37. In this way he abides contemplating mind-objects as mind-objects internally, or he abides contemplating mind-objects as mind-objects externally, or he abides contemplating mind-objects as mind-objects both internally and externally. Or else he abides contemplating in mind-objects their nature of arising, or he abides contemplating in mind-objects their nature of vanishing, or he abides contemplating in mind-objects their nature of both arising and vanishing. Or else mindfulness that *there are mind-objects* is simply established in him to the extent necessary for bare knowledge and mindfulness. And he abides independent, not clinging to anything in the world. That is how a bhikkhu abides contemplating mind-objects as mind-objects in terms of the five hindrances.

2. (The Five aggregates)

38. Again, bhikkhus, a bhikkhu abides contemplating mind-objects as mind-objects in terms of the five aggregates affected by clinging. And how does a bhikkhu abide contemplating mind-objects as mind-objects in terms of the five aggregates affected by clinging? Here a bhikkhu understands: *Such is material form; such its origin, such its disappearance; such is feeling, such its origin, such its disappearance; such is perception, such its origin, such its disappearance; such are the formations, such their origin, such their*

disappearance; such is consciousness, such its origin, such its disappearance.

39. In this way he abides contemplating mind-objects as mind-objects internally, or he abides contemplating mind-objects as mind-objects externally, or he abides contemplating mind-objects as mind-objects both internally and externally. Or else he abides contemplating in mind-objects their nature of arising, or he abides contemplating in mind-objects their nature of vanishing, or he abides contemplating in mind-objects their nature of both arising and vanishing. Or else mindfulness that *there are mind-objects* is simply established in him to the extent necessary for bare knowledge and mindfulness. And he abides independent, not clinging to anything in the world. That is how a bhikkhu abides contemplating mind-objects as mind-objects in terms of the five aggregates affected by clinging.

3 (The Six Bases)

40. Again, bhikkhus, a bhikkhu abides contemplating mind-objects as mind-objects in terms of the six internal and external bases. And how does a bhikkhu abide contemplating mind-objects as mind-objects in terms of the six internal and external bases?

Here a bhikkhu understands the eye, he understands forms, and he understands the fetter that arises dependent on both; and he also understands how there comes to be the arising of the unarisen fetter, and how there comes to be the abandoning of the arisen fetter, and how there comes to be the future non-arising of the abandoned fetter.

He understands the ear, he understands sounds, and he understands the fetter that arises dependent on both; and he also understands how there comes to be the arising of the unarisen fetter, and how there comes to be the abandon-ing of the arisen fetter, and how there comes to be the future non-arising of the abandoned fetter.

He understands the nose, he understands odours, and he understands the fetter that arises dependent on both; and he also understands how there comes to be the arising of the unarisen fetter, and how there comes to be the abandoning of the arisen fetter, and how there comes to be the future non-arising of the abandoned fetter.

He understands the tongue, he understands flavours, and he understands the fetter that arises dependent on both; and he also understands how there comes to be the arising of the unarisen fetter, and how there comes to be the abandoning of the arisen fetter, and how there comes to be the future non-arising of the abandoned fetter.

He understands the body, he understands tangibles, and he understands the fetter that arises dependent on both; and he also understands how there comes to be the arising of the unarisen fetter, and how there comes to be the abandoning of the arisen fetter, and how there comes to be the future non-arising of the abandoned fetter.

He understands the mind, he understands mind-objects, and he understands the fetter that arises dependent on both; and he also understands how there comes to be the arising of the unarisen fetter, and how there comes to be the abandoning of the arisen fetter, and how there comes to be the future non-arising of the abandoned fetter.

41. In this way he abides contemplating mind-objects as mind-objects internally, or he abides contemplating mind-objects as mind-objects externally, or he abides contemplating mind-objects as mind-objects both internally and externally. Or else he abides contemplating in mind-objects their nature of arising, or he abides contemplating in mind-objects their nature of vanishing, or he abides contemplating in mind-objects their nature of both arising and vanishing. Or else mindfulness that *there are mind-objects* is simply established in him to the extent necessary for bare knowledge and mindfulness. And he abides independent, not clinging to anything in the world. That is how a bhikkhu abides contemplating mind-objects as mind-objects in terms of the six internal and external bases.

4. (The Seven Enlightenment Factors)

42. Again, bhikkhus, a bhikkhu abides contemplating mind-objects as mind-objects in terms of the seven enlightenment factors. And how does a bhikkhu abide contemplating mind-objects as mind-objects in terms of the seven

enlightenment factors? Here, there being the mindfulness enlightenment factor in him, bhikkhu understands: *There is the mindfulness enlightenment factor in me*; or there being no mindfulness enlightenment factor in him, he understands: *There is no mindfulness enlightenment factor in me*; and he also understands how there comes to be the arising of the unarisen mindfulness enlightenment factor, and how the arisen mindfulness enlightenment factor comes to fulfilment by development.

There being the investigation-of-states enlightenment factor in him, a bhikkhu understands: *There is the investigation-of-states enlightenment factor in me*; or there being no investigation-of-states enlightenment factor in him, he understands: *There is no investigation-of-states enlightenment factor in me*; and he also understands how there comes to be the arising of the unarisen investigation-of-states enlightenment factor, and how the arisen investigation-of-states enlightenment factor comes to fulfilment by development.

There being the energy enlightenment factor in him, a bhikkhu understands: *There is the energy enlightenment factor in me*; or there being no energy enlightenment factor in him, he understands: *There is no energy enlightenment factor in me*; and he also understands how there comes to be the arising of the unarisen energy enlightenment factor, and how the arisen energy enlightenment factor comes to fulfilment by development.

There being the rapture enlightenment factor in him, a bhikkhu understands: *There is the rapture enlightenment factor in me*; or there being no rapture enlightenment factor in him, he understands: *There is no rapture enlightenment factor in me*; and he also understands how there comes to be the arising of the unarisen rapture enlightenment factor, and how the arisen rapture enlightenment factor comes to fulfilment by development.

There being the tranquility enlightenment factor in him, a bhikkhu understands: *There is the tranquility enlightenment factor in me*; or there being no tranquility enlightenment factor in him, he understands: *There is no tranquility enlightenment factor in me*; and he also understands how there comes to be the arising of the unarisen tranquility enlightenment factor, and how the arisen tranquility enlightenment factor comes to fulfilment by development.

There being the collectedness enlightenment factor in him, a bhikkhu understands: *There is the collectedness enlightenment factor in me*; or there being no collectedness enlightenment factor in him, he understands: *There is no collectedness enlightenment factor in me*; and he also understands how there comes to be the arising of the unarisen collectedness enlightenment factor, and how the arisen collectedness enlightenment factor comes to fulfilment by development.

There being the equanimity enlightenment factor in him, a bhikkhu understands: *There is the equanimity enlightenment factor in me*; or there being no equanimity enlightenment factor in him, he understands: *There is no equanimity enlightenment factor in me*; and he also understands how there comes to be the arising of the unarisen equanimity enlightenment factor, and how the arisen equanimity enlightenment factor comes to fulfilment by development.

43. In this way he abides contemplating mind-objects as mind-objects internally, or he abides contemplating mind-objects as mind-objects externally, or he abides contemplating mind-objects as mind-objects both internally and externally. Or else he abides contemplating in mind-objects their nature of arising, or he abides contemplating in mind-objects their nature of vanishing, or he abides contemplating in mind-objects their nature of both arising and vanishing. Or else mindfulness that *there are mind-objects* is simply established in him to the extent necessary for bare knowledge and mindfulness. And he abides independent, not clinging to anything in the world. That is how a bhikkhu abides contemplating mind-objects as mind-objects in terms of the seven enlightenment factors.

5. (The Four Noble Truths)

44. Again, bhikkhus, a bhikkhu abides contemplating mind-objects as mind-objects in terms of the Four Noble Truths. And how does a bhikkhu abide contemplating mind-objects as mind-objects in terms of the Four Noble Truths? Here a bhikkhu understands as it actually is: *This is suffering*; he understands as it actually is: *This is the origin of suffering*; he understands as

it actually is: *This is the cessation of suffering*; he understands as it actually is: *This is the way leading to the cessation of suffering.*

(INSIGHT)

45. In this way he abides contemplating mind-objects as mind-objects internally, or he abides contemplating mind-objects as mind-objects externally, or he abides contemplating mind-objects as mind-objects both internally and externally. Or else he abides contemplating in mind-objects their nature of arising, or he abides contemplating in mind-objects their nature of vanishing, or he abides contemplating in mind-objects their nature of both arising and vanishing. Or else mindfulness that *there are mind-objects* is simply established in him to the extent necessary for bare knowledge and mindfulness. And he abides independent, not clinging to anything in the world. That is how a bhikkhu abides contemplating mind-objects as mind-objects in terms of the Four Noble Truths.

(CONCLUSION)

46. Bhikkhus, if anyone should develop these four foundations of mindfulness in such a way for seven years, one of two fruits could be expected for him: either final knowledge here and now, or if there is a trace of clinging left, non-return.

Let alone seven years, bhikkhus. If anyone should develop these four foundations of mindfulness in such a way for six years...for five years...for four years...for three years...for two years...for one year, one of two fruits could be expected for him: either final knowledge here and now, or if there is a trace of clinging left, non-return.

Let alone one year, bhikkhus. If anyone should develop these four foundations of mindfulness in such a way for seven months...for six months...for five months...for four months...for three months...for two months...for one month...for half a month, one of two fruits could be expected for him: either final knowledge here and now, or if there is a trace of clinging left, non-return.

Let alone half a month, bhikkhus. If anyone should develop these four foundations of mindfulness in such a way for seven days, one of two fruits could be expected for him: either final knowledge here and now, or if there is a trace of clinging left, non-return.

47. So it was with reference to this that it was said: "Bhikkhus, this is the direct path for the purification of beings, for the surmounting of sorrow and lamentation, for the disappearance of pain and grief, for the attainment of the true way, for the realisation of nibbāna - namely, the four foundations of mindfulness."

That is what the Blessed One said. The bhikkhus were satisfied and delighted in the Blessed One's words.

Dhamma Talk

This is a fundamental doctrine of the Buddha. It is essential to understand what the Buddha says in this phenomenal discourse. He categorizes the four foundations of mindfulness into these four: body, feelings, mind, and mind-objects. If anyone were to be mindful of any aspect of this conditioned existence, divided into these four as the Buddha says, let alone all that time; within one week, one will attain Arahantship. And if there is any clinging, non-return.

The Buddha breaks these down into further exercises to establish *Right mindfulness*. There is a reason why it is helpful to observe the arising and passing away of these different categories of conditioned existence in every moment.

The body

Take the body for example. There are different ways in which the Buddha talks about looking at the body in a way that is not clinging, void of any craving, and completely dispassionate. The body itself, in that sense, has no self. What we attach to it is the sense of self in every moment, with the idea that there is a permanent self within the body. If it were not so, you would not feel threatened by certain things that are said about your body. In other words, when someone says something about this body of ours, we first should understand that this body is merely made up of different components of causes and conditions. It is made up of various organs, various cells. Each cell has its own function and creates its own waste products.

We must understand; if there is an independent, unchanging, permanent sense of self, how could we link it to any aspect of this body, which itself is made up of all these different components of causes and conditions? Where in the cell, which arises and passes away, can you find the self? Where in the byproducts of the body can you find the self? Where in the movement of the body can you find the self; is it before the movement, is it in the movement, is it after the movement, where in it can you find the self? It is all coming from a series of causes and conditions. This is important to understand.

The Buddha divides the body into different categories, like the four great elements. To modernize these four great elements to today's understanding, we can see it from the scientific perspective of

a solid state
a liquid state
a gaseous state and
a plasma state.

The body, in that regard, is made up of all these different kinds of states, on the molecular and the atomic level. The body is created from the consumption of food, the consumption of air, built up from the consumption of water and it is dependent upon these things for its survival.

So, to project onto it any sense of self will ultimately and invariably create suffering, because once the body is built up, it can also break down. If it does not have sufficient food, air, or water, the body will break down. Therefore, the Buddha also talks about the body as what it really is. It is a corpse. It is just a walking corpse that is built up by all these different components and factors. To say that there is also a soul residing within the body, where within that body will you find the soul? Is it within the feelings and sensations that arise within the body, within the thoughts that arise in the body, or within the mental phenomena that arise in the body? It cannot be because they arise and pass away too.

Feeling or Sensation

Let us now take the feelings or sensations. If you take feeling personally, that then creates craving. The taking personal of feeling is craving itself. The Buddha explains it in such a way that he talks about just plainly understanding what sort of feeling is arising, without projecting onto it any sense of self. So, for example, if the body is feeling tired, there is the understanding of reality as it is, which is that the body is tired. But to project onto it *I am tired and therefore this is causing me tiredness*. Or, *I have made myself tired*, or anything related to that, starts to create stories. The creation of these stories further goes down into clinging. And this clinging attaches some sense of self to that body. Then, this creates a reactionary response, idea, concept, or speech. Once you crave, or in other words, as soon as you take the sensations that arise personally- whether it is hunger, thirst, tiredness, any biological aspect or sensation of the body, or even emotional states that are rooted within the mind -, you start to create ideas, situations, and stories internally around those feelings. Which then lead to clinging. And this leads to building up and accumulating of tendencies. These tendencies then create some form of an identity, which is linked and rooted with these associations, with the sensations that are arising and passing away in the body. When that happens, your mindfulness is no longer there. When your mindfulness is no longer there, then you react out of ignorance, out of delusion, out of conceit, out of craving.

However, if you just understand that this body is tired, or if there is irritation arising in the mind and you just simply understand the reality that there is irritation in the mind, which is the beginning of mindfulness. That is the start of recognizing the bodily and mental states in yourself, so to speak. And when you recognize, you can *stop* the arising of craving by understanding that there is just this irritation, or there is just tiredness. Or there is just this happiness or energy within the mind and the body. Therefore, it was not caused by a sense of self, but caused by external or internal factors.

If you understand this, then you let go of the personalization of that feeling and just allow that feeling or sensation to be there, let it pass away and observe it passing away. This recognition aspect is the beginning of the meditation practice, which are the 6R's. It is also the start of the process of the four right efforts, or right effort. How? You see that irritation is arising in the meditation, and that it is a hindrance that creates distractions and generates a destructive mind. Therefore, you recognize that you are no longer on your vehicle of meditation - mettā, or any of the other brahmavihāras. You then understand that you are distracted and release the attention, away from that distraction. Then, you relax any kind of irritation, or personalizing, of that distraction; *I was distracted,* or *why did this distraction happen,* or any other variant thereof. Meaning, either taking it personally, saying that *I* was distracted, or having aversion toward it. In other words, saying *why did I get distracted,* or *I shouldn't have been distracted,* and all kinds of ideas and stories that might follow. Release your attention from anything that arises from such distractions, and then relax that craving in the form of those stories and ideas, of taking it personally. Once you are aware of this, you notice whether you are smiling or not. Next, you bring up the wholesome object, which could be mettā or any of the other brahmavihārās. Finally, you continue.

But what is important to understand is that first you need to have that base of mindfulness. First you need to know where your mind is, within the meditation. If it is continually observing the brahmavihārās, you are fine. If it is doing anything other than observing the brahmavihārā, then you should use the 6R's/the four right efforts and return to your object of meditation.

When it comes to these five hindrances, you only need to understand that they are present within you. Do not try to analyze *why* they came about. Just know that they arose, let them go and then come back to your object of meditation.

The theory of why these hindrances came about can be understood later, through talks and understanding the suttas. But within the context of the meditation and the mindfulness, it is important to understand to not cling to them. To abandon any form of clinging to them, feeding them your attention with questions like; *why did this happen,* or *how did this arise.* Instead, let them go and return to your object. Realize that the hindrance came about, and let it go.

Thoughts

Let us take thought itself. Thoughts arise and pass away. If it were not so, you would have the very same thought from birth until death. However, within one microsecond you have a dozen thoughts, so in all of that, where is a permanent sense of self? This is what needs to be understood and contemplated, to really penetrate the understanding of the three characteristics of existence.

Mind states

The Buddha also talks about the mind states. You understand if the mind is irritated or distracted. Again, with mindfulness, you recognize that this is the state of the mind, release your attention from such a state, relax the craving that has arisen, create a wholesome state through the re-smile and then return to your object of meditation.

The Five Hindrances and the Five Precepts

Let's briefly talk about the hindrances and their relation to the precepts.

Ill Will

Ill will arises when you cultivate a mindset that is rooted in ill will, through intentionally harming any beings with action, speech, or thought. Cultivating such an intention causes the hindrance of ill will to arise. That is why it is important to keep the precept of abstaining, refraining, from intending to harm any being in thought, speech, or action.

Restlessness

The hindrance of restlessness arises, rooted in conceit. It comes up when you cultivate an idea of taking what is not given. That does not only mean physical possessions. It also means looking for attention where it is not due, taking credit for something where it is not due. Looking for your needs to be fulfilled when they cannot be fulfilled in that moment. Rather than letting it go, you look for it and therefore project onto it a sense of self. Thereby stealing, in that sense, others emotional needs and their peace of mind. The only thing you are responsible for, in terms of your own emotional needs, is to cultivate them for yourself. To look for it outside of your mind and therefore steal that kind of peace of mind from others to satisfy the sense of self, will also cause restlessness. And that is rooted in conceit, which is to say, taking it personal, taking these things to be I, me, or mine.

Doubt

Then you have doubt, or skeptical doubt. This can manifest as doubt in yourself, doubt in the meditation, doubting *am I doing this right, is this working, what is going on.* This arises from cultivating an attitude of falsifying, meaning, using false speech and in essence tricking others. By doing so, you start to distrust others. And thereby, you do not trust your own capabilities. This translates into the meditation as doubt of whether you are doing something right or not.

Sloth & Torpor

Sloth & torpor arises from indulging in intoxicants.

You could say that if you take stimulants, it creates restlessness. And it would create restlessness in that moment. But on a long-term basis it translates into a dull mind. It dampens that mind's ability to be mindful and to be collected within the meditation.

Intoxicants does not just mean drugs and alcohol. Intoxicants and indulgences also translate into taking something more than is required, or more than satisfying your needs. It could be indulging in the media, in news, the internet, technology and even something as little as drinking tea or coffee. Seen from a neuro- scientific perspective, you create disturbances within the neurotransmitters in the brain. You create an imbalance of dopamine and serotonin, which - within the meditation, within right collectedness -, normally comes about in certain increases within the first and second jhāna. Dopamine and serotonin arise when you feel joy, bliss, and rapture within the first and second jhāna. However, if you indulge in things outside of the mind's capacity to feel these kinds of pleasure within jhāna, you destabilize your ability, the mind's ability, to come back to these jhanic states. And as you get deeper and higher into these states, you will not be able to balance them in such a way that you can basically enter other states at will. Whether that's cessation, or nibbāna itself as an object, so to speak.

Sensual Desire and Lust

Sensual craving arises from breaking the precept of sexual misconduct. But this also further translates into sensual misconduct. Once you take personal the sensory experiences that arise in the mind and through the five physical senses, you start clinging to it. You create this unsatisfiable desire and are always looking for more and more, to satisfy this never-ending craving for sensory experiences. And this creates heedlessness. Sexual misconduct is such that if you indulge in sexual activities, it creates harm for yourself and harm for the other individual. And it, too, creates heedlessness in your mind. This will create pain, both for yourself and for the other person. And thereby you act in sexual misconduct and attached a sense of self to the sexual pleasure to the point that it blinds your ability to be mindful of your own feelings and emotions, and the other individual's feelings and emotions. Which creates an attachment that further roots you into craving, ignorance, and conceit.

So, these are the five hindrances and their inverse relation with following, or not following, of the five main, basic precepts.

Seven Enlightenment Factors

The enlightenment factors are essential to cultivate a mind that will lead you to nibbāna. These seven are played with, so to speak, as you go into higher and deeper states of jhāna and understand where mind is in every given moment. As you get higher into the jhānas, within the meditation, the mind continues to become clarified and purified. You come to a point where the mind is so tranquil and so quiet, that you can use that mind as your vehicle of meditation. In other words, mind is looking at mind itself, without any thoughts or hindrances arising in those moments.

Sloth & Torpor and Boredom

Sometimes, restlessness or sloth & torpor can occur. To return to the balanced state of mind, you can generate some of the seven enlightenment factors, if necessary. If sloth & torpor arises, first you use the enlightenment factor of mindfulness to detect that there is sloth & torpor in the mind. Then you generate minute amounts of joy, rapture. Sloth & torpor arises because mind starts to get 'bored'. This boredom arises because mind is used to states of excitement and delight from sensory experiences. Because those are no longer feeding mind, there is this sense of boredom, which creates either sloth & torpor or restlessness.

Bring up a little interest in the object and generate the enlightenment factor of energy. This is to create some form of effort to remain in a balanced state. You can also generate the investigative principle, the enlightenment factor of investigation, which comes about when you understand that there is sloth & torpor. Ask or allow the mind to inform what is going on, and thereby let the mind intuit if it requires the joy or the energy. By doing so, you balance back into a neutral state, between sloth & torpor and restlessness.

Restlessness and Trying Too Hard

Restlessness primarily arises when there is this personalizing of taking away not only physical possessions that are not given, but also emotional, mental, and social needs.

But within the practice of the meditation itself, these restless thoughts, this restless energy, arise because you are trying too hard. So, this restlessness arises because the mind hasn't had any sensory experiences for so long, within the duration of the sit, and boredom arises. And then, you try too hard by focusing, rather than observing the meditation object. The balancing enlightenment factors for this start, again, with mindfulness because it is with this that you recognize that there is restlessness. Whatever situation arises, the starting point is always mindfulness, observation. A recognition that mind is, for example, in a restless state. To balance this restless state, you bring about the enlightenment factor of tranquility, which is to relax that state of mind, to relax that restlessness by pulling back the focus, so to speak. Because essentially, the mind is focusing too hard, rather than being collected, which is the other factor you need for the quiet mind. If you pull back, if you relax the mind and come back to just observing in a relaxed state, you are essentially bringing up the tranquility enlightenment factor. This is how you do it.

The equanimity enlightenment factor means not being affected by that restless state. Not taking it personally and saying *oh, I am restless, oh, I got into restlessness*, and all these ideas and stories around it. You accept the reality as it is. Okay, there is restlessness, so now the mind is going to back away. The equanimity is the ability to accept the situation as it is, without being affected through craving, aversion, clinging, conceit, or delusion. Finally, you have the enlightenment factor of collectedness, which is to say that you unify the mindset around your object. At this point, you understood that the mind was focusing too hard, so you pull back through tranquility and you allow the situation to be as it is through equanimity, you use the 6R's and then you return to a collected state, by just simply observing the brahmavihāra, or whatever your object is.

This is how the seven enlightenment factors come into play, especially in the higher jhānas. Eventually, as you continue with your object, you slant, slope toward nibbāna, toward seclusion and you have the awakening of enlightenment. This is how the entire process works. In all of that, whether they are the mental objects of hindrances, or the mental objects of the enlightenment factors; don't cling to them. Don't take any aspect of it personal.

If you see that you are restless and you bring up an enlightenment factor, don't come from it with the attitude that *I need to bring up this enlightenment factor* or *I am going to bring up this enlightenment factor*. There is just the simple intention that there is going to be tranquility. So, there is the intention of pulling back. You will feel, through the mind and through the practice, that there is a withdrawing of that focus and coming back to observation. Then, there is the intention of creating minute amounts of equanimity, which is to say the intention of just letting it be and not being involved in it. And next, the intention of being collected, unifying your attention around the object, rather than being one-pointed and focused on it.

This also extends beyond the meditation to everyday life, with the body, the mind and the mental phenomena that arise. Along with the phenomena that arise outside of this body, in the form of visual or auditory experiences, experiences of smell, taste, touch on the skin, and even thoughts. They all should be understood as arising from a series of causes and conditions.

If you look at it closely, to project any sense of self to any aspect within the body, within sensations, within feelings and sensations within the mind, and within phenomena, both internal and external, is delusional.

If you look closely, you will understand that, because of the arising and passing away, these things are therefore impermanent. Since they come from a series of causes and conditions, there cannot be an independent self attached to any aspect of this conditioned existence. Therefore, you let go. And in letting go, you no longer cling and grasp. And by not clinging and grasping, the mind is freed.

Daily Reflection Day 2

Additional Suttas to read

SN46.35 - Yonisomanasikāra Sutta (how proper attention brings about the awakening factors and destroys the hindrances)

SN46.53 – Aggi Sutta (balancing mind with the seven factors)

The Four Aspects of Conditioned Existence

The Buddha points out four broad categorizations to contemplate and observe. This powerful and simple way of the mindful observation of the reality of our situation in relation to the body, feeling, mindset, and phenomena provides you the ability to take a pause between the reception of stimuli and what you respond with, which would then habitually be rooted in right intention.

Body (Kaya)

The body is comprised of trillions of cells, trillions of microorganisms, and micro biomes. It is a composite of various chemicals, atomic structures and neurons and nerves and other elements that various physicians of various concentrations can pinpoint that are always changing according to a situation in any given microsecond.

The body is dependent upon and affected by countless external and internal factors that are always in flux to be in some form of balance, but in all of that, where is there a sense of self? Is there a self that controls which genes are passed down, and which are activated? Is there a self that controls when white blood cells move into action, when an infection invades the body? Or are these dependent on causes and conditions? Is the self found in the skin cells we shed, or in the bacteria that make up the digestive micro biome?

Reflect on how the body can function without a need for a homunculus, a singular, unchanging, and controlling self. A condition arises and the body changes. Did such a self decide when the body hit puberty, or did it decide when it would stop growing? Did it decide the body's metabolism, or the inherited genetic conditions the body faces? Or were these dependent upon various circumstances, external stimuli, input, actions, and reactions - in short, upon causes and conditions?

When the body moves, observe how that movement occurs through a series of processes starting in the mind, and through the neurons that fire. Is the self found in any aspect of these processes? Was the intention to move itself caused by a self, or was there a self in that intention? If such was the case and the self is considered permanent, then why does it change with every movement and every changing intention behind that movement? In walking, in lying down, in sitting, in standing, in eating, in any biological process that arises, try to pinpoint a self. Is it there, or are these dependent upon a series of conditions and causes?

Go as deep as you intend to, with different levels of the body, starting at the skin and organs, all the way down to the electrons and quarks making up the body. Everything is a composite of smaller parts, and even those smaller parts are made up of even smaller parts, and so on.

Feeling (Vedanā)

Feeling is dependent upon contact. All that is dependent, arises and passes away. Feeling that arises does so, dependent upon neuronal, hormonal, and genetic causes and conditions. Simply put, in using the example of the eye, light hits the photoreceptors, and a signal in the form of neurons firing creates an image in the brain. Likewise, for each of the five physical senses. The thoughts that arise, are a result of various external and internal stimuli that then cause neurons to fire, and through which a thought arises.

Reflect first on the physical feeling. In daily activities and daily meditation, when this feeling arises, observe it. Does the feeling arise with a sense of self, or do we superimpose that sense of self upon it seemingly before or after the fact?

Does the painful feeling arise because we perceive it as such right after, and because it is conditioned by our past experiences, memory, and associations?

Likewise, when a pleasant feeling arises, is the feeling itself inherently pleasant, or do we project onto it our personal perceptions based on past experiences, memory, and associations?

And when a purely neutral feeling arises, do we still attach some sense of control or sense of self upon that feeling? If so, observe if that sense of self arises before the feeling, or after the fact? Or is it in the feeling itself? If the sense of self arises based around the feeling, then it would mean such a self ceases with the passing away of that feeling. In other words, such a self would not be a singular, independent, and permanent self.

Pay attention to each feeling and observe how the perception, that labels that feeling, immediately arises. Why was it that particular perception? What is it based on? Observe feeling as an outsider looking in, like a scientist looking through a microscope. Remain as impersonal as possible, and purely observe without attaching the need to personalize the feeling.

When thoughts arise, observe, and see how such thoughts arose. Did they arise dependent on, and affected by, other sensory stimuli? Were they brought on by another thought? Thoughts arise and pass away in the same way as all feeling does. If it were not so and we would say thoughts are self, then the thoughts that do arise would never pass away. The very fact that your mind is observant of multiple thoughts in just one moment, shows the fleeting nature of thoughts in general. How then could we attach a sense of permanent, independent self to thoughts, which are impermanent, in flux, always arising and passing away, affected by and dependent on other factors?

Mindset and Mood (Citta)

A mindset is a collection of similar thoughts, concepts, and beliefs that come in and out of your life. It may last a few seconds, or it may last lifetimes. Nevertheless, it too is impermanent. Since mindsets are made up of various thoughts of one kind, they are dependent on those thoughts for their existence.

When these thoughts pass away, so does the mindset. *Moods are similar in the way of emotions.* They are a collective of similar emotions, which are thoughts, heavily taken to be personal and affecting and being affected by other physical stimuli within the body. For example, when the body is tired, mind can become restless. Or when the body is tense and too active, it may produce anxiety in the mind. By observing and letting go the unwholesome causes rooted in the state of the body, it also produces a beneficial effect on the mind. Conversely, when you let go of the unwholesome causes rooted in the mind, it also produces a beneficial effect on the body.

Upon waking up, are you aware of the first thought that arose in the mind? What kind of emotional coloring did it resonate and how did that thought then culminate into a mindset and mood? Moreover, did that mindset and mood change, as stimuli affected it in a way, to either become pleasant, unpleasant, or neutral?

During meditation, is the mindset one of peace and tranquility? Does the mood consist of joy and equanimity? Or is the mindset hazy and in unease? Was the preceding mood filled with craving and resistance?

While listening to a dhamma talk, is the mood relaxed or tensed? Is the mindset open or closed? While attending to bodily needs, is the mindset observant and clear or distracted, allowing for changing moods? When reading, is the mindset loose and liberated, or is it rigid and stressed? Is the mood one of clarity, or is it one of confusion?

In general, is your mindset and mood filled with craving, aversion, or taken to be personal? Are they seen as being collected or distracted, rooted in form or in the formless realms during sitting meditation, limited and closed, or limitless and spacious, tranquil, or restless, experiencing release in jhāna or beyond, or still unreleased of craving, conceit and ignorance?

Observe how mindsets and moods change. See how the very nature of change in mindset and mood denotes their inability to be taken as self. They arise and they pass away. To observe them is to see that the very observing denotes separateness between mindset/mood and the "observer." In that sense, even the observed body, feeling and phenomena in general cannot be taken to be self.

> *The observer too is not self, because the observer is dependent on its object of observation. It changes, dependent on the change in object and observation.*

Phenomena (Dhamma)

All is phenomena. What we perceive, and the perception itself are phenomena. The hindrances are phenomena. The six senses, their receptors, and their stimuli, are phenomena. The five aggregates are phenomena. The seven factors of awakening are phenomena. The four noble truths are phenomena.

Observing when these phenomena arise in mind, dominate it, cease, and are no longer present in mind, provides clarity into the realities of impermanence, unsatisfactory nature of these phenomena, and of no inherent, permanent, independent self attached to them.

In every moment, see if any of the hindrances of sensual desire, ill will, sloth and torpor, restlessness, or uncertainty are present or not present. Use the 6R's if they are, whether during a sitting meditation, walking meditation, yoga, or if they are present in the mind in general. Remember to see if mind craves, in the form of taking the hindrance personal, delighting in it, avoiding it, or fighting it. If so, come back to the 6R practice.

The five aggregates constitute the way in which all phenomena are experienced, through contact in form, which results in feeling, which then results in perception, which then influences formations, and which gives rise to the next consciousness, which ties up in form and feeling, and thus the cycle goes on. Notice this cycle and the awareness of each of these, and if there is craving rooted to any of them, or if mind takes any of them personally as a self. If you begin to identify with any of these aggregates, 6R and come back to your object of meditation.

Observe the six senses. Watch and be aware of any craving, resistance, or sense of ownership and control that might arise, and that might be present or not present when any of the stimuli contact the receptors. The same for thought. Is the thought superimposed with craving or sense of self, or is it void of it, being observed impersonally and without involvement? For example, when the nose contacts the aroma of good food, does that make the mind relish in that aroma? When you enter the shower and turn on the hot water on a cold day, or cool water on a muggy day, does the mind immediately take relief in that, through the body? Is there a sense of self in that relishing and relief? Start to see the impersonal process in the senses, and that they are not tied to a self.

Understand by paying attention and seeing if the seven factors are present. Observe what levels of each factor are present, and if one factor is too much or too little in terms of degree, whether there is too much joy, or too much tranquility, or whether there is not enough equanimity.

Observe that when the factors are present, you are in a jhāna, whether sitting in meditation, walking, practicing yoga, or eating. The degree to which the factors are present, denotes the level of jhāna.

The four noble truths are to be understood, analyzed, penetrated, and experienced through insight and wisdom. Observe if mind comprehends them intellectually, is able to analyze them through discussion and study, penetrate them in right collectedness, and experience them in right liberation. In short, you should see if mind comprehends suffering, abandons craving, realizes its cessation, and fulfills the eightfold path.

The Five Precepts and the Five Hindrances

There is an invariable connection between following or not following the five precepts, and the arising or non-arising of the five hindrances. The origin of the five hindrances is not following the five precepts, and the cessation of the five hindrances is keeping the five precepts. In short, there is an inverse relationship between the five precepts and the five hindrances.

Harming and Ill Will

When you intentionally harm (with speech, action, or thought) or kill another living being, you cultivate the hindrance of ill will. This is because you act from ill will whenever there is an intention to harm.

Stealing and Restlessness

When you intentionally take what is not given, you cultivate the hindrance of restlessness. This is because you have developed a view through such action that causes the mind to always be in a state of paranoia – as you take from others in a way that is unwholesome, by essentially having the intention to take away what is not given freely (time, resources, credit, attention, needs, etc.), this only deepens the hold of conceit. Through this conceit, there is the subtlest fear and worry that your own "possessions" - or on a broader level what you may consider to be a need from the sense of conceit (both tangible and intangible, physical, mental and emotional)-, will be taken away in the same way.

Sexual/Sensual Misconduct and Sensual Desire

When you indulge in sensual (and particularly sexual) pleasures to the point of heedlessness and misconduct, you cultivate the hindrance of sensual desire. This is because you indulge the senses to the point that you identify in their pleasure and become prone to misconduct, to acting in a way that causes harm to another being and to yourself.

Lying and Doubt

When you use false speech, you cultivate the hindrance of doubt. This is because if you develop an attitude of tricking others with false speech, you continue to create a view to doubt others of their trustworthiness. This translates to doubt in your own capabilities and capacities, both in daily living and in meditation.

Intoxicants and Sloth & Torpor

When you use intoxicants, you cultivate the hindrance of sloth and torpor. This is because if you indulge in alcohol, drugs, or overindulge in the use of social media, phones, the internet, and even coffee or tea in general, it creates surges of various neurotransmitters, including dopamine and serotonin. You lose the ability to stay balanced. This makes you seek happiness outside of yourself and become dependent on these things to make you happy. Even if there is indulgence in a stimulant, which may produce energy in the short-term, and in fact causes restlessness immediately after its use, the long-term effect is dullness of mind. The overuse and dependence on anything that creates imbalances in your thoughts, thus dulls the mind and dampens its abilities to cultivate wholesome qualities.

The Seven Factors of Awakening

The seven factors of awakening are present when the five hindrances are absent. They arise in different degrees, depending on the nature of the mindset.

In a mind that observes and remembers to 6R and comes back to object of meditation, **observation (mindfulness)** is present.

When such observation is developed further, **investigation** arises.

This continuance of investigation of the state of your mind provides you the capacity and information required to use **right effort (energy)** to bring mind to a wholesome state if necessary.

When this happens, **joy** arises.

When joy arises, it remains and then fades into **relaxation (tranquility)**.

This provides you with a mind free of distractions, and thus there is **collectedness**.

This grows into **equanimity** to understand reality as it is, without craving, resistance, or superimposition of self.

As you deepen your practice, you become more aware of which factor is present, which is too active, and of which one is not enough. Then, you start to balance each of the factors into alignment in small amounts until it clicks, and awakening occurs. This is done through intending the factors required and keeping them present with attention rooted in reality, until mind returns to a balance between laziness and restlessness

Open, flowing attention rooted in reality (*yoniso manasikara*) fuels each of the seven factors of awakening and has release as its fruition. Unsteady attention or not paying attention at all (*ayoniso manasikara*) makes you distracted and when you are distracted, it fuels the hindrances.

When sensual craving, ill will, and restlessness are present in the mind, bring up the factors of collectedness, equanimity, and relaxation through intention, and maintain through attention rooted in reality. When sloth, torpor and uncertainty are present in the mind, bring up the factors of investigation, right effort, and joy through intention, and maintain through attention rooted in reality. In both cases, observation is necessary for the bringing up of the other factors.

The Factors and the 6R's

When you RECOGNIZE that you are distracted, you have brought up the factors of observation and investigation.

When you RELEASE that attention from distraction, you have brought up the factor of right effort.

When you RELAX tension and craving, you have brought up the factor of tranquility (relaxation).

When you SMILE (or RE-SMILE), you have brought up the factor of joy.

When you RETURN to your object of meditation, you have brought up the factor of collectedness.

When you REPEAT the process of the 6R's, you are not resisting, delighting, or taking the hindrance personal. You understand that there is a hindrance, and you remain unaffected upon observing, and thus have brought up the factor of equanimity.

Questions

"How do I bring up an intention without personalization ('I am') in it?"

Answer:

It is a matter of phrasing it in a suitable way. If you mentally, verbally, say *I am generating a wholesome state*, instead, first take the *I* out of the equation.

When you begin the meditation and bring up that wholesome state, you usually say: "*May I be happy.*" So, there is already a sense of *I* in there. Once you let go of that verbalizing - which is when the mind feels tense if it tries to verbalize -, you bring up an image, or something else that generates that wholesome state. But in doing that, you should no longer attach to that memory as *your* memory. For example, if it is a happy memory, you understand that this memory came about as a series of causes and conditions. Detach that *me, my,* and *I* from it and allow it to generate the wholesome quality of mind. When there is that wholesome quality of mind, look at it from a detached perspective. Look at it as *now there is a wholesome state*. It is again using mindfulness, and instead of saying *I am in a wholesome state*, there is a wholesome state present within mind.

So, don't start with *I am meditating,* or *I am going to meditate.* Close your eyes, relax, and use mindfulness in saying *the body is presently in this condition, the mind is now in this.* If it requires relaxing, you relax the mind and bring up a wholesome state, in whatever way it works. Whether it is a harmonious image or a wholesome memory, do whatever works for that mind. Something that creates a smile on the face. And approach it with the mindfulness that, *now this creates a wholesome state*, instead of saying, thinking, or projecting that *I* am now feeling wholesome. It is a matter of disconnecting the sense of doership, disconnecting the sense of self, and any words like I, me, or mine, related to a sense of self. Be very objective, just like a scientist, and say, think or understand that there is currently present a harmonious, wholesome state of mind. Allow that to be observed, but don't say *I* am observing this. Instead, there is observing going on.

Outside of the meditation too, whenever a feeling arises, like tiredness in the body, you will notice that you project with a sense of self - with the inherent conceit -, that *I* am tired.

If one has a released mind, they can say *I am tired*, but essentially mean the body is tired. They don't project a sense of self in using the word *I*. They understand that the body is tired, but they do not suffer from that tiredness. They just merely understand that there is tiredness.

Whereas if you say *I am tired*, with the conceit rooted in that word *I*, you will not only feel tired, but you will feel other things related to that tiredness, and thus cause yourself suffering.

As a simple exercise, detach that word *I* from whatever is arising. Little by little, you will understand that this is just an impersonal phenomenon happening. Superimposing the *I* is where the suffering arises. But if it is just a phenomenon arising, because of a series of impersonal causes and conditions, that means it will also pass away. It is the taking things personal in day-to-day life, that you attach permanency, a sense of eternalism, to what is arising. And so, the mind attends toward the arising, and the moments between the arising and passing away. There is the arising of something, then the plateau, and then the cessation. If the mind continues to use the word *I* from a deep-rooted sense of conceit or sense of self, it will be focused on creating a permanent sense in that plateau.

So, in day-to-day life, when feeling, or anything else, arises, make it an exercise of mindfulness to detach any sense of *I* through that phenomenon. Whether it happens to the body or to the mind, through sensations, or through external phenomena. By doing so, you will understand that this is all impersonal and that will translate in the meditation as; *okay, the mind is this way right now*. If there is a need to 6R, generate the wholesome quality of mind.

When, on the deeper level of meditation, there is the intention to bring up any of the seven enlightenment factors, the intention is simply the thought of it that carries the intention. Don't say *I require this particular enlightenment factor,* or *my mind requires this enlightenment factor.* There is just a need for this enlightenment factor to arise. In the very seeing of that, the intention is in some sense pushed. Thereby, there will be that balance, because the mind is so purified at that point, so tranquil, that very minute forms of intention will affect it quite quickly. But the intention itself should not have that personalizing.

"How can I see reality as it is in daily life?"

Answer:

Phrases like *understanding reality as it is; taking reality as it is; seeing reality as it is* don't mean that you accept or let go in a manner that leads to non-action. This could create further negative components in your life. Once you see reality as it is, you do not project a sense of self or craving onto it. Craving would mean saying *right now, I don't like this reality,* or *I really like this reality and I want more of it,* or just the idea that this reality affects *me.* If you take it personally, it needs to be rooted out. That is what needs to be understood. The actions you take when you don't take things personally, come from clarity that is void of craving.

Craving is the personalizing, either through desire or attachment, wanting more of it, or through ill will or aversion, not wanting more of it. And finally, craving is taking it to be personal. It affects some sense of a permanent self.

When craving arises, it automatically clouds the mind and creates a chain reaction of clinging and becoming. This subsequently leads to suffering. Accepting reality as it is, means to see it as it is, by letting go any kind of attachment or aversion that might have already arisen in that situation. You let go by using the 6R's, thereby relaxing the tension from that craving. From this letting go comes clarity of mind, a clear mind. When you relax that tension, which is the craving in the mind and body, there is an open space within the mind, a sense of spaciousness that is like a clear, blue sky. It is void of any thoughts, or only wisps of thoughts. From that mind you act.

Accepting reality is first understanding what the reality *is*, in your own mind. Do you personalize what is going on right now? If you do, let go of that, relax the craving and then from that mind, there will be clarity. From this clarity, there will be an insight into how you should act. And, of course, you will act according to the brahmavihāras and rooted within the eightfold path. You exercise right speech, if required, where you speak or don't speak, according to the situation. You act and behave according to the situation, which creates a wholesome state for everyone involved. So, when you understand what the reality of the situation is in your mind, once you see that there is personalizing going on, you let go of that personalizing. And then, when you find that clear mind, you will understand how to act, according to the situation.

"How can I practice the Four foundations of Mindfulness?"

Answer:

Within the context of the first foundation of mindfulness, the body, there are many different types of exercises:

- Ānāpānasati, which is understanding you breathe in long or short, and then the tranquilizing aspect of breathing in and breathing out.
- looking at the different components of the body in relation to the four great elements.
- the different aspects within the body, the organs and processes that function within the body.
- the practice of seeing the body as a corpse.

All these practices are for various types of people with different kinds of mentalities or mindsets. These are recommended practices to root out certain ideas in the mind of what the body is. But at the end of every exercise, the Buddha says it can also be just the mindfulness that this is the body (or the mind, the feeling, or the mind object), for the bare knowledge of what is arising and passing away.

For example, in the arising and passing away, there is the bare knowledge that there is now present a particular hindrance. This is the practice and exercise of mindfulness. It is the beginning of the recognize step, the remembering aspect, and thereby the right collectedness aspect, which will root out the hindrance through the rest of the 6R process, or through the rest of the four right efforts.

It is important to understand where you are in the present moment, both in the meditation and in day-to-day life. For example, you might be aware that there is currently anger in the mind. Or irritation, lethargy, or hunger in the body. By saying and understanding that *there is something present in this body or in this mind*, you step back from the sense of *I*.

What is important here is that, when the Buddha finishes the insight aspect of each category - of body, feeling, mind, and mental object -, he says to look at the arising and passing away and root out and abandon the clinging aspect of it.

These recommended practices – e.g., the foulness aspect of the body, or the Ānāpānasati - are cultivated for certain mindsets. It roots out certain desires that are related to the body, where you mistake the body as self. But there is an easier way by just understanding there is present this body and letting go of any notions around the body. Or, right now there is this mind, mindset, mental object, or feeling, and taking any notions of sense of self away from those things.

It is about abandoning the clinging of each category, as the Buddha says in the summary of the exposition. The delight, desire and lust that arise from these components, need to be abandoned.

First, the mindfulness is to be aware what condition is the mind in, related to any of these four aspects of conditioned existence. And then, accordingly, root out any personalizing, any craving, and any ignorance that might arise from the mind.

In daily life you can be aware, in that moment, that there is currently this emotional or mental state present. Once you understand it, you let go of any personalizing and craving of it, and then you act from there.

Within the meditation context, you are aware that you are distracted, or that one of the enlightenment factors is currently weak in the mind. It is just a bare knowledge that this is so, and a coming back to what is required for the meditation, or what is required for the situation in your daily life.

Mindfulness is remembering where you are, in relation to the present situation. And that is categorized in the present conditions of body, feeling, mind, and of mental objects.

Meditator's Reflections

Hindrances

What is a hindrance? If we assume mind is an information processing machine (which is a big assumption) whose purpose is to process incoming signals to help us navigate in the environment, mind needs to help us orientate ourselves through our senses, make decisions, and motivate us to act on those decisions. What is interesting is when you look at the Dhamma through this lens, the theory is complete, the Dhamma explains all of it.

When a hindrance arises, mind runs a cost-benefit analysis that is important enough to rise to conscious awareness, and basically says, "give me what I maximally want with the least amount of energy. Give me a plan, plot a course for me, tell me how to invest this time or what to do next." Part of meditation is to retrain mind to want different things, and not be fooled into wanting things that won't make us permanently or even partially happy. So, the process is about changing aspects of our lives (the precepts and the Eightfold Path) along with our thoughts that completely reprograms us in different ways.

The hindrances can be seen as motivational prompts from our inner GPS:

- Sensual desire is about how to get things, people, or events we want. Greed.
- Aversion is about how to get rid of the people, things or events that no longer make us happy. Ill will.
- Restlessness is about planning for future wants. Remorse is about learning about the past.
- Sloth and Torpor is about not thinking that the meditation is worth investing in, so not committing to it with a suitable level of energy.
- Doubt is about whether the investment of energy we are making will pay dividends for us.

The way these GPS signals work is that they provide a pressure in mind, which creates an imbalance, and we then act to balance the imbalance. For example, we are hungry, we feel pressure, either mental or physical to eat, and once we have eaten the pressure goes away. Which is why there is pressure or tension related to thought, at times. The thought has a degree of direction to it. It's there to guide behavior and to motivate.

For me it's freeing to be able to say that thought is just a misguided signal from my GPS and rather than act on it, or consider it important, I can alleviate this pressure by doing a 6R and letting it go, not get attached it to, and letting it flow through without creating pressure that results in unwise action. There are levels of attachment. When we are super attached, we act on that thought somewhat attached and it creates pressure in us, and not attached and we don't invest attentional capital.

- Meditator from California, USA

Seven Factors of Awakening

Bringing into balance the seven factors of awakening has been a powerful way to guide the mind into jhāna and to gradually fall into deeper states of meditation. In daily life, placing awareness on the factors has helped me stay balanced when the mind starts to sway.

- Meditator from British Columbia, Canada

Mindfulness is the key quality of bringing all factors together and balance with other factors as two wings. When the sloth and torpor occurred, I needed to bring up more mindfulness (Observation) and investigation (Understanding) and energy (Application) and joy.

When the restlessness occurred, I would bring up the equanimity, *samādhi* (Collectedness), and tranquil mind (Relaxation) together with mindfulness. My experience is that the seven factors of enlightenment would be practiced all the way in the meditation, especially during the state of neither perception nor perception.

- Meditator from Hong Kong

Brahmavihārās

Using the Brahmavihārās as a vehicle of meditation has been a rich and healing experience. The mind wants to rest in these emotions, it needs to bathe in these positive qualities, and awareness arises out of these states of mind.

- Meditator from British Columbia, Canada

Loving Kindness (Mettā): I usually feel Mettā in my chest area. It feels warm and cozy. There is happiness in it too. It can grow like a bit of a balloon and move up to the face area. Typically, it will seep out by itself toward the direction or person/being I intended to send it out to. This feeling always makes me smile, satisfied and happy. The Loving Kindness feeling itself does not choose any being; it will touch it without any discretion. It was back in February of 2021 when a challenging group of individuals was doing nasty things to many people in my mother country. So naturally, I have that disliking to those individuals. To my surprise, some of them did come up in my daily loving-kindness meditation sessions, and the feeling of Mettā touches them without any boundary and discrimination. The feeling of Mettā is an invincible yet peaceful and beautiful state of mind.

Compassion (Karuna): This is lighter than Mettā feeling for me. The feeling of Mettā has some thickness to it. But, on the other hand, Karuna is more expendable and lighter than Mettā. But it still feels warmhearted with dilation to it. I remembered how much of an incredible feeling that was for the very first time I experienced it mindfully.

Joy (Muditā): This is always very prominent state of mind for me. I always feel intense happiness with a very uplifting quality. There could be a feeling that I am almost floating out of my seat. Sometimes joy arises with warmness in the body. I normally experience the joy accompany with blistering flickers of arising and passing away of consciousnesses in this state.

Equanimity (Upekkhā): The balanced feeling is impossible to not notice. I feel very steady. Mindfulness becomes unshakeable. Nothing is essential or a significant deal anymore at this state. I am not interested in the outside world or any things arising and passing away as much at this point. So, the mind is tranquil and not trying to look for anything outside.

- Meditator from Toronto, Canada

Loving-kindness (Mettā) is the key factor to bring up the four faces of *Brahmavihārās*. At the beginning of practice, I need to cultivate the mind and radiate Loving-kindness until there was a breaking barrier state while the energy moved up to the head. During that stage, I experienced the expansion of the consciousness, and it spontaneously changed to Compassion and radiated to the immeasurable space. The feeling became calmer and the Compassion links with all beings and my mind became united without separation from the universe.

By continuously practicing, the feelings then turned into empathetic joy (Muditā) which caused the sharp sensation of the sense doors, and I could feel the flickering of the consciousness in either one of the sense doors. Afterward, I experienced the very tranquil, balanced mind that is the fourth part of the Brahmavihārās, Equanimity (Upekkhā) in the space of

Nothingness (which is really nothing and looked like an empty screen in front of me). After that, the mind turned into Neither Perception nor Non-perception, which felt like semi-awake and semi-sleep mode, and I needed to sit long enough to allow a deeper mental standstill and continuously watching the mind.

- Meditator from Hong Kong

Day 3:
Right Collectedness

Suttas

MN 111 Anupada Sutta - One by One As They Occurred
Translation by bhikkhu Bodhi.

Thus, have I heard. On one occasion the Blessed One was living at Sāvatthī in Jeta's Grove, Anāthapiṇḍika's Park. There he addressed the bhikkhus thus: "Bhikkhus." - "Venerable, sir," they replied. The Blessed One said this:

"Bhikkhus, Sāriputta is wise; Sāriputta has great wisdom; Sāriputta has wide wisdom; Sāriputta has joyous wisdom; Sāriputta has quick wisdom; Sāriputta has keen wisdom; Sāriputta has penetrative wisdom. During half a month, bhikkhus, Sāriputta had insight into states one by one as they occurred. Now Sāriputta's insight into states one by one as they occurred was this:

Here, bhikkhus, quite secluded from sensual pleasures, secluded from unwholesome states, Sāriputta entered upon and abided in the first jhāna, which is accompanied by applied and sustained thought, with rapture and pleasure born of seclusion.

And the states in the first jhāna - the applied thought, the sustained thought, the rapture, the pleasure, and the unification of mind; the contact, feeling, perception, volition, and mind; the zeal, decision, energy, mindfulness, equanimity, and attention - these states were defined by him one by one as they occurred; known to him those states arose, known they were present, known they disappeared. He understood thus: *So indeed, these states, not having been, come into being; having been, they vanish.* Regarding those states, he abided unattracted, unrepelled, independent, detached, free, dissociated, with a mind rid of barriers. He understood: *There is an escape beyond*, and with the cultivation of that [attainment], he confirmed that there is.

Again, bhikkhus, with the stilling of applied and sustained thought, Sāriputta entered and abided in the second jhāna, which has self-confidence and singleness of mind without applied and sustained thought, with rapture and pleasure born of concentration.

And the states in the second jhāna - the self-confidence, the rapture, the pleasure, and the unification of mind; the contact, feeling, perception, volition, and mind; the zeal, decision, energy, mindfulness, equanimity, and attention - these states were defined by him one by one as they occurred; known to him those states arose, known they were present, known they disappeared. He understood thus:...and with the cultivation of that [attainment], he confirmed that there is.

Again, bhikkhus, with the fading away as well of rapture, Sāriputta abided in equanimity, and mindful and fully aware, still feeling pleasure with the body, he entered upon and abided in the third jhāna, on account of which noble ones announce: "He has a pleasant abiding who has equanimity and is mindful."

And the states in the third jhāna - the equanimity, the pleasure, the mindfulness, the full awareness, and the unification of mind; the contact, feeling, perception, volition, and mind; the zeal, decision, energy, mindfulness, equanimity, and attention - these states were defined by him one by one as they occurred; known to him those states arose, known they were present, known they disappeared. He understood thus:...and with the cultivation of that [attainment], he confirmed that there is.

Again, bhikkhus, with the abandoning of pleasure and pain, and with the previous disappearance of joy and grief, Sāriputta entered upon and abided in the fourth jhāna, which has neither-pain-nor-pleasure and purity of mindfulness due to equanimity.

And the states in the fourth jhāna - the equanimity, the neither-painful-nor-pleasant feeling, the mental unconcern due to tranquility, the purity of mindfulness, and the unification of mind; the contact, feeling, perception, volition, and mind; the zeal, decision, energy, mindfulness, equanimity, and attention - these states were defined by him one by one as they occurred; known to him those states arose, known they were present, known they disappeared. He understood thus:...and with the cultivation of that [attainment], he confirmed that there is.

Again, bhikkhus, with the complete surmounting of perceptions of form, with the disappearance of perceptions of sensory impact, with nonattention to perceptions of diversity, aware that *space is infinite*, Sāriputta entered upon and abided in the base of infinite space.

And the states in the base of infinite space - the perception of the base of infinite space and the unification of mind; the contact, feeling, perception, volition, and mind; the zeal, decision, energy, mindfulness, equanimity, and attention – these states were defined by him one by one as they occurred; known to him those states arose, known they were present, known they disappeared. He understood thus:...and with the cultivation of that [attainment], he confirmed that there is.

Again, bhikkhus, by completely surmounting the base of infinite space, aware that *consciousness* is infinite, Sāriputta entered upon and abided in the base of infinite consciousness.

And the states in the base of infinite consciousness – the perception of the base of infinite consciousness and the unification of mind; the contact, feeling, perception, volition, and mind; the zeal, decision, energy, mindfulness, equanimity, and attention - these states were defined by him one by one as they occurred; known to him those states arose, known they were present, known they disappeared. He understood thus:.. .and with the cultivation of that [attainment], he confirmed that there is.

Again, bhikkhus, by completely surmounting the base of infinite consciousness, aware that *there is nothing*, Sāriputta entered upon and abided in the base of nothingness.

And the states in the base of nothingness - the perception of the base of nothingness and the unification of mind; the contact, feeling, perception, volition, and mind; the zeal, decision, energy, mindfulness, equanimity, and attention - these states were defined by him one by one as they occurred; known to him those states arose, known they were present, known they disappeared. He understood thus:...and with the cultivation of that [attainment], he confirmed that there is.

Again, bhikkhus, by completely surmounting the base of nothingness, Sāriputta entered upon and abided in the base of neither-perception-nor-non-perception.

He emerged mindful from that attainment. Having done so, he contemplated the past states, which had ceased and changed, thus: *So indeed, these states, not having been, come into being; having been, they vanish.* Regarding those states, he abided unattracted, unrepelled, independent, detached, free, dissociated, with a mind rid of barriers. He understood: *There is an escape beyond* and with the cultivation of that [attainment], he confirmed that there is.

Again, bhikkhus, by completely surmounting the base of neither-perception-nor-non-perception, Sāriputta entered upon and abided in the cessation of perception and feeling. And his taints were destroyed by his seeing with wisdom.

"He emerged mindful from that attainment. Having done so, he recalled the past states, which had ceased and changed, thus: *So indeed, these states, not having been, come into being; having been, they vanish.* Regarding those states, he abided unattracted, unrepelled, independent, detached, free, dissociated, with a mind rid of barriers. He understood: *There is no escape beyond,* and with the cultivation of that [attainment], he confirmed that there is not.

Bhikkhus, rightly speaking, were it to be said of anyone:

"He has attained mastery and perfection in noble virtue, attained mastery and perfection in noble concentration, attained mastery and perfection in noble wisdom, attained mastery and perfection in noble deliverance," it is of Sāriputta indeed that rightly speaking this should be said.

Bhikkhus, rightly speaking, were it to be said of anyone:

"He is the son of the Blessed One, born of his breast, born of his mouth, born of the Dhamma, created by the Dhamma, an heir in the Dhamma, not an heir in material things" it is of Sāriputta indeed that rightly speaking this should be said.

Bhikkhus, the matchless Wheel of the Dhamma set rolling by the Tathagata is kept rolling rightly by Sāriputta."

That is what the Blessed One said. The bhikkhus were satisfied and delighted in the Blessed One's words.

Dhamma talk for MN 111

Suppressing the hindrances

This is a very important sutta to understand through Sāriputta's experience, because - as the Buddha said - Sāriputta attained wisdom by going into the jhānas in the correct manner. There is a way of going into jhānas in which someone has a one-pointed concentration or one-pointed focus. Whenever there is one-pointed focus, the mind gets suppressed, as well as any hindrances that might arise. Therefore, not allowing them to come to be, so that they come face to face with the mind, so to speak, and then can be let go of. Suppressing the hindrances is like the metaphor of a beach ball which you push under water. Upon releasing it, it jumps back up and splashes out in the same way as the hindrances do by using one-pointed concentration, or one-pointed focus.

When someone suppresses the hindrances in that incorrect jhāna, they still experience other factors, like the bliss, rapture, joy, and other factors in the higher jhānas. But at the same time, they can't let go of the hindrances, because there is no opportunity for them to arise. When they come out of the meditation, they will notice that the mind is quite deep and silent for perhaps a few minutes to a few hours, maybe throughout the day. But when the effect of such a meditation wears off, they are back in the same place as they were when they first started the meditation. Perhaps even worse off, because quite a lot of hindrances start to arise, and then they have no way of dealing with them. So, there will not be a real tangible, perceptible change in personality from the meditation, that is long-lasting, sustainable, and noticeable throughout day-to-day life.

But in right collectedness, there are certain factors that are involved in the correct form of jhāna. Particularly right mindfulness. When you generate the wholesome quality of mind through one of the brahmavihāras, you also allow a space for the mind to observe that brahmavihāra. When you give mind that space, you allow it to flow. You will see the different factors of the jhāna, and the different elements within each jhāna, as Sāriputta rightly pointed out.

You will notice that in the rūpa jhānas, the form jhānas – which are the first four jhānas -, there is still perception of form. In other words, there is still the contact of the form with the outside world. You will notice that sensory experiences are still present within the correct form of jhānas. If you suppress the mind, you also suppress the sensory experiences and if, even for a second, your mindfulness slips, or you stop paying attention and something distracts you from outside, it will cause irritation and further distraction.

But if you keep your mind spacious and open, and any sensory experience arises, you let go of it. You understand it was there and then it goes away, and you let go of any attachment to it, through your attention. And you use the 6R's, or the four right efforts, to come back to your object of meditation. You do this through the unification of mind, what I call a unified mindset. It is an attention that is *rooted in reality*. This means that you pay attention to the reality as it unfolds, even while in jhāna. You pay attention to the mind observing, using right mindfulness to observe your vehicle of meditation. But you do not allow the mind to grasp onto the object, to focus to such an extent that it does not let go of the object of meditation. When this would happen, it would invariably create craving by holding on to the object. And it would create restlessness because the mind is trying too much. When you put in too much energy, it will create a lot of restless thoughts. In an incorrect form of jhāna, you will not be able to let go of them.

However, with the unification of mind, a unified mindset, attention is rooted in reality as it unfolds. It is accepting, understanding, and seeing what is unfolding, while within the jhāna. The attention is around the object, the loving-kindness, compassion, or another brahmavihāra you may be using. When the attention is around it, it allows a space within mind for the distractions or hindrances to come to be. When those arise, you have the process of right effort to be able to let go of them. So, you effectively use the four right efforts to come into right mindfulness and continue that observation.

The collectedness that naturally arises, when you are observing and 6R'ing distractions, is what is the fruit of that practice. In that collected mind, that right collectedness, the jhānas start to arise. In each jhāna you are aware of what is going on in relation to the five aggregates, in relation to your mentality-materiality. As Sāriputta notes within his experiences, the perception of form is still there, up until the fourth jhāna. The perception of the other aggregates is still present as well. It is only after you enter infinite space that you lose a sense of the body, a sense of form, because you start to experience that infinite spaciousness. Within that experience, you are still aware and mindful, and aware of the other four aggregates. There are sensations that arise internally, which you are conscious of. There is still perception in the fifth, sixth, and seventh jhāna. And consciousness, insofar as the experiences of the mind are concerned. Consciousness is tied to the mental experiences that might arise within jhāna, from the fifth onwards. And the formations that are there – bhikkhu Bodhi translated them as volition - give rise to thoughts and might give rise to certain hindrances. You need to *recondition* these formations. Every time the hindrances arise, they arise not only due to not having followed the precepts in the past, but because the fruition of that comes through by the formations. So, when hindrances arise, you experience the formations and the effects of them. When you let go of them instead of fighting them, trying to stop them, instead of trying to suppress them, you recondition the formations. They, and the strength of those hindrances, are weakened bit by bit, until they finally are no longer present in that meditation. You also understand where your mindfulness is, regarding the meditation. If you practice right collectedness, you are aware of the different mental factors that are present, and that is the use of right mindfulness. That means that in each of the jhānas, you are aware of what kind of state the mind is in.

Compassion

Within the fifth jhāna, the loving-kindness transforms into compassion. It is a different quality of feeling which is much lighter, and you understand what this compassion truly means within that practice.

In compassion, you see the other person's suffering. You understand that the other person, or other beings, are suffering, but you do not allow the mind to identify with their suffering. You are there as a support in words, actions, and thoughts, which creates a wholesome state of being for them. You also understand that they require their own space and time as it were, for them to learn from that experience, so that they themselves can grow out of that suffering. It would be unjust, it would be wrong and unfair for you to try to take them out of that suffering. In doing so, you would not allow them the ability to gain the insights required to come out of that suffering. So, instead of being a crutch, you provide emotional and physical support in whatever way is required. But don't try to take them out of the suffering, insofar as attaching a sense of self to it. You allow the person, the being, to come out of it.

Empathetic Joy

As you get into the sixth jhāna, this experience of compassion flowers into empathetic joy.

The empathetic joy that arises, is the ability to celebrate the successes of that person, or being, coming out of that suffering. And generally, being able to experience celebration and happiness for the general well-being and successes that others have experienced throughout the universe.

Equanimity

This then flowers into what is equanimity, within the seventh jhāna. This equanimity is likened to the metaphor of a grandparent; if you notice parents with their children, they have a certain level of attachment that clouds their judgment. When a child is acting a certain way, they project the care and concern for that child onto them. But through that, they might be so attached that they are unable to allow that child to express and be itself. Whereas a grandparent, who has already experienced being a parent, allows the child to flower and be themselves, even if the child is, let's say, mischievous, playing around, or acting out. They have been through it already, so they are watching the child from an objective perspective, in that regard. There is still concern for that child, but there is no sense of attachment or clinging to it that will cloud their judgment. So, they have developed a certain type of wisdom to be able to know when the child requires certain attention, or when the child needs to be left alone.

Using that metaphor of a grandparent, the equanimity is not that you are detached from things and situations. The very word *detachment* denotes that you were first attached and therefore needed to detach. Equanimity is not detachment. It is more of observing reality as it is happening without attaching a sense of self to it. Not personalizing it, not craving for it, without being aversive against it. It is understanding the reality as it is. Whether it is a positive or a negative element, the mind remains undisturbed and quiet. In the quietness and stillness of the jhāna of nothingness, the mind abides with equanimity. At this point mind is so refined, that just a mere intention - and that intention alone - is what sets out the radiating of the equanimity, within the seventh jhāna. That intention is like a pebble which you drop into a cool, clear lake, which creates a ripple effect of that intention, creating equanimity and sending it outward.

When you get to the seventh jhāna, there is a point where there is only the mindfulness of nothingness. There is still the experience of perception, of the formations, and of the sensory experiences within the mental plane. The no-thingness is the nothingness of external sensory experiences. Now the mind has turned into itself. It basically uses its own self as an object. At that point, there are no coarse thoughts, images, or formations to deal with. Whatever arises might arise in the background, but by the time you are in the seventh jhāna of nothingness, your mindfulness has become so sharp that it automatically lets go of those thoughts, those distractions or proto distractions, in the background, while the mind stays with equanimity.

The Quiet Mind

There comes a moment when the mind becomes so quiet and relaxed, that even the intention becomes tense. At that point you understand that you need to take this quiet mind as your object of meditation. This is the base of neither-perception-nor-non-perception, the eighth jhāna. When you do that, you enter such a level of stillness that it is like a lucid, deep sleep. It is like you are aware within deep sleep. In that state, there may arise in the background certain thoughts and images. If you pay attention to them and get caught up with them, you are no longer in neither-perception-nor-non-perception, since you used perception and therefore are no longer within that realm. You then should 6R and return into this tranquil mind, and allow mind to further relax, to further unravel to its innermost depths.

Then, you start to see certain formations, but in seeing them, your mindfulness has become so sharp that it 6R's them or lets go of them completely and automatically. Your job at this point is to just continue to observe.

The seven Enlightenment Factors

At a certain point, using mindfulness, you might notice that the mind starts to go one side or another; it either becomes a little too sluggish, tending toward sloth & torpor, or if you are trying too hard in some way, creating too much energy and effort, it becomes restless. This is when you intend, very subtly, to balance the mind with the use of the enlightenment factors.

In the case of sloth & torpor, you *intend* a little bit of joy, a little bit of interest, with energy and investigation into the dhammas. You still use your mindfulness to be aware if your mind starts to slope toward sloth & torpor.

For restlessness you generate, very subtly tranquility, equanimity, and collectedness.

The very fact that you can do this, shows that you are in a unified mindset, a collected mindset, rather than a mindset that is basically using focus, one-pointed concentration. Because, if you would use one-pointed concentration, you would not be aware of any of these states arising and passing away, even within the very subtlest jhāna of neither-perception-nor-non-perception.

When you get to the eighth jhāna. what you should do even *more* so - and it is emphasized *more* so -, is to observe. You let the mind continue to 6R when required, but now your entire attention is on observing the quietude of mind, the bright, radiant, luminous mind that you have taken as your object of meditation. Allow mind to rest in it.

Review

If you have not completely let go and you come out of the eighth jhāna, it is important to spend a few minutes to use your *retrospective lens*, so to speak. Look back at what might have occurred that your mindfulness didn't pick up, because of its subtleness. Whatever might arise when looking back; let go of it. These are very subtle formations, perceptions, thoughts, ideas, concepts, and imageries. They are related to your life here and now in this lifetime, and possibly previous lifetimes. But whatever they may be, what is important is to let go of them. It is all about letting go.

Cessation of Perception and Feeling

There will be a certain point where mind lets go of the subtlest of subtlest formations, the subtlest of subtlest perceptions, of all concepts. And in the balancing of the enlightenment factors so that you are in a stable mindset - within the quietude of that bright, radiant, luminous, silent mind -, having let go, you then enter the cessation of perception and feeling. In this cessation, there is a blank. There is nothing, there is no perception, there is no feeling, there is no consciousness. All experience ceases and you will only know that you were in it, *after* you come out of it.

After mind emerges from the cessation, the mind is so pristine, so inclined toward seclusion and nibbāna, that it will experience certain things that are the signatures of the nibbāna experience. When that happens, you will have let go of certain fetters, depending upon what level of awakening you might already be at. Until, at the very last, final fruition, you have completely uprooted all the taints, destroyed all fetters, and attained Arahantship.

This seeing with wisdom begins upon the emergence of cessation of perception and feeling. After coming out of it, it is not important to *see*, in the sense of the visual things that might occur. What is more important to understand is the state of the mind afterwards. After emerging from it, observe how mind responds to situations, how mind perceives the reality as it is now.

It is only then that you understand that the fetters have been destroyed, what level you are at. When you have the final fruition, the experience that you have is of full wisdom and understanding of the four noble truths. You fully understand the links of dependent origination. And you have cut off any ability for the mind for the emergence of rebirth, for re-becoming, to occur.

The only way you know that something has changed in the personality, is post-meditation. Observe how mind responds in situations after having this experience, and accordingly you will understand where you are at.

The first and foremost thing to understand within the meditation practice, is to make sure that the mind is open, that there is awareness, mindfulness, which is completely open and relaxed so that the insights - that will for sure arise from the emergence of cessation of perception and feeling - can come and create a change in personality. You will understand the links of dependent origination, in whatever way they might arise, after this cessation. You will see with wisdom what Sāriputta also saw with wisdom.

Daily Reflection Day 3

Additional Suttas to Read

SN46.54 – Mettāsahagata Sutta (brahmavihārās and the four spheres)

Attention Rooted in Reality (*Yoniso Manasikara*)

Reality is more than the present moment. The present moment is just a concept. If you only adhere your attention to the present moment, then you have missed the point of right collectedness, which is to understand and see reality as it is, rooted in right view.

There is the flowing, steady, and open attention, rooted in reality, which is the fuel for the seven factors of awakening and leads to release.

> *Then there is the attention that is haphazard, distracted, and while it may seem to be rooted in the present moment without thought, it is closed and tense, rooted in the delusion of open presence. This is because as you try to stay in the moment, you begin to attach a sense of self and there is delineation between what reality is as it is, and what you perceive through the idea of the present moment, conditioned by previous moments, interactions, and reactions to those moments. As one meditator puts it, "One is always too late, when one tries to be in the present moment. The harder you try, to more you move downward in the flow of dependent origination, while to see reality as it is, one needs to move 'up', i.e., let go of craving."*

Every time you *try* to do something, you will already have missed the point. Instead of this, pull back the focus, relax it, and just watch. This is seeing reality unfold. This is one aspect of such attention. In right mindfulness, with attention rooted in reality, see the present moment of the four aspects of conditioned existence, and use investigation. See if any of the three delusions – taking each aspect to be personal; taking it to be permanent; and taking it to be deeply and eternally satisfying – are present in mind upon the seeing.

In doing this, you then, through right effort, could root out such unwholesome qualities and come to intellectual understanding of the three symptoms of reality – impermanence of causes and conditions, their unsatisfactoriness, and the impersonal nature of all phenomena, including nibbāna.

The next step is how you respond to that reality. This determines whether you allow the link of craving to bind you further down, or if you see through with wisdom and understanding, let go if that craving arises, and continue to see the three symptoms of reality of each situation.

Fruition of Attention Rooted in Reality

This then is attention rooted in the three symptoms of reality. This is attention rooted in right view. It first comes through intellectual knowledge, right mindfulness, and right collectedness. But then when that right vision is experienced - namely seeing firsthand the four noble truths, through which the three symptoms of reality of existence are always attended to without personalized intellectualization, striving, or analysis, and rather is automatic and informed by right view -, then such attention continually flows from wisdom.

Being in the present moment is just the beginning of attention rooted in reality. It is not forced. It is relaxed into and then it is open, nurturing, loving, and accepting of reality. It sees what hindrances may arise, but rather than trying to stop them upon that seeing, the 6R's are implemented and you have practiced right effort in order to bring up the seven factors of awakening.

Right collectedness is when the seven factors are present. In other words, in jhāna, mind is rooted in mindfulness, investigation, right effort, joy, tranquility, collectedness, and equanimity.

> *These factors balance themselves with flowing attention that is rooted in reality, when you get deeper through the jhānas and the higher planes of perception.*

Here then, with such attention, you are naturally in the present moment, and more importantly, you are open and allowing the mind to unravel itself so that insights arise without force. The nature of insights is that they are not forced or contemplated. They arise in a flash when the conditions are right. The work at first, in right collectedness, is to nurture the ground in which insights can arise, through the nutriment of attention rooted in reality.

In short, intellectual understanding through analysis and reflection first gives you conviction, which informs attention. Such conviction, if fully cultivated, developed, and realized, can destroy the fetter of doubt altogether, and such attention, when open and accepting in right mindfulness, then activates the seven factors, where you then practice right collectedness. Finally, these factors blossom into right liberation, when right knowledge is realized. That is when the work is complete.

Unified Mindset (Citta-Ekaggata)

Especially when you are in the form jhānas, there will be sounds, smells, wind or breeze if meditating outside, and perhaps insects that will make contact with the body. All five aggregates and the four aspects of conditioned existence remain active in jhāna. In the planes of perception beyond the fourth, the contact with the physical body becomes less and less pronounced, to the point of imperceptibility. You may still perceive contact, but as mind enters deeper and subtler levels of perception in the higher jhānas, it is almost non-existent. You begin to fine-tune your attention to the contact that arises within the mind, in the form of thoughts, but if those thoughts do not keep you from watching your object, those thoughts will fall apart due to insufficient nutriment, i.e., attention.

One-pointed focus is not the objective or a component of this practice. In one-pointed focus, you utilize maximum concentration upon the object to the point that all contact ceases, without understanding the causes and conditions prior to and after such ineffective cessation. This suppresses the mind's ability to relax and observe and respond. Suppression of mind does not release the hindrances but leads to them arising back with full force when you come out of this form of meditation. It may manifest through the senses and perception, creating wrong views, intensifying craving and deepening ignorance and conceit.

> *It is like forcing a ball underwater. What happens? As soon as you let go, the ball jumps out of the water due to the suppressive pressure.*

In Sāriputta's experience of each jhāna, there are other factors and phenomena he observes, all the way up to the dimension of nothingness. Depending on the jhāna, he experiences and perceives the factors tied to a particular jhāna, which differentiates the quality of each jhāna. What is common in all jhānas, up to the dimension of nothingness, is the presence of mentality and its functions – which are the faculties and processes of contact, feeling, perception, intention, and attention rooted in reality. The awareness of materiality is present up until the fourth jhāna, after which it becomes less perceptible. The other factors common to every jhāna that are also present up to nothingness, are unified mindset, application, observation, and equanimity. Further commonalities also include each of the seven factors in varying degrees.

Beyond nothingness, when Sāriputta enters the dimension of neither-perception-nor-non-perception (NPNNP), he does not report seeing anything, here the factors and phenomena have almost ceased – perceptions in the form of formations may arise, but when you see them, you are not in that dimension of NPNNP anymore. Mind 6R's automatically and it rests in the quietness of this dimension once again for quite some time, until another small, subtle disturbance might arise, at which time mind releases it yet again. In this dimension, there may be formations and perceptions, that mind may not be quite able to understand at the time of sitting meditation.

Rather, the experience within this dimension is one that you can only understand *after* emerging from it, with observation and investigation of what had occurred within it. It is like a state in which you are in lucid deep sleep. If you emerge from this dimension without attaining cessation, then you should reflect on what arose and 6R anything that might arise. This cultivates the retrospective mind that arises post-cessation.

With cessation, however, you cannot even report back what occurred in that state at all. You are only able to recollect what occurred prior to and after cessation. Whatever that experience is that arises after cessation, it should be reported to the teacher for further discussion.

The key point to take away is that, if you were to practice with one-pointed focus, you would not even be able to look back with vivid clarity at the phenomena that may have arisen, even in the coarser jhānas where physical contact can still be felt, let alone the dimension of NPNNP. Moreover, your attention would no longer be rooted in reality, but suppressed by the force of concentration. At that point, attention would no longer even be present.

It is not one-pointed focus that is required, nor is one-pointed focus a factor of the more coarsely perceptible jhānas, i.e., the first to fourth jhānas and up to the dimension of nothingness. Rather, what it is instead is the extension, the flowering, and the effect of an attention rooted in reality that has been refined beyond collectedness. In other words, once attention fuels the factors, it is refined and transformed through each factor until it becomes not one-pointed focus, but rather a unified mindset. All these wholesome factors deepen with every jhāna attained.

> *While collectedness is where attention is comfortably on the object without attaching to it with identification and craving, unified mindset is where attention no longer is scattered or diffused. In other words, when sensory experiences arise, they are felt but attention does not get scattered by feeling. Instead, it rests comfortably within the realm of its object. It is unified around its object, not with it. This is because unified mindset remains open to what arises in the way of phenomena. However, such a mindset does not break apart or becomes distracted in jhāna.*

Background thoughts

The practical experience of this is emphasized here again – when any thoughts or any other feeling seem to be in the background while observing, and they do not distract mind from its object, you do not need to 6R. Those wisps of feeling will dissipate with no fuel of attention nourishing them. Such attention remains undisturbed. It is a unified mindset because, while the attention is rooted in the reality of what arises, it does not react to it and mind continues to observe the object, undisturbed. It understands what has arisen is there, but your attention is not distracted, only aware of what arises, while through collectedness it continues to observe the object of meditation. Of course, when these factors fade away due to a hindrance arising, and thus distracting the mind, right effort through the 6R's is to be used.

Watch, Don't Get Involved

A unified mindset begins with and is a fruition of a wholesome intention when the seven factors and right mindfulness, right effort and right collectedness are practiced.

The meditation starts with an intention to bring up the object. That intention is carried forward by attention rooted in reality and right mindfulness. When that attention is steady, the seven factors come into being. When those factors are brought up, you are in right collectedness. When you are here, you are in jhāna, and the unified mindset has naturally come to be through this process. It remains a factor of the jhānas, up until the dimension of neither-perception-nor-non-perception. In this whole process, mind watches without getting involved. When mind is relaxed, it has the ability to watch through a unified mindset, but as soon as it gets involved through focus, hindrances will arise, craving has arisen, and you are no longer in a jhāna.

Just watch the mind as if you are seeing a new show for the first time, that you've wanted to watch. You allow everything - the characters, the storyline, the themes, the dialogue, the music, the emotions- to arise, but your attention does not get transfixed at one aspect, at the expense of losing out on the other qualities of the show. You watch with interest, but you don't get lost in your own thoughts about it. It is fresh in every moment, because you are experiencing something new all the time, for the duration of that show.

In the same way, with an attitude that every sitting will be different, you can keep your mind alert but unhindered, interested but not attached, attentive but not one-pointed, and open to new phenomena that arise, but unaffected by them through not taking them personal, craving, or pushing them away. Just think, *let's see what comes up today*, let go of the expectations, and dive in with the tools of right mindfulness, right effort, right collectedness, and attention rooted in reality. Watch as the seven factors arise with a unified mindset, as you 6R. The factors or the hindrances may arise in one way in one sitting and in another way in another sitting. Every sitting, every meditation during walking, yoga practice, or eating will be different. That's what makes it interesting.

Questions

Relationship between Relax step and next jhāna

"Is there a relationship between the hindrance and the transition to the next jhāna?

For example, when you're in the first jhāna and a hindrance comes up, or mind attaches itself to something and you 6R, is that letting go a steppingstone for mind to move into the second jhāna?"

Answer:

If you spend some time with the relax step, independently of the other steps, you will experience the spacious reality of mind, where, for those few moments, there are no thoughts. When you effectively practice the relax step, in conjunction with the rest of the 6R's, you have an experience of mundane nibbāna, because at that moment, you let go of any factors, causes and conditions for craving. And therefore, any factors, causes and conditions for suffering. So, when you relax that craving, you actually experience the third noble truth of cessation of suffering. Having done so, you also relax and let go of certain factors of the jhāna, which will then allow you to proceed to further jhānas.

More than that, I want to add that there is the ability to experience the supramundane nibbāna, the full-blown nibbāna, within or after any of the jhānas. In other words, even within the first or the second jhāna, if there is this level of insight that can arise after having let go, one can experience wisdom. One can have the experience of nibbāna.

In the letting go process, you essentially let go of all factors, of all causes and conditions of craving, and thereby all factors within that particular jhāna. By doing so there is the opportunity, the potential, of not only moving up into a higher jhāna with certain intention, but also the potential for having cessation of perception and feeling, even after the first or second jhāna. And more so, the potential for nibbāna to arise.

"It is mentioned that unworldly painful feelings may arise in the jhānas, called meditation pain, generated by the mind.

In the arūpa jhānas, where the experience of contact and the body is strongly reduced, can there still arise a meditation pain. Can meditation pain also occur in the first four jhānas, or is it restricted to arūpa jhānas?"

Answer:

It can happen even in the first four jhānas, where there is the perception of form. But the meditation pain in and of itself is wholly mental. What you will notice is that, as soon as you effectively let go of your attention from that pain, it ceases. It may take some time; it may take a few cycles of the 6R's for your attention to fully detach from that meditation pain. But that pain in and of itself is not physical, though it *appears* to be physical. For example, it seems to be in the chest or the knee, shoulders, or the neck, but it is purely mental.

Certain pain can arise, especially in the head, if the mind is trying too hard. If there is too much effort going on, more craving arises which then creates more tension in the mind and body.

Having said that, this kind of meditation pain generally appears more in the higher jhānas. The reason is that one is sitting for so long that the mind gets deeper and deeper, and therefore starts to lose perception of form. So, at the deeper layers of mind, the meditation pain that arises is purely on a mental level. For that, you just need to 6R if the attention continues to be on that pain. Just treat that meditation pain as any other hindrance and let go of it. Eventually, it will cease.

Meditator Reflections

What are the Jhānas?

- Some say that the jhānas are signs of progress, indications of where you are on the path. So-called markers on the path to liberation.
- Others say that the jhānas are teaching tools or learning aids that allow you to climb the awakening ladder. They help in focusing and quietening the mind. So, they are tools to help us on our journey.
- Others say that the jhānas are levels of wisdom, or levels of insight. They are related to the ability to see things clearly. So, they are based on insight or wisdom.
- Some say that the jhānas are levels of letting go. So, they are related to reduced levels of attachment. In the early stages, they are related to physical relaxation. In the later levels, they are related to mental relaxation.
- Others say that the jhānas are the rewards or fruits of right effort. The benefits of good practice. The rewards of mindfulness.

I would say that the jhānas are all of these things. They are guides, teaching tools, insight enablers, levels of letting go, and rewards, but at the core they are the result of allowing relaxation to restructure and deactivate the information processing modules of the mind. As one relaxes mind more and more, modules switch off until mind is left with only bare experience with nothing being added to sensory experience. And then ultimately mind switches off during Cessation. So, the path of the jhānas is about relaxing the conditioning of mind that leads to suffering.

- I would describe them as being steps or milestones on the path to awakening. Almost like gas stations or refueling stops that one has to go through to remain fully fueled for the journey towards awakening. That way they are somewhat independent of other topics, and you can just teach them in isolation and get a lot of value from the teachings to early students. Once the students have been through the journey once, they can come back and learn them at a deeper level.

The first four jhānas are likely related to neurotransmitter levels in the brain that are related to pleasure and motivation. After a while your joy, motivation, and engagement changes. The final four jhānas (arūpa jhānas or ayatanas) are likely related to mental modules being turned off. As each module is deactivated, one's experience changes.

A good example of this is the fourth jhāna, when one loses a sense of where one's body parts are. Infinite Space is about the vestibular system that is related to our sense of orientation and space. etc. Our relationship and orientation to space changes.

- Meditator from California, USA

One benefit of jhāna practice is that there is nowhere, no state of being that chisels out the four noble truths with such clarity. When one experiences this deep ease, fullness, contentment, openness, and release, it becomes very clear that anything that causes tension in the mind or body is painful. The contrast between well-being and dis-ease becomes very well defined, very strong, and understanding flows out of this.

- Meditator from British Columbia, Canada

Day 4:
Right Action

Suttas

MN9 Sammādiṭṭhi Sutta – Right View
Translation by Bhikkhu Bodhi.

Thus, have I heard. On one occasion the Blessed One was living at Sāvatthī in Jeta's Grove, Anāthapiṇḍika's Park. There the venerable Sāriputta addressed the bhikkhus thus: "Friends, bhikkhus."—"Friend," they replied. The venerable Sāriputta said this:

"One of Right view, one of Right view," is said, friends. In what way is a noble disciple one of Right view, whose view is straight, who has unwavering confidence in the Dhamma, and has arrived at this true Dhamma?

"Indeed, friend, we would come from far away to learn from the venerable Sāriputta the meaning of this statement. It would be good if the venerable Sāriputta would explain the meaning of this statement. Having heard it from him, the bhikkhus will remember it."

"Then, friends, listen and attend closely to what I shall say."

"Yes, friend," the bhikkhus replied. The venerable Sāriputta said this:

THE WHOLESOME AND THE UNWHOLESOME

"When, friends, a noble disciple understands the unwholesome and the root of the unwholesome, the wholesome and the root of the wholesome, in that way he is one of Right view, whose view is straight, who has unwavering confidence in the Dhamma and has arrived at this true Dhamma.

And what, friends, is the unwholesome, what is the root of the unwholesome, what is the wholesome, what is the root of the wholesome? Killing living beings is unwholesome; taking what is not given is unwholesome; misconduct in sensual pleasures is unwholesome; false speech is unwholesome; malicious speech is unwholesome; harsh speech is unwholesome; gossip is unwholesome; covetousness is unwholesome;

ill will is unwholesome; wrong view is unwholesome. This is called the unwholesome.

And what is the root of the unwholesome? Greed is a root of the unwholesome; hate is a root of the unwholesome; delusion is a root of the unwholesome. This is called the root of the unwholesome.

And what is the wholesome? Abstention from killing living beings is wholesome; abstention from taking what is not given is wholesome; abstention from misconduct in sensual pleasures is wholesome; abstention from false speech is wholesome; abstention from malicious speech is wholesome; abstention from harsh speech is wholesome; abstention from gossip is wholesome; uncovetousness is wholesome; non-ill will is wholesome; Right View is wholesome. This is called the wholesome.

And what is the root of the wholesome? Non-greed is a root of the wholesome; non-hate is a root of the wholesome; non-delusion is a root of the wholesome. This is called the root of the wholesome.

When a noble disciple has thus understood the unwholesome and the root of the unwholesome, the wholesome and the root of the wholesome, he entirely abandons the underlying tendency to lust, he abolishes the underlying tendency to aversion, he extirpates the underlying tendency to the view and conceit *I am*, and by abandoning ignorance and arousing true knowledge he here and now makes an end of suffering. In that way too a noble disciple is one of Right view, whose view is straight, who has unwavering confidence in the Dhamma, and has arrived at this true Dhamma."

NUTRIMENT

Saying, "Good, friend," the bhikkhus delighted and rejoiced in the venerable Sāriputta's words. Then they asked him a further question: "But, friend, might there be another way in which a noble disciple is one of Right view...and has arrived at this true Dhamma?"—"There might be, friends.

When, friends, a noble disciple understands nutriment, the origin of nutriment, the cessation of nutriment, and the way leading to the cessation of nutriment, in that way he is one of Right view…and has arrived at this true Dhamma.

And what is nutriment, what is the origin of nutriment, what is the cessation of nutriment, what is the way leading to the cessation of nutriment? There are four kinds of nutriment for the maintenance of beings that already have come to be and for the support of those about to come to be. What four? They are: physical food as nutriment, gross or subtle; contact as the second; mental volition as the third; and consciousness as the fourth. With the arising of craving there is the arising of nutriment. With the cessation of craving there is the cessation of nutriment. The way leading to the cessation of nutriment is just this Noble Eightfold Path; that is, Right view, Right intention, Right speech, Right action, Right livelihood, Right effort, Right mindfulness, and Right collectedness.

When a noble disciple has thus understood nutriment, the origin of nutriment, the cessation of nutriment, and the way leading to the cessation of nutriment, he entirely abandons the underlying tendency to greed, he abolishes the underlying tendency to aversion, he extirpates the underlying tendency to the view and conceit *I am*, and by abandoning ignorance and arousing true knowledge he here and now makes an end of suffering. In that way too a noble disciple is one of Right view, whose view is straight, who has unwavering confidence in the Dhamma, and has arrived at this true Dhamma."

THE FOUR NOBLE TRUTHS

Saying, "Good, friend," the bhikkhus delighted and rejoiced in the venerable Sāriputta's words. Then they asked him a further question: "But, friend, might there be another way in which a noble disciple is one of Right view…and has arrived at this true Dhamma?"—"There might be, friends.

When, friends, a noble disciple understands suffering, the origin of suffering, the cessation of suffering, and the way leading to the cessation of suffering, in that way he is one of Right view…and has arrived at this true Dhamma.

And what is suffering, what is the origin of suffering, what is the cessation of suffering, what is the way leading to the cessation of suffering? Birth is suffering; ageing is suffering; sickness is suffering; death is suffering; sorrow, lamentation, pain, grief, and despair are suffering; not to obtain what one wants is suffering; in short, the five aggregates affected by clinging are suffering. This is called suffering.

And what is the origin of suffering? It is craving, which brings renewal of being, is accompanied by delight and lust, and delights in this and that; that is, craving for sensual pleasures, craving for being, and craving for non-being. This is called the origin of suffering.

And what is the cessation of suffering? It is the remainderless fading away and ceasing, the giving up, relinquishing, letting go, and rejecting of that same craving. This is called the cessation of suffering.

And what is the way leading to the cessation of suffering? It is just this Noble Eightfold Path; that is, Right view...Right collectedness. This is called the way leading to the cessation of suffering.

"When a noble disciple has thus understood suffering, the origin of suffering, the cessation of suffering, and the way leading to the cessation of suffering...he here and now makes an end of suffering. In that way too a noble disciple is one of Right view...and has arrived at this true Dhamma."

AGEING AND DEATH

Saying, "Good, friend," the bhikkhus delighted and rejoiced in the venerable Sāriputta's words. Then they asked him a further question: "But, friend, might there be another way in which a noble disciple is one of Right view...and has arrived at this true Dhamma?"—"There might be, friends.

When, friends, a noble disciple understands ageing and death, the origin of ageing and death, the cessation of ageing and death, and the way leading to the cessation of ageing and death, in that way he is one of Right view...and has arrived at this true Dhamma.

And what is ageing and death, what is the origin of ageing and death, what is the cessation of ageing and death, what is the way leading to the cessation of ageing and death? The ageing of beings in the various orders of beings, their old age, brokenness of teeth, greyness of hair, wrinkling of skin, decline of life, weakness of faculties—this is called ageing. The passing of beings out of the various orders of beings, their passing away, dissolution, disappearance, dying, completion of time, dissolution of the aggregates, laying down of the body—this is called death. So, this ageing and this death are what is called ageing and death. With the arising of birth there is the arising of ageing and death. With the cessation of birth there is the cessation of ageing and death. The way leading to the cessation of ageing and death is just this Noble Eightfold Path; that is, Right view...Right collectedness.

When a noble disciple has thus understood ageing and death, the origin of ageing and death, the cessation of ageing and death, and the way leading to the cessation of ageing and death...he here and now makes an end of suffering. In that way too a noble disciple is one of Right view...and has arrived at this true Dhamma."

BIRTH

Saying, "Good, friend," the bhikkhus delighted and rejoiced in the venerable Sāriputta's words. Then they asked him a further question: "But, friend, might there be another way in which a noble disciple is one of Right view...and has arrived at this true Dhamma?"— "There might be, friends.

When, friends, a noble disciple understands birth, the origin of birth, the cessation of birth, and the way leading to the cessation of birth, in that way he is one of Right view...and has arrived at this true Dhamma.

And what is birth, what is the origin of birth, what is the cessation of birth, what is the way leading to the cessation of birth? The birth of beings in the various orders of beings, their coming to birth, precipitation in a womb, generation, manifestation of the aggregates, obtaining the bases for contact—this is called birth. With the arising of being there is the arising of birth. With the cessation of being there is the cessation of birth. The way leading to the cessation of birth is just this Noble Eightfold Path; that is, Right view...Right collectedness.

When a noble disciple has thus understood birth, the origin of birth, the cessation of birth, and the way leading to the cessation of birth...he here and now makes an end of suffering. In that way too a noble disciple is one of Right view...and has arrived at this true Dhamma."

BEING

Saying, "Good, friend," the bhikkhus delighted and rejoiced in the venerable Sāriputta's words. Then they asked him a further question: "But, friend, might there be another way in which a noble disciple is one of Right view...and has arrived at this true Dhamma?"—"There might be, friends.

When, friends, a noble disciple understands being, the origin of being, the cessation of being, and the way leading to the cessation of being, in that way he is one of Right view...and has arrived at this true Dhamma.

And what is being, what is the origin of being, what is the cessation of being, what is the way leading to the cessation of being? There are these three kinds of being: sense-sphere being, fine-material being, and immaterial being. With the arising of clinging there is the arising of being. With the cessation of clinging there is the cessation of being. The way leading to the cessation of being is just this Noble Eightfold Path; that is, Right view...Right collectedness.

When a noble disciple has thus understood being, the origin of being, the cessation of being, and the way leading to the cessation of being...he here and now makes an end of suffering. In that way too a noble disciple is one of Right view...and has arrived at this true Dhamma."

CLINGING

Saying, "Good, friend," the bhikkhus delighted and rejoiced in the venerable Sāriputta's words. Then they asked him a further question: "But, friend, might there be another way in which a noble disciple is one of Right view...and has arrived at this true Dhamma?"—"There might be, friends.

When, friends, a noble disciple understands clinging, the origin of clinging, the cessation of clinging, and the way leading to the cessation of clinging, in that way he is one of Right view... and has arrived at this true Dhamma.

And what is clinging, what is the origin of clinging, what is the cessation of clinging, what is the way leading to the cessation of clinging? There are these four kinds of clinging: clinging to sensual pleasures, clinging to views, clinging to rules and observances, and clinging to a doctrine of self. With the arising of craving there is the arising of clinging. With the cessation of craving there is the cessation of clinging. The way leading to the cessation of clinging is just this Noble Eightfold Path; that is, Right view...Right collectedness.

When a noble disciple has thus understood clinging, the origin of clinging, the cessation of clinging, and the way leading to the cessation of clinging...he here and now makes an end of suffering. In that way too a noble disciple is one of Right view... and has arrived at this true Dhamma."

CRAVING

Saying, "Good, friend," the bhikkhus delighted and rejoiced in the venerable Sāriputta's words. Then they asked him a further question: "But, friend, might there be another way in which a noble disciple is one of Right view...and has arrived at this true Dhamma?"—"There might be, friends.

When, friends, a noble disciple understands craving, the origin of craving, the cessation of craving, and the way leading to the cessation of craving, in that way he is one of Right view... and has arrived at this true Dhamma.

And what is craving, what is the origin of craving, what is the cessation of craving, what is the way leading to the cessation of craving? There are these six classes of craving: craving for forms, craving for sounds, craving for odours, craving for flavours, craving for tangibles, craving for mind-objects. With the arising of feeling there is the arising of craving. With the cessation of feeling there is the cessation of craving. The way leading to the cessation of craving is just this Noble Eightfold Path; that is, Right view...Right collectedness.

When a noble disciple has thus understood craving, the origin of craving, the cessation of craving, and the way leading to the cessation of craving…he here and now makes an end of suffering. In that way too a noble disciple is one of Right view… and has arrived at this true Dhamma."

FEELING

Saying, "Good, friend," the bhikkhus delighted and rejoiced in the venerable Sāriputta's words. Then they asked him a further question: "But, friend, might there be another way in which a noble disciple is one of Right view…and has arrived at this true Dhamma?"—"There might be, friends.

When, friends, a noble disciple understands feeling, the origin of feeling, the cessation of feeling, and the way leading to the cessation of feeling, in that way he is one of Right view…and has arrived at this true Dhamma.

And what is feeling, what is the origin of feeling, what is the cessation of feeling, what is the way leading to the cessation of feeling? There are these six classes of feeling: feeling born of eye-contact, feeling born of ear-contact, feeling born of nose-contact, feeling born of tongue-contact, feeling born of body-contact, feeling born of mind-contact. With the arising of contact there is the arising of feeling. With the cessation of contact there is the cessation of feeling. The way leading to the cessation of feeling is just this Noble Eightfold Path; that is, Right view… Right collectedness.

When a noble disciple has thus understood feeling, the origin of feeling, the cessation of feeling, and the way leading to the cessation of feeling…he here and now makes an end of suffering. In that way too a noble disciple is one of Right view…and has arrived at this true Dhamma."

CONTACT

Saying, "Good, friend," the bhikkhus delighted and rejoiced in the venerable Sāriputta's words. Then they asked him a further question: "But, friend, might there be another way in which a noble disciple is one of Right view…and has arrived at this true Dhamma?"—"There might be, friends.

When, friends, a noble disciple understands contact, the origin of contact, the cessation of contact, and the way leading to the cessation of contact, in that way he is one of Right view…and has arrived at this true Dhamma.

And what is contact, what is the origin of contact, what is the cessation of contact, what is the way leading to the cessation of contact? There are these six classes of contact: eye-contact, ear-contact, nose-contact, tongue-contact, body-contact, mind-contact. With the arising of the sixfold base there is the arising of contact. With the cessation of the sixfold base there is the cessation of contact. The way leading to the cessation of contact is just this Noble Eightfold Path; that is, Right view…Right collectedness.

When a noble disciple has thus understood contact, the origin of contact, the cessation of contact, and the way leading to the cessation of contact…he here and now makes an end of suffering. In that way too a noble disciple is one of Right view…and has arrived at this true Dhamma."

THE SIXFOLD BASE

Saying, "Good, friend," the bhikkhus delighted and rejoiced in the venerable Sāriputta's words. Then they asked him a further question: "But, friend, might there be another way in which a noble disciple is one of Right view…and has arrived at this true Dhamma?"—"There might be, friends.

When, friends, a noble disciple understands the sixfold base, the origin of the sixfold base, the cessation of the sixfold base, and the way leading to the cessation of the sixfold base, in that way he is one of Right view…and has arrived at this true Dhamma.

And what is the sixfold base, what is the origin of the sixfold base, what is the cessation of the sixfold base, what is the way leading to the cessation of the sixfold base? There are these six bases: the eye-base, the ear-base, the nose-base, the tongue-base, the body-base, the mind-base. With the arising of Mentality-Materiality there is the arising of the sixfold base. With the cessation of Mentality-Materiality there is the cessation of the sixfold base. The way leading to the cessation of the sixfold base is just this Noble Eightfold Path; that is, Right view…Right collectedness.

When a noble disciple has thus understood the sixfold base, the origin of the sixfold base, the cessation of the sixfold base, and the way leading to the cessation of the sixfold base...he here and now makes an end of suffering. In that way too a noble disciple is one of Right view...and has arrived at this true Dhamma."

MENTALITY-MATERIALITY

Saying, "Good, friend," the bhikkhus delighted and rejoiced in the venerable Sāriputta's words. Then they asked him a further question: "But, friend, might there be another way in which a noble disciple is one of Right view...and has arrived at this true Dhamma?"—"There might be, friends.

When, friends, a noble disciple understands Mentality-Materiality, the origin of Mentality-Materiality, the cessation of Mentality-Materiality, and the way leading to the cessation of Mentality-Materiality, in that way he is one of Right view...and has arrived at this true Dhamma.

And what is Mentality-Materiality, what is the origin of Mentality-Materiality, what is the cessation of Mentality-Materiality, what is the way leading to the cessation of Mentality-Materiality? Feeling, perception, volition, contact, and attention—these are called mentality. The four great elements and the material form derived from the four great elements—these are called materiality. So, this mentality and this materiality are what is called Mentality-Materiality. With the arising of consciousness there is the arising of Mentality-Materiality. With the cessation of consciousness there is the cessation of Mentality-Materiality. The way leading to the cessation of Mentality-Materiality is just this Noble Eightfold Path; that is, Right view...Right collectedness.

When a noble disciple has thus understood Mentality-Materiality, the origin of Mentality-Materiality, the cessation of Mentality-Materiality, and the way leading to the cessation of Mentality-Materiality...he here and now makes an end of suffering. In that way too a noble disciple is one of Right view...and has arrived at this true Dhamma."

CONSCIOUSNESS

Saying, "Good, friend," the bhikkhus delighted and rejoiced in the venerable Sāriputta's words. Then they asked him a further question: "But, friend, might there be another way in which a noble disciple is one of Right view...and has arrived at this true Dhamma?"—"There might be, friends.

When, friends, a noble disciple understands consciousness, the origin of consciousness, the cessation of consciousness, and the way leading to the cessation of consciousness, in that way he is one of Right view...and has arrived at this true Dhamma.

And what is consciousness, what is the origin of consciousness, what is the cessation of consciousness, what is the way leading to the cessation of consciousness? There are these six classes of consciousness: eye-consciousness, ear-consciousness, nose-consciousness, tongue-consciousness, body-consciousness, mind-consciousness. With the arising of formations there is the arising of consciousness. With the cessation of formations there is the cessation of consciousness. The way leading to the cessation of consciousness is just this Noble Eightfold Path; that is, Right view...Right collectedness.

When a noble disciple has thus understood consciousness, the origin of consciousness, the cessation of consciousness, and the way leading to the cessation of consciousness ...he here and now makes an end of suffering. In that way too a noble disciple is one of Right view...and has arrived at this true Dhamma."

FORMATIONS

Saying, "Good, friend," the bhikkhus delighted and rejoiced in the venerable Sāriputta's words. Then they asked him a further question: "But, friend, might there be another way in which a noble disciple is one of Right view...and has arrived at this true Dhamma?"—"There might be, friends.

When, friends, a noble disciple understands formations, the origin of formations, the cessation of formations, and the way leading to the cessation of formations, in that way he is one of Right view...and has arrived at this true Dhamma.

And what are formations, what is the origin of formations, what is the cessation of formations, what is the way leading to the cessation of formations? There are these three kinds of formations: the bodily formation, the verbal formation, the mental formation. With the arising of ignorance there is the arising of formations. With the cessation of ignorance there is the cessation of formations. The way leading to the cessation of formations is just this Noble Eightfold Path; that is, Right view...Right collectedness.

When a noble disciple has thus understood formations, the origin of formations, the cessation of formations, and the way leading to the cessation of formations...he here and now makes an end of suffering. In that way too a noble disciple is one of Right view...and has arrived at this true Dhamma."

IGNORANCE

Saying, "Good, friend," the bhikkhus delighted and rejoiced in the venerable Sāriputta's words. Then they asked him a further question: "But, friend, might there be another way in which a noble disciple is one of Right view...and has arrived at this true Dhamma?"—"There might be, friends.

When, friends, a noble disciple understands ignorance, the origin of ignorance, the cessation of ignorance, and the way leading to the cessation of ignorance, in that way he is one of Right view...and has arrived at this true Dhamma.

And what is ignorance, what is the origin of ignorance, what is the cessation of ignorance, what is the way leading to the cessation of ignorance? Not knowing about suffering, not knowing about the origin of suffering, not knowing about the cessation of suffering, not knowing about the way leading to the cessation of suffering—this is called ignorance. With the arising of the taints there is the arising of ignorance. With the cessation of the taints there is the cessation of ignorance. The way leading to the cessation of ignorance is just this Noble Eightfold Path; that is, Right view...Right collectedness.

When a noble disciple has thus understood ignorance, the origin of ignorance, the cessation of ignorance, and the way leading to the cessation of ignorance...he here and now makes an end of suffering. In that way too a noble disciple is one of Right view…and has arrived at this true Dhamma."

TAINTS

Saying, "Good, friend," the bhikkhus delighted and rejoiced in the venerable Sāriputta's words. Then they asked him a further question: "But, friend, might there be another way in which a noble disciple is one of Right view, whose view is straight, who has unwavering confidence in the Dhamma, and has arrived at this true Dhamma?"—"There might be, friends.

When, friends, a noble disciple understands the taints, the origin of the taints, the cessation of the taints, and the way leading to the cessation of the taints, in that way he is one of Right view, whose view is straight, who has unwavering confidence in the Dhamma, and has arrived at this true Dhamma.

And what are the taints, what is the origin of the taints, what is the cessation of the taints, what is the way leading to the cessation of the taints? There are these three taints: the taint of sensual desire, the taint of being, and the taint of ignorance. With the arising of ignorance there is the arising of the taints. With the cessation of ignorance there is the cessation of the taints. The way leading to the cessation of the taints is just this Noble Eightfold Path; that is, Right view, Right intention, Right speech, Right action, Right livelihood, Right effort, Right mindfulness, and Right collectedness.

When a noble disciple has thus understood the taints, the origin of the taints, the cessation of the taints, and the way leading to the cessation of the taints, he entirely abandons the underlying tendency to lust, he abolishes the underlying tendency to aversion, he extirpates the underlying tendency to the view and conceit *I am*, and by abandoning ignorance and arousing true knowledge he here and now makes an end of suffering. In that way too a noble disciple is one of Right view, whose view is straight, who has unwavering confidence in the Dhamma, and has arrived at this true Dhamma."

That is what the venerable Sāriputta said. The bhikkhus were satisfied and delighted in the venerable Sāriputta's words.

Dhamma Talk MN 9

Right view starts with knowing what is wholesome and what is unwholesome. This is the beginning of right view. This is the right view of one who is still in training, of one who has begun the path. Once you understand what is unwholesome and what is wholesome, you can enter the path and with this initial right view be able to walk the different steps of the eightfold path, which culminate into right collectedness.

Here, Sāriputta starts with the unwholesome and the wholesome. Understanding what is the unwholesome, which arises from not following the precepts. They come in the form of hindrances in the mind, whether it is in meditation or outside of it. When you know the root of this unwholesomeness, you can understand how to recognize and let go of the arising of the unwholesome.

Once you begin to follow the precepts and practice right intention, right speech, right action, and right livelihood, you start to develop the right view even further. This develops and cultivates a mindset that inclines toward the wholesome. Once you cultivate and follow the precepts, and you continually do this with right intention, right action, right speech, and right livelihood, the mind is ripe for being mindful in the correct manner, having right mindfulness within the meditation and in your daily life.

Mindfulness

Once you develop and generate the wholesome by understanding and using right effort - which is to cultivate an attitude and intention of harmlessness, of loving-kindness, of the brahmavihārās, and of letting go -, you can be mindful correctly. You understand in any given moment where mind is, what the body feels, what mental states arise and pass away. Such mindfulness allows you to go deeper into the meditation, thereby entering right collectedness, which are the jhānas and the higher jhānas. It is after this, with the right mindfulness, that you realize bit by bit how mind works and how to bring it back to a wholesome state. To a state that is rooted in the ultimate right view, which is the understanding and experience of the four noble truths. This happens both in the meditation and in daily living, through this pure awareness, right mindfulness. Don't force onto it any projections of what needs or does not need to be done. In other words, in any given present moment, just be purely conscious and aware of what arises in the mind, the body, the mental states, and sensations or feelings. Once you do this, you are aware of what sensations arise, and you understand *there is a sensation arising, there is an arising of this feeling.*

It might be that your mindfulness is not yet sharp enough to see the feeling and understanding the arising of it as impersonal - therefore not worth holding on to and causing suffering through ignorance. And you get caught up in craving, clinging, being, or any other of the links of dependent origination further down. But there should still be some level of mindfulness, where you are able to recognize that this has arisen and understand that it was caused by something prior to this.

In other words, when you understand that there was a getting caught up in feeling, and then in craving, you can see that it was the taking this personal that caused the craving. Craving means taking something personal. Or attaching a sense of self to it, with desire and lust for it. It is the *I want* attitude, or *I want more of it*, or the *I don't want it* attitude. Taking the feeling personal in these ways causes the craving. You then use the third noble truth, which is the letting go.

So, first you recognize that this craving has arisen. Then you release the attention from it and let go of it. You relax the tension caused by that craving, and then understand that there was a slight misperception of what that feeling was. The feeling is impersonal and impermanent. Therefore, it is not worth holding on to, or to consider it to be something that will provide lasting happiness.

When you practice the 6R's in this way, you know what first arose in the mind. Then you know its origin, and you can let go of the cause of that arising. By letting go of it you experience a mundane nibbāna, the letting go of, and not grasping onto, whatever the causes and conditions caused it to arise in the present moment.

You do this by practicing the 6R's, or right effort. Essentially, this comes to be when you understand and follow the eightfold path. This is the way leading to the cessation of that craving, and therefore to the cessation of that suffering. The eightfold path goes hand in hand with the 6R practice, or with the practice of using right effort.

In other words, you use right intention and right mindfulness within the context of right collectedness during meditation and in day-to-day living. Mindfulness should be developed to the point where, when a feeling arises, that underlying tendency to attach a sense of self must be let go of. The underlying tendency that either wants more of it, or that averts from it, that does not want more of it, should be let go. That tendency is craving for another reality, instead of understanding the reality of the situation as it is. This needs to be let go through right effort. First, you understand what arises through right mindfulness and then you effectively apply these different steps of the path. You let go and stop grasping it. Then, the understanding of the four noble truths gets developed.

Don't cultivate and develop this mindfulness by pushing. Do not develop it in such a way that you *force* the mind to see what is going on. Instead, allow the mind to unravel, to unfold, and then see what arises. In that arising - in any given moment, whether in the meditation or in daily living -, you apply the principles of the four Noble Truths. In essence, you apply and understand; the arising itself; the origin of that arising; and the cessation of it. Then you use the 6R's/right effort, combined with right mindfulness and right intention, to let go of the cause of whatever has arisen. In that letting go and not grasping, you experience nibbāna.

As you go deeper into the higher states of meditation and mindfully stay with your mind, you will see increasingly deeper layers of the mind. These layers include the links of dependent origination.

So, you start with what has arisen, understand it, let it go, and then understand the origin of it. Then, bit by bit, the mind gets even deeper. You know how craving arose, you let go of that craving, and you understand that the cause of that craving was taking the arisen feeling personal. You then look at that feeling and if it causes you to sway from the observation of your object, you let go of that distraction and return to observing. This is practicing what is known as attention rooted in reality. In Pali this is called *yoniso manasikāra*. It is understanding reality as it is, through the source point of what has arisen. By doing so, you are also applying the awakening factor of investigation; you know that something has arisen, you let mind unravel so that it sees for itself what caused the arising. You let go of it and then get deeper, until you get to the level of formations. Generally, you will start to see these, in increasingly subtler forms, in the seventh and eighth jhāna. Then, you should use the seven enlightenment factors to stay with the balanced mind. You use the factors of investigation of principles, and mindfulness.

This way you begin to let go of ever subtler formations, until you now practice the art of letting go; almost automating letting go until whatever arises immediately is let go of. You understand how it arose, and then come to the cessation of that arising, the cessation of craving. This cessation is the third noble truth, which is *nirodha*. It's the cessation of perception and feeling. On the mundane level of day-to-day living, the third noble truth can be experienced as well. Every time you understand what has arisen, let go of it, and then let go of the origin of it, you come to deeper levels of stillness within the mind. Then, you can experience that nibbāna from having let go, from non-grasping.

The Taints

When in the eighth jhāna these subtler formations arise, do not allow your mind to get distracted and come out of the jhāna completely distracted. Just understand that it has arisen, release your attention from it and let it go. In this process of letting go, you weaken those formations. They are rooted in the taints, which then influences the causal link of ignorance. This causes the entire flow of dependent origination and ends in suffering. Don't allow the mind to get distracted by these. Instead, let go of the formations, which recondition s the mind, weaken ns the fetters and the taints, the defilements. I like to call them viruses or projections of sensual craving.

They influence the craving that arises, by taking personal the feeling. It is a feedback loop between the taint/defilement/projection of sensual craving, and the link of craving within dependent origination. And similarly, the craving for existence, or being, which is also the accumulated tendencies. Clinging solidifies into the accumulated tendencies. One takes these personal and then says that. This further strengthens the fetter of conceit, and thereby influences and strengthens those Formations. These will continue to fuel the fetter of conceit. They are rooted in the defilement and projection of the craving for being, craving for existence, for holding onto a sense of self, some form of identity.

Finally, you have ignorance, which is the ignorance of the four noble truths. Not able to apply what we just talked about; the principles of the four noble truths in whatever is arising. By not knowing them, you further feed the defilement and projection of ignorance. This solidifies and strengthens the fetter of Ignorance, which influences those particular formations. These will make you create choices that will then create and strengthen more formations, deepening that ignorance.

A released mind

When you understand how mind works and what arises in it, and you apply the four noble truths in this way, you weaken the fetters of ignorance. You break them and destroy the taint of ignorance.

When this happens, there will be formations that arise in a released mind, but when they arise, they are no longer fettered by craving, conceit, or ignorance. These three fetters are influenced and strengthened by the defilements and projections;

- sensual craving
- being, or craving for existence, holding on to a sense of identity
- the taint of ignorance.

When these projections are destroyed, the fetters - which continued to influence the formations - are also destroyed. Then, whatever formations arise, are pure. These arising formations will be influenced by the contact that arises, but it will no longer be taken to be *yourself*, no longer be taken as personal. Through wisdom this ultimate, elevated, perfected right view of having cultivated and experienced the four noble truths, replaces that link of ignorance. This influences the formations, the consciousness that is activated through those formations, the mentality-materiality through which that consciousness flows, the six sense bases, and the feeling, the experience of the six sense bases.

A released mind always understands feeling to be not me, not myself, not mine. Therefore, it doesn't even have to let go of it. It is just the pure experience of it, which makes it impossible for any of the links of craving, clinging, being, birth, aging and death to arise. Suffering is completely destroyed when the four noble truths are fully realized. The mind is now established in this right view/right view.

Daily Reflection Day 4

Right View (Samma Diṭṭhi)

There is Suffering but Life is Not Suffering

Everything that is conditioned, is bound to fall apart. Existence itself is conditioned and the elements within existence, by the nature of conditioning, will fall apart as well. Therefore, don't take it so seriously. We're all getting out of this life through the same process. What matters is how well we can accept this reality.

That does not mean life itself is suffering. If life were suffering, then why do we smile at the joys that life provides us? Why do we laugh at the happy memories? Why do we even have happy memories? Why then would we smile in the meditation?

There is suffering, but it is not what is conventionally conceptualized. Life is a series of fragmented moments in reality. What we make of it, allows us to see it in one way that binds us to a mode of craving, ignorance, and suffering. Or in another way in which we don't take things personally and we understand that anything that is acquired in this lifetime will not exist forever, even if such acquisitions seem to outlive us.

> *There is an end to everything conditioned, including our relationships, assets, and memories.*

Say you enjoy a certain food. You relish it while consuming it. The chef says they've prepared another portion of the same food for you to consume. You've had your fill, but the craving in you says, "let's eat it." So, you do. And you enjoy it, but not as much as in the beginning. You've eaten more than your fill. The chef comes back again and gives you another helping. This time you won't eat it. But it is your favorite, the chef insists. What changed now? At first, you did not pay attention to your body and the senses, and allowed craving to take over, and that gave rise to suffering. In seeing this, you had the wisdom to decline the third helping through understanding what had happened. Perhaps, with that understanding, when the chef cooks for you another day, you will know what your fill is and not crave more.

165

You can smell the flowers, you can lie around on the beach, or you can take a walk in the park, and enjoy it. How you see this enjoyment, is what matters. You are fulfilled in that moment and craving will not arise. If you identify with the senses aroused through the situation, then craving takes over and you lose sense of what is correct and effective and, in the end, there will be suffering from one consequence or another. If you enjoy something in that moment, with the understanding that this too shall pass, and that it is only this, whether good or bad, and that it is not personal but came about through a series of causes and conditions, then after having gone through it, you move on.

> *Look at every **moment** as an opportunity, as a choice.*

You can see what arises as something to be taken personal, affecting some sense of self which is not there, and that it will last and always satisfy, or be a danger, to that sense of "you." Or you can see it as having come about through choices that were conditioned by prior choices that led you to that moment, but in it there was no permanent self. And that whatever arises now will change, good or bad, and it won't be forever or be wholly satisfying on every level.

A mindset coming to alignment with right view understands life as an impersonal series of choices and situations. And in that impersonal series, you know to let go of the notion of control, or any sense of self. Doing so, wisdom will arise, and mind will know the reason why you let go – doing so helps on a deeper level in your meditation where it comes naturally to the mind to let go of hindrances, craving, and the need to push or control. Thus, you can easily stay with your object.

How Suffering Comes to Be

The root of suffering is craving. Craving is the reaction of taking personal any stimuli that are felt through contact. However, if wisdom and right mindfulness replace craving, there will be no suffering. Wisdom arises through the realization of right view, through the eradication of ignorance of the four noble truths.

This ignorance conditions your perspective, your reality, and craving is the automated response to all feeling that arises, upon which you establish the falsehood of all that occurs as *mine*.

Conceit is the fetter that corrupts the formations through the projection of *being*. This projection gives rise to the accumulation of tendencies through clinging to a false sense of self, which then turns into being, which is an amalgam of those accumulated tendencies. This is the sense *I am*.

Hence, these projections – of ignorance, being, and craving – are to be uprooted through the practice of the eightfold path. Through the momentum of underlying tendencies, which have been accumulated and conditioned over time, the projections push forth and fetter the formations that then condition the rest of the links of dependent origination.

Dependent origination

Ignorance – Not comprehending the four noble truths. Rooted within the projections. Feeds the projections and is fed by the projections – they are interdependent.

Formations – Kammic impulses that influence intentions and are in turn influenced by choices made in every present moment. Brought on through accumulated tendencies, which fuel the momentum of their rising, having first been conditioned by ignorance. They can also activate via the process of contact in any given moment.

Consciousness – *Cognition, the bare collection of information.* Established through the framework of mentality-materiality and measured by, and measures, experiences of the senses. Without these factors, cognition remains unlinked and cannot be sustained.

Mentality-Materiality – Mentality comprises of the neurological faculties for feeling, perception, intention, contact, and attention.

Materiality is the physical body, and the conceptualization of the physical world.

Six Sense Bases – The sense receptors, nerves and neurons that receive input from external and internal stimuli.

Contact – The process of stimuli interacting with the receptors.

Feeling – When the receptors, nerves and neurons are stimulated. This includes *interoception*, which is sensing the internal pleasure and pain within mind and body, *proprioception*, which is sensing movement and position of the body, and *exteroception*, which is sensing the stimuli of the five physical senses. Here, the feeling is just the bare feeling. The noting of whether any bare feeling is pleasant, painful, or neutral, is the start of the process of perception.

Craving – Taking the impersonal activity of sensory experience as personal and reacting out of a sense of self through perception and conceptualization. (*I want more of it, I can't take any more of it, I made it happen. This is my pleasure. This is my pain. This is my neutrality. This hurts me and I want it to stop. This gives me pleasure, so give me more. I wish I didn't have to experience this anymore; I wish I had this instead*)

Clinging – The process of accumulating habits, beliefs, views, and tendencies and creating the sense of self (*this is me, this is mine, this is who I am because..., this is why I am like this, I used to be like this, I'm going to be this someday, I'll never be good enough,*), sensory experiences (*I like it/don't like it because of..., that hurt me so I don't like it, that aroused me so I'm making it mine*), rituals (*I do this because it will lead me to salvation*), and views in general (*I vote so-and-so party because I believe..., I support this cause because I believe..., I never liked that person because they belong to that group, I'll never be like my...*)

Being – *Accumulated beliefs solidify a sense of self, a personality, kamma to be experienced through that person.* Bundles of kamma taken to be personal and as a personality, with a deeply rooted sense of self. The crystallizing of self into a framework of existence that their choices and kamma (or actions) have brought them into. (*I am the CEO of..., I am a Buddhist, I am a member* *of this club, I am the head of the household, I built this place with my bare hands, I am a citizen of..., I am a human. I'm all alone. I'm successful. I'm rich. I'm poor. I'm not good enough. I'm the best... in the world. I'm the worst... in the world. I'm neutral... I am...)*

Birth – *Taking your actions personal,* feeling connected to actions and situations as self. Fruition of kamma taken personally. Self is completely cooked through, becoming fully established in being. (*I love myself. I hate myself. I won. I lost. I did this. I didn't do this. I am doing this. I'm buying that phone. I got married. I got a divorce.*)

Ageing, Suffering, Death – The fruition of your actions taken personally. (*Why did this happen to me? Why does it have to end? I didn't get what I wanted. This isn't how I imagined it. Why did they leave me? Why did they have to die? When will I die? Will I be alone? Who's going to be there for me?*)

Cessation of Suffering

How you consider the feeling that arises, will determine whether craving arises. When feeling arises, perception arises. With these two, there is the consciousness of that feeling and perception, the cognizance, the bare knowing intertwined with the feeling and perception.

For example, you see a banana. The seeing of the object, the banana, is the feeling. When the photons meet the receptors in the eye, then that is contact. The knowing of this, the awareness of this, arises dependent on the contact, feeling, and the banana, and that is the cognition, consciousness. Once the banana is visible, the mind attaches the name "banana" to it. All the concepts (*"yellow" "fruit" "sweet" "healthy" "potassium"* and so on) attached around that word – this is perception.

Perception arises out of memory, through recognizing – re-cognizing – meaning you have seen a banana before, and through the formations of having seen it via cognition, you are able to name it accordingly. This perception is what conceptualizes, based on learning and memory through the cognizing tied with feeling.

If the body feels physical hunger, you may see the "banana" as a means to end that hunger and that will be the end of it. But if you preoccupy the mind with the ideas around the banana and that this yellow fruit will, does, or did satisfy *me*, the false sense of self, that is where craving arises.

This is due to inattention, or not paying attention rooted in reality. If you feel, or have a feeling, there should be a pause – remember, respond, don't react – and in that pause attention rooted in reality manifests, and you let go of the idea that the arisen feeling is self or belongs to any sense of self. The feeling came about through a series of causes and conditions and now you do not put any self to the enjoyment in that feeling but remain fulfilled.

You then go a step further and make it an exercise to see feeling with attention rooted in the three symptoms of reality, seeing that whatever arises is not going to last forever, is not going to keep you satisfied completely or infinitely, and that indeed it is all impersonal. With this seeing, you automatically let go even before craving can arise, and in this way, you are at peace, letting the feeling be, having seen with clarity.

This reconditions formations through perception that is the attention rooted in reality. You weaken the fetters of craving, conceit, and ignorance in the formations that arise. This process uses right effort to continuously let go. The more this is done, the easier it is for you to experience letting go on an automatic level in the higher jhānas, and finally at an attainment event post-cessation.

The Four Noble Truths and the 6R's

When you RECOGNIZE, you have seen that there is suffering, in the form of a hindrance and being distracted in meditation. In daily activities, you RECOGNIZE craving, clinging, and the links thereafter that have arisen. In both instances, this happens through attention rooted in reality. In meditation, you see you were distracted, because breaking a precept has weakened your attention. In daily life, you see the cause of craving, which is that you took the link of feeling to be personal. Hence, the noble truths of suffering and its cause are understood through the RECOGNIZE step.

When you RELEASE and RELAX, you let go of the cause of the suffering and in doing so, there is the cessation of suffering. In the meditation, you RELEASE your attention from the hindrance and RELAX the tension caused by it, hence the cessation of the hindrance, and craving arising from it. Likewise, in daily living when craving arises by taking something personal, you RELEASE from taking the feeling to be personal and RELAX the immediate tension that has arisen, hence the cessation of that craving.

When you SMILE (or RE-SMILE), you come back to a wholesome state of mind, and when you RETURN to your object of meditation, and REPEAT, when necessary, you are following the eightfold path to cessation. When doing these steps in the meditation, you are practicing right mindfulness and right collectedness. In daily living, when craving has been let go and you smile and return to an attitude cultivated by the brahmavihāras and following the precepts, and you continue to stay there, you are practicing right view, right intention, right speech, right action, and right livelihood. In both cases, you are practicing right effort through the whole 6R process.

Questions

"Are all aspects of the Sammādiṭṭhi Sutta Right View?"

Answer:

All aspects are *sammā diṭṭhi* – right view - because it's replacing the unwholesome with the wholesome. This is arguably the most important part of that sutta. The more you understand how to cultivate the wholesome and uproot the unwholesome, the more you're establishing right view, because you're using right intention. The more you do that, the more you are embedding mind with right view.

There are levels of right view, which is the mundane right view and the supramundane right view. The mundane right view is in relation to the precepts, keeping the precepts, knowing that our actions have consequences, that there is kamma and rebirth, and so on and so forth. When you know that, you understand that it's important to cultivate wholesome mindsets, wholesome qualities of mind, wholesome actions, and wholesome speech, because that will result in wholesome rebirth in the next moment, etcetera.

Once you start to see this, you're starting to practice right effort, right intention, right speech, right action, and right livelihood. This is all done when you have right mindfulness, when you're observing in every moment the choices that you have available to you. With the right mindfulness, you're making the choices that are rooted in right view. So, already you're taking care of most of this eightfold path, and that culminates in right collectedness, where you then take it into your meditation practice, go through the jhānas and then experience nibbāna.

It always starts with cultivating the wholesome, uprooting the unwholesome. Once you do that, you are starting to bring in choices and situations for yourself, that lead you towards the right view. Every time you make a wholesome choice, you recondition the formations for the next moment. So, you weaken the fetters in the formations that create the conceit, the ignorance, and the craving, and you strengthen the formations that help you to make more wholesome choices in future moments. The more you do this in your daily living, the more it translates to a better meditation in your sitting practice. That allows you to let go of even deeper and subtler formations, as you get higher and higher into the levels of meditation. Until you finally can destroy some of the fetters.

There is a chance you can destroy all the fetters at once, but you need a mind that is quite sharp, quite deep, and a very deep understanding of right view for that to occur. It might happen in different stages.

However, it will happen, the most important part is that you should follow the eightfold path in this way, which is always rooted in cultivating the wholesome, uprooting the unwholesome, establishing right view bit by bit. Recondition the formations through right speech, right action, and right livelihood, with right intention in mind, and use right mindfulness. And then allow all of that to come to fruition in right collectedness.

When right view is fully established, it continues to influence the formations, which are now pure; they're purified of the fetters from the projections of craving, being and ignorance. That then unlocks, so to speak, the two path factors, or the fruition of the path; the right knowledge and right liberation. You know that the projections are no longer active and will no longer be active. Through that knowledge, you have the experience of the liberation of mind, *vimutti*, of nibbāna.

"Why does Sāriputta, in this sutta, talk from the perspective of an actual birth and death of a body, versus the millions of dependent originations arising and passing away?"

Answer:

Birth can be looked at in two different ways. Death is just determination of life, the termination of the bodily processes, and the mental processes. That's the dissolution of the body, let's make sure that we're clear on that.

Birth can be seen as birth of action, which is the kamma coming into play, where you are having a sense of self that you are doing something. That's the birth of action in one regard, and that happens continuously through just one lifetime. It can happen a trillion times because of the different actions that are happening with the intention.

Then the birth of, let's say, a being. Being is basically *bhava*, which is really the accumulated tendencies. When you see the idea of a sense of self, it's all just this bundle of kamma. It's a bundle of different associations, a bundle of different ideas, concepts, and mindsets, which create the sense of self. It's all these tendencies that you take together, and that's the accumulated tendencies that creates this sense of being. But you take that all away and there is no being, there is no permanent being there. It's always changing, so when you have that sense of being, and act from that sense of being. there is the birth of action.

In the case of rebirth on the macro level, where you're looking at dependent origination from that viewpoint, there is the being that is being conceived in the womb, in the case of a human birth. In the previous life, because of the formations that arise at the point of death, in the deep layers of mind, there is craving or attachment to one of those formations. The consciousness that is carried forward through those formations then intends for rebirth. That creates the intention for rebirth. Then, those formations are carried forth by that consciousness, which spontaneously links at the point of conception, which will then create the mentality-materiality. In this case, it's the fetus that grows in the womb. And there is already a sense of being and the formations start to grow, and different formations start to come into being, based on the experience of the fetus in the womb. So, there is still craving, there is still clinging because of the sensory inputs that arise when the six sense bases develop, during the nine-month process of the conception of that being, of the making up of that being. That is 'being', that is becoming. Now that being is becoming, that's the process of becoming a *bhava*. And then, birth happens, which then creates the birth of that being into this physical world. That's one way to look at it through the process of macro level rebirth.

Meditator Experiences

On First Jhāna

The first jhāna can best be described as glee, or excitement. So, I start with Mettā to myself, 6R-ing whenever mind wanders. About ten minutes into the practice, I can start to feel a ting of electricity in the hands. A very slight tingling, barely noticeable. I start getting excited by this.

It's a sign I am on the right path, and it motivates me to continue. Very soon the tingling changes to warmth, my hands start to feel warm, like I put them into warm water, or those hot oven mitts. Then they start to become hot. Not boiling but noticeably hot.

Now I sink into the feeling. It's very pleasant. And if I want to go further, I will start to feel the tingling on the back of my feet, then go up my legs, then go into my buttocks, and if I am patient, I can kind of get my whole body glowing with this warm tingling glow. It can be very pleasant. But what it does is focus the mind on the warmth. The hands physically feel hot, I have measured them with a thermometer, and they are the same temperature as normal, so the heat and glow are totally an experiential phenomenon. What is interesting is it's the first clear example of how mind can create pleasure.

Mental proliferation starts backing off, and mind becomes still. I am only getting a thought every minute or so, and it's less tense. So, for me it's a sign, it's a steppingstone, it's a tool to help me get to the next stage. And it also gives me confidence the Buddha was right.

- Meditator from California, USA

The experience of the first jhāna is that of strong mettā, also known as loving-kindness. This radiated outward from my head in a way that was physically felt. It was strong and went out in all directions in waves. There was also a strong vibratory aspect to the meditation, like rapidly oscillating, high-energy waves. There was a strong sense of joy, almost to the point of laughter. It was very pleasant and energizing. When I opened my eyes after the meditation, I had a big smile on my face that wanted to persist.

- Meditator from Missouri, USA

The feeling of Joy arose quite strongly and lasted for around thirty minutes continuously. Watching it start to drop away, a natural feeling of Anicca (perception of impermanence) arose and mind used the 6R's, which deepened the feeling of letting go.

- Meditator from Australia

On Second Jhāna

The best way to describe it is a sense of joy at being alive, a vitality, and a feeling of wellbeing, safety, and security. If mind wanders from this sense of goodness, I 6R it, and return to the feeling of well-being in my chest. Pretty soon the warmth in my chest grows, it opens, and I feel healthy and vital and just in a good place. Rather than force my breathing, I just let go and let the machine breathe. It feels goodness is filling my chest and entire body and I'm radiating it There is still some movement of mind, but the volume is getting turned down a lot, and rather than external worldly thoughts it's more internally focused thoughts on the vital feeling. The feeling is so pleasant that it's easy to focus on it and mind wants to go there. Here the 6R's are lighter, they are still effortful but less so.

- Meditator from California, USA

Everything went still and the mind was quiet, yet the joy was a little stronger and a more natural Mettā for a spiritual friend arose and less tension noticed in the head.

- Meditator from Australia

There is still the experience of mettā, but it has "cooled off" a bit, and doesn't have the strong, vibratory presence. The experience is that the joy is still present, but that's it's slowed down, or matured into something that is more stable, has more depth, and is expansive. There is a sense of lightness with the second jhāna. It feels as if the high-energy waves from the first jhāna have morphed into something deeper, slower, with more substance to them.

- Meditator from Missouri, USA

Day 5:

The Five Aggregates

Suttas

Majjhima Nikāya 109 - Mahapunnama Sutta - The Greater discourse on the Full moon night

Translation by Bhikkhu Bodhi.

1. THUS, HAVE I HEARD. On one occasion, the Blessed One was living at Sāvatthī in the Eastern Park, in the Palace of Migara's Mother.

2. On that occasion - on the Uposatha day of the fifteenth, on the full-moon night - the Blessed One was seated in the open surrounded by the Sangha of bhikkhus.

3. Then a certain bhikkhu rose from his seat, arranged his upper robe on one shoulder, and extending his hands in reverential salutation toward the Blessed One, said to him: "Venerable sir, I would ask the Blessed One about a certain point, if the Blessed One would grant me an answer to my question." - "Sit on your own seat, bhikkhu, and ask what you like." So, the bhikkhu sat on his own seat and said to the Blessed One:

4. "Are these not, venerable sir, the five aggregates affected by clinging; that is, the material form aggregate affected by clinging, the feeling aggregate affected by clinging, the perception aggregate affected by clinging, the formations aggregate affected by clinging, and the consciousness aggregate affected by clinging?"

"These, bhikkhus, are the five aggregates affected by clinging; that is, the material form aggregate affected by clinging...and the consciousness aggregate affected by clinging."

Saying, "Good, venerable sir," the bhikkhu delighted and rejoiced in the Blessed One's words. Then he asked him a further question:

5. "But, venerable sir, in what are these five aggregates affected by clinging rooted?"

"These five aggregates affected by clinging are rooted in desire, bhikkhu."

6. "Venerable sir, is that clinging the same as these five aggregates affected by clinging, or is the clinging something apart from the five aggregates affected by clinging?"

"Bhikkhu, that clinging is neither the same as these five aggregates affected by clinging, nor is the clinging something apart from the five aggregates affected by clinging. It is the desire and lust in regard to the five aggregates affected by clinging that is the clinging there."

7. "But, venerable sir, can there be diversity in the desire and lust regarding these five aggregates affected by clinging?"

"There can be, bhikkhu," the Blessed One said. "Here, bhikkhu, someone thinks thus: *May my material form be thus in the future; may my feeling be thus in the future; may my perception be thus in the future; may my formations be thus in the future; may my consciousness be thus in the future.* Thus, there is diversity in the desire and lust regarding these five aggregates affected by clinging."

8. "But, venerable sir, in what way does the term 'aggregates' apply to the aggregates?"

"Bhikkhu, any kind of material form whatever, whether past, future, or present, internal or external, gross or subtle, inferior or superior, far or near - this is the material form aggregate. Any kind of feeling whatever...far or near - this is the feeling aggregate. Any kind of perception whatever...far or near – this is the perception aggregate. Any kind of formations whatever... far or near - this is the formations aggregate. Any kind of consciousness whatever...far or near - this is the consciousness aggregate. It is in this way, bhikkhu, that the term 'aggregate' applies to the aggregates."

9. "What is the cause and condition, venerable sir, for the manifestation of the material form aggregate? What is the cause and condition for the manifestation of the feeling aggregate... the perception aggregate...the formations aggregate...the consciousness aggregate?"

"The four great elements, bhikkhu, are the cause and condition for the manifestation of the material form aggregate. Contact is the cause and condition for the manifestation of the feeling aggregate. Contact is the cause and the condition for the manifestation of the perception aggregate. Contact is the cause and condition for the manifestation of the formations aggregate. Mentality-Materiality is the cause and condition for the manifestation of the consciousness aggregate."

10. "Venerable sir, how does personality view come to be?"

"Here, bhikkhu, an untaught ordinary person, who has no regard for noble ones and is unskilled and undisciplined in their Dhamma, who has no regard for true men and is unskilled and undisciplined in their Dhamma, regards material form as self, or self as possessed of material form, or material form as in self, or self as in material form. He regards feeling as self...perception as self...formations as self...consciousness as self, or self as possessed of consciousness, or consciousness as in self, or self as in consciousness. That is how personality view comes to be."

11. "But, venerable sir, how does personality view not come to be?"

"Here, bhikkhu, a well-taught noble disciple, who has regard for noble ones and is skilled and disciplined in their Dhamma, who has regard for true men and is skilled and disciplined in their Dhamma, does not regard material form as self, or self as possessed of material form, or material form as in self, or self as in material form. He does not regard feeling as self...perception as self...formations as self...consciousness as self, or self as possessed of consciousness, or consciousness as in self, or self as in consciousness. That is how personality view does not come to be."

12. "What, venerable sir, is the gratification, what is the danger, and what is the escape in the case of material form? What is the gratification, what is the danger, and what is the escape in the case of feeling...in the case of perception...in the case of formations...in the case of consciousness?"

"The pleasure and joy, bhikkhu, that arise in dependence on material form - this is the gratification in the case of material form. Material form is impermanent, suffering, and subject to change - this is the danger in the case of material form. The removal of desire and lust, the abandonment of desire and lust for material form - this is the escape in the case of material form. The pleasure and joy that arise in dependence on feeling...in dependence on perception...in dependence on formations...in dependence on consciousness - this is the gratification in the case of consciousness. Consciousness is impermanent, suffering, and subject to change - this is the danger in the case of consciousness. The removal of. desire and lust, the abandonment of desire and lust for consciousness - this is the escape in the case of consciousness."

13. "Venerable sir, how does one know, how does one see, so that in regard to this body with its consciousness and all external signs, there is no I-making, mine-making, and underlying tendency to conceit?"

"Bhikkhu, any kind of material form whatever, whether past or present, internal or external, gross or subtle, inferior or superior, far or near - one sees all material form as it actually is with proper wisdom thus: *This is not mine, this I am not, this is not my self.* Any kind of feeling whatever... Any kind of perception whatever...Any kind of formations whatever...Any kind of consciousness whatever...one sees all consciousness as it actually is with proper wisdom thus: *This is not mine, this I am not, this is not my self.* It is when one knows and sees thus that in regard to this body with its consciousness and all external signs there is no I-making, mine-making, or underlying tendency to conceit."

14. Then, in the mind of a certain bhikkhu this thought arose: *So, it seems, material form is not self, feeling is not self, perception is not self, formations are not self, consciousness is not self. What self, then, will actions done by the not-self affect?*

Then the Blessed One, knowing in his mind the thought in the mind of that bhikkhu, addressed the bhikkhus thus: "It is possible, bhikkhus, that some misguided man here, obtuse and ignorant, with his mind dominated by craving, might think that he can outstrip the Teacher's Dispensation thus: "So, it seems, material form is not self...consciousness is not self. What self, then, will actions done by the not-self affect?" Now, bhikkhus, you have been trained by me through interrogation on various occasions in regard to various things.

15. Bhikkhus, what do you think? Is material form permanent or impermanent?" - "Impermanent, venerable sir." - "Is what is impermanent suffering or happiness?" - "Suffering, venerable sir." - "Is what is

184

impermanent, suffering, and subject to change fit to be regarded thus: *This is mine, this I am, this is my self?*" - "No, venerable sir."

"Bhikkhus, what do you think: Is feeling...perception...formations... consciousness permanent or impermanent?" - "Impermanent, venerable sir." - "Is what is impermanent suffering or happiness?" - "Suffering, venerable sir." - "Is what is impermanent, suffering, and subject to change fit to be regarded thus: *This is mine, this I am, this is my self?*" - "No, venerable sir."

16. "Therefore, bhikkhus, any kind of material form whatever, whether past, future, or present...all material form should be seen as it actually is with proper wisdom thus: *This is not mine, this I am not, this is not my self.* Any kind of feeling whatever... Any kind of perception whatever...Any kind of formations whatever...Any kind of consciousness whatever...all consciousness should be seen as it actually is with proper wisdom thus: *This is not mine, this I am not, this is not my self.*

17. Seeing thus, a well-taught noble disciple becomes disenchanted with material form, disenchanted with feeling, disenchanted with perception, disenchanted with formations, disenchanted with consciousness.

18. Being disenchanted, he becomes dispassionate. Through dispassion [his mind] is liberated. When it is liberated there comes the knowledge: *It is liberated.* He understands: *Birth is destroyed, the holy life has been lived, what had to be done has been done, there is no more coming to any state of being.*"

That is what the Blessed One said. The bhikkhus were satisfied and delighted in the Blessed One's words. Now while this discourse was being spoken, through not clinging the minds of sixty bhikkhus were liberated from the taints.

Dhamma Talk-MN 109

As you deepen your practice both in meditation and in daily life, you will see with wisdom that the links of dependent origination are the flow that affect the five aggregates. There is this link between the five aggregates and dependent origination. You can liken dependent origination to a river and the five aggregates to the riverbed. As it flows, if it has craving, clinging, conceit rooted in any of the links, starting from formations, these fetters tie into the five aggregates. So, the five aggregates are likened to be the stationary aspect of how we experience things, though they change in every moment. The links of dependent origination also continuously flow. This incessant flow, this continual change and cycle of the links of dependent origination, arising and passing away, influences the five aggregates. Looking at each of the five aggregates with wisdom, you will see that to consider any of them - starting with form – as a self, is looking through delusion.

Five aggregates

Form

The form that the Buddha talks about, is the material form of the four great elements. In modern and scientific terminology, they are the four states of matter. These constantly influence the body; the body changes continuously. If it were not so, when you were born, you would not grow, the bones wouldn't fuse, the organs wouldn't grow and change, the cells in the body wouldn't change, and so on and so forth.

As the Buddha says: if something is impermanent, should you consider it to create happiness or suffering? In other words, if something is impermanent, should we consider it to be something that can provide us with long-lasting happiness? If you just watch and observe, you will see that there is no point in holding on to something that is impermanent. It arises and passes away in a matter of moments, likewise with feeling, our sensations, which arise and pass away, dependent upon causes. And since they arise and pass away, dependent on so many different causes and conditions in every given moment, you cannot consider feelings, these sensory experiences, to be permanent. Therefore, they are not worth holding on to.

Formations

This formation aggregate is the receptacle, if you will, of the flow of formations in every given moment. This aggregate is a repository of formations, which is continually changing. Likewise for the aggregate of consciousness, the aggregate of perception, of feeling, and of course of the body, or material form.

Feeling and Perception

When you look at the perceptions that arise, these are conditioned by contact, as the Buddha says. When feeling arises, it is *conjoined* with perception and cognition, consciousness.

Perceptions are rooted in memory and learning. When you saw the color blue for the first time, and you didn't yet know what color it was, you learned through your elders, parents, teachers, or through society in general, that it was 'blue'. The concept of 'blue' then is ingrained in the memory. Whenever you see this color, there is the recognition aspect of the mind, rooted in that memory, and it arises through formations. So, these formations too arise from contact. When you have contact, formations arise that are based on that contact. They then activate a certain consciousness, which then flows through mentality-materiality. Through that mentality-materiality, it is experienced and reckoned through the sensory experiences. Then, the feeling that arises is conjoined with the perception. So, there is an interdependence, an interlinking, an interconnection between feeling, perception, and consciousness.

Consciousness

The Pali word for consciousness is *viññaṇa*. It means the consciousness that discerns, the consciousness that discriminates. It discriminates the different sensory experiences that you have. Therefore, this consciousness that arises is always tied, through mentality and materiality, to the sensory experiences that arise.

There are twelve types of consciousness:

There are the consciousnesses that are tied to the eyes, the ears, the nose, the tongue, the body, and the mind. These are tied to the *internal* six sense bases.

There are also the consciousnesses that are tied to the visual forms, the auditory experiences, the olfactory experiences through the nose, the experience of taste in the tongue, the experience of touch through the skin, and the experience of thought and feeling through the mind. These are tied to the *external* six senses, the experiences. The consciousnesses that arise, are dependent upon these sensory experiences. These experiences we already understand to be impermanent because they arise and pass away, dependent on other causes and conditions, particularly contact. Therefore, we cannot consider such consciousness to be permanent. We also cannot consider them undivided, which is to say an independent, undivided, unchanging consciousness that is eternal.

Every second, up to two million consciousnesses arise and pass away. You cannot consider long-lasting happiness within them. Likewise with formations, perception, feeling, material form and the body. Therefore, you cannot consider any sense of self that can arise from these five aggregates. Or that any of the five aggregates that arise from a sense of self can be permanent, satisfying, and unchanging. There is no permanent self in any of these, including the links of dependent origination.

You will understand the links of dependent origination with increasingly more wisdom and insight. And finally, after ignorance is destroyed, you will realize that the formations flow through, which activate consciousnesses, which then are rooted in this mentality-materiality, making up the five aggregates.

In other words, the formations are a process, which are received through the aggregate of formations. There is the faculty of the *ability* for the Formations to arise, and there is a process of them arising. There is, within mentality-materiality, the faculty for consciousness to be rooted into, and then experienced through the six sense bases, which is also rooted within the mentality-materiality. Then, there is the process of feeling and perception which is rooted within the faculties of feeling and perception, within mentality. Finally, there is the process of contact, which is rooted in the mentality, in the faculty of contact.

Mentality-Materiality

To simplify, within the mentality part of the link of materiality-mentality, you have these five faculties:

feeling
perception
contact
intention
attention

The process of formations gets rooted, through consciousness, into intention.

The process of feeling and perception gets rooted through the faculties of feeling and perception, which also include the six sense bases themselves.

Then there is the material form, which makes up the materiality of mentality-materiality.

When an experience arises, for example seeing the color blue, there are mental formations that are connected to the association of what that color is. This provides the consciousness to arise, which gets rooted through the mentality-materiality. That is, through the faculties of mentality, and through the form that is rooted in materiality. This is then experienced at the process of contact, through the six sense bases, particularly through the eyes. When that arises, the process of feeling gets activated through the faculty of feeling, within the mentality part of mentality-materiality. This gives rise to perception. Perception is the recognition that this is 'blue'. It arises through the faculty of perception that is rooted in mentality.

This all occurs within less than a moment. It is the firing of the neurons and the synapses in which the formations arise. Then, within microseconds, there is the recognition that this is 'blue'.

There are much more complex and complicated aspects of reality. For example, when watching a movie, there are moving pixels, colors, and images, but you are also listening to auditory experiences, and perhaps even feeling on the skin - if you pay attention to the air-conditioned room, or whatever it might be. In any given moment, a myriad of consciousnesses, feelings and perceptions arise.

What arises thereafter is based on right mindfulness. If, with mindfulness, you understand that whatever arises – past, present, or future; internal or external; subtle or gross - is not me, not mine, not myself, you will not personalize the experience that arises and is felt. Therefore, you will not crave more of it, or feel uncomfortable and try to detract from it through aversion.

If you see this with wisdom and mindfulness, craving will not arise. Therefore, the clinging that is attributed to the five aggregates affected by clinging - that desire and lust and even aversion that arises from the experience of the five aggregates - will be let go of, abandoned and will be seen through with wisdom. The more you do this, the more you condition the mind in daily practice, in daily life.

Within the meditation, these five aggregates are present. But as the practice deepens and you enter the higher jhānas, the experience of these aggregates becomes increasingly subtle, until at the point between nothingness and neither-perception-nor-non-perception, they are not felt and experienced. Though they are present, they are not tended to with mind's attention.

The base of Nothingness

In the sixth jhāna of infinite consciousness, you will see the different consciousness experiences. These are tied to a particular sense, or maybe even multiple senses. Then you begin to look at the gaps in between each arising and passing away. You deepen your practice to the point that you only tend toward that gap. As that gap widens, you sink into that nothingness and there is the perception of nothingness, the perception of being in the seventh jhāna of nothingness. There is also the contact of having a perception of 'no-thingness', the feeling of being in nothingness, and the consciousness that arises from seeing that nothingness. However, since you are so deeply rooted in the higher jhānas, while being there with right collectedness, there is little contact in the way of the physical form. Now, the experiences of the external reality - in relation to the physical senses and form - are no longer, or very rarely, perceivable. Within the experience of nothingness, you have the internal experiences of the four mental aggregates, discounting the material form.

The base of Neither-perception-nor-non-perception

How do you enter neither-perception-nor-non-perception? Your mind starts to quiet down, just merely observing the radiating of equanimity, with the small intention that sends it out. At a certain point, the mind becomes so quiet that you take this mind as the object.

Here is what you should understand in taking the tranquil mind as an object; do not allow the projection of a sense of self in that mind. In other words, see that mind as another effect of a series of causes and conditions, and therefore don't take that as 'self', just merely observe it. In allowing the mind to be a not-self aspect, you abandon any kind of projection that would create subtle craving, conceit, and ignorance, related to observing that mind.

Disenchantment and Dispassion

Once this happens, a disenchantment and dispassion arise, in which concepts that might arise, no longer interest that mind. The mind automatically abandons and lets go through automatically 6R'ing. Mind has become so deep at that point, that the *intention* of just the 6R's automates it. You start to disregard and become disenchanted with any perception and formation that might arise. There is a shift that can be felt as a sinking, or looking away, from the mind that is tranquil. The luminous, radiant, bright, tranquil mind that you have taken as an object, but as an impersonal object.

Once disenchantment arises from that, you enter neither-perception-nor-non-perception. At this point there might arise very subtle formations and perceptions. There might be disconnected thoughts. Allow the mind to continually let go of them and remember - when required - to balance the enlightenment factors. There comes a point where there is such stillness, that no formations, or very, very, very subtle formations arise, few and far in between their arising and passing away. Observing this stillness, you just merely intend relaxing that, letting go of that, without paying attention to it. You just stay with that stillness.

Signless Collectedness

At a certain point, disregarding whatever might arise in such a still mind, you come to, what some of the suttas describe as *signless collectedness*. Here, you disregard all signs that arise, because you become disenchanted with, and dispassionate for them. This happens because you have understood that everything that arises and passes away is impermanent, and therefore not worth holding on to. You disregard them and no longer project any sense of self toward any kind of formation that arises.

In the stillness, disregarding all signs, there is that state of signless collectedness, which is the border line between the eighth jhāna of neither-perception-nor-non-perception and the total cessation of perception and feeling. When you see that even the stillness should be taken as not self, and you disregard even this stillness and any concepts of nibbāna that might arise, or any concepts of stillness that might arise, and let go of even that, you have let go of even the most subtle levels of formation, perception, feeling and consciousness. Then, you enter the cessation of perception, feeling and consciousness. When you emerge from it, you experience nibbāna.

In almost every sutta, in some way or another, there is an emphasis to let go and of not grasping. Not even grasping at that border line of signless collectedness. You allow the mind to even let go of that, and you understand that even this is fabricated. Even this is made up of formations. Therefore, in letting go you decondition the mind of any concepts, you 'un-condition' it. From this un-conditioning, un-forming, un-birthing, un-creating of it, you let go completely. In that process, you abandon all grasping and enter nibbāna.

Daily Reflection Day 5

The Five aggregates and Dependent origination

The five aggregates are interconnected with the links of dependent origination.

> *The first six links after ignorance –formations, consciousness, mentality-materiality, the six sense bases, contact, and feeling – encompass the five aggregates.*

While the flow of dependent origination is like a river, the five aggregates are like the riverbed. The river flows within the bounds of the riverbed and its banks. The riverbed is never the same as the river flows. Moss, dirt, pebbles, fish, and rocks traverse it through the flow of the river and can touch, or get left behind, on the riverbed.

In the same way, through the flow of dependent origination, depending on whether there is craving, conceit, and ignorance, the five aggregates, as vessels for such a flow, can become contaminated with those fetters.

However, once new water, that of right knowledge, and the force of this water, right effort, flows down, the elements that were on the riverbed wash away, and the riverbed, as well as the river itself, become pristine.

Faculties and Processes

There are faculties and there are processes. The faculties for feeling, perception, intention, contact, and attention are the factors of mentality, while form comprises materiality. These together make up the fourth link of mentality-materiality in dependent origination.

Then there are processes, the activities, of contact in the fifth link, feeling in the sixth link, and perception, which is tied to that process of feeling. Formations are processes that condition the faculty for intention within mentality-materiality, and through that faculty are brought to fruition, through thought, speech, or action. Consciousness is a process that can only be detected when it mingles with mentality-materiality, and felt through the processes of contact, feeling, and perception, and through the six sense bases.

Form

Form is the materiality within mentality-materiality, or what may be considered as the mind-body complex. Form consists of, and contains, the faculties related to feeling, perception, intention, contact, and attention, and that includes the six sense bases. In other words, mentality is contained within materiality. At the same time, mentality also affects materiality, based on how feeling and perceptions through contact and attention determine your intentions, and how those intentions may cause you to act.

For example, you may see (or feel/perceive/cognize) that the body, which is form, is becoming unhealthy, and based on this, you decide, intend, to make changes. You act on those changes and the body, through the actions you intend, is transformed. In more minute ways, the body continues to be in flux, whether a sickness enters it and thus the body is different from what it was before the sickness, or when cells shed to give way to new cells that perform the same work, in which case the body is now comprised of new composites, causes and conditions, or any other internal or external contact and change that affects it.

The form aggregate continues to change in every microsecond, dependent upon causes and conditions, and so mentality and materiality, and the processes it affects, are both interdependent and interpenetrative, leading each other through change. The proof of such change is on a macro level – in which your body matures from infancy to puberty to adulthood to old age – as well as on a micro level, in the way the body's cells shed and experience autophagy, and the way your internal systems are affected by one another, as well as external factors. In this continually changing and transformative environment, you cannot attach a sense of self to pertain to any aspect of the form aggregate, both on the macro level and the micro level. It functions purely on various factors that arise and pass away, dependent upon causes and conditions.

Feeling

Feeling includes sensory experiences tied to the six sense bases, the receptors, neurons, and nerves that allow the reception of the outside world. They also include any feeling within the body, and your awareness of movement, conditioned by intention. These experiences are what influence and condition the faculty for feeling within mentality.

At the same time, these experiences are dependent upon the faculty for feeling, which includes the six sense bases. Physical feeling arises and ceases at lightning pace, at a rate of up to 11 million bits per second by some contemporary estimates, through photons, auditory waves, odor molecules, flavor molecules, and tangibles. Although only a miniscule amount of that information is registered in your normal, waking state, according to some research, this process is experienced at the most microscopic level in the dimension of infinite consciousness. How each consciousness is registered at this level, is determined by which formations tied to a particular sense base are stronger, both in momentum and quantity.

Every bit of sensory data received, is one iota of sensory experience, sensory cognition, and sensory perception, which arise and cease in every successive microsecond. This arising and ceasing within the feeling faculty, continually changes its structure and ability at a minute level. Over time the effects of such changes may become noticeable.

The body and its various facets, including the sense faculties, begin to wane as the years go on – another example of impermanence. For example, the eyes grow weary, there isn't much sharpness in the ears, or your body itself weakens. Perhaps, the mind itself slows down through diminished ability to decipher at a normalized pace. In this way, the processes of the various sorts of feeling themselves, change in quality and reception through the ever-changing faculty for feeling. At the same time, enough rest, healthy nutrition, and other activities may sharpen the faculties, as well as the reception of feeling.

Perhaps external damage may cause them to be impaired. You may have been born into this lifetime with one set of sensory receptors that is compromised in its ability to function. Besides the senses, even while at rest, there is internal activity of the organs that continues to change the way you feel – this includes the heart rate, blood pressure, body temperature, digestion, nerve pain, and so on.

Whatever may arise, you can see with reflection that the feeling aggregate, which contains all forms of feeling that includes sensory experiences and other feeling within and throughout the body, as well as the faculty for feeling within mentality, is susceptible to change from your choices and intentions, as well as from external factors that are also dependent on and made up of composites, causes and conditions.

Perception

The process of perception is rooted in learning and memory, which are components of the faculty for perception. When you first become conscious of an object – whether it is a thing, person, place, name, concept, idea, belief, or any sort of information – there is the bare cognition (consciousness) of it. This is tied to that object, when there is contact with mentality-materiality through the six sense bases – that is the feeling process.

> *When you learn what that object is, it is now new information that becomes stored in your memory, through formations. These formations then condition your mind, based on that new piece of information.*

When you then see (cognize through consciousness, or cognition), the formations activate the cognition. This turns into recognition (recollection or remembering) or re-cognition, which is the process of perception.

Such perception can then, through the process of intention, which is rooted in the faculty for intention, take the feeling that arose as personal, pleasurable, or painful to a sense of self, pertaining to or affecting a self, or arising from a self, or anything around the sense of self. This perception then gives rise to mental proliferation, in which you obsess over and in turn recondition the formations that will cause your next choice or process of intention - that is rooted in the faculty for intention in mentality-materiality - to be the dominant, automatic response to stimuli.

However, through attention rooted in reality, which is wise perception, through learning and remembering the concepts related to the dhamma, you then recondition the formations so that your intentions and choices in the next moment start to experience with wisdom that the feeling that arose is not self, not possessing a self, or not felt by a self, or pleasurable or painful to a sense of self.

The more you perceive through continuous attention rooted in reality, through right mindfulness, via the faculties for perception, intention and attention, the more the formations become reconditioned. Those formations, fettered by craving, conceit and ignorance, weaken, since there is no longer any attention via contact to provide them nutriment. In this way, during an attainment event, during the process of contact, when there is complete letting go, these fetters break apart and fade away, never to return to condition your mind into saṃsāra.

When this change occurs through the process of perception, it also changes the faculty for perception.

> *Memory is provided new neural pathways that replace the old ones and the kammic impulses (formations) that give rise to the old ones, no longer function, or barely function, depending on the attainment level and strength of those impulses.*

This is the effect of the work done through right effort, right mindfulness, right collectedness, and attention rooted in reality.

That is not to say you forget what a banana is, for example. Rather, you see the banana for what it is – an impersonal object, which means there is no sense of self to relate it to, which would otherwise make you crave for it. Reflect on this, regarding your more emotional memories. In one fully released, such memories continue to exist, but there is no longer an emotional resonance with taking any of it personal.

Even after this new attainment arises, the perception aggregate – that are the perception processes and faculty – is continues to be subject to change through new information being collected, but still seen with wisdom, as you encounter new situations, places, people, and objects. That wisdom doesn't take any process of or around that contact to be self or pertaining to any sense of self. This is rooted in right view.

Formations

The formations aggregate consists of formations as a process, and intention, as both a process and a faculty within the subset of mentality. Formations, as a process, are kammic impulses that activate through the process of contact, and through the media of neurons and synapses and the signals that traverse through them.

These formations condition the cognition, which will then take root in an intention faculty that is either corrupted by the fetters of craving, conceit, and ignorance within the formations conditioning it, or one that is pure and void of any sense of self, craving or delusion. The conditioning of such an intention occurs in every given present moment, where you act with attention rooted in reality, through right effort of the 6R's and right mindfulness, and thus, bit-by-bit, it eats away at the fetters through such right intentions.

> *How you perceive the feeling determines the next set of formations that will arise, and these formations will then condition your process and faculty for intention.*

The cycle repeats and with each repetition, there is transformation of the faculty for intention, which then strengthens the process of choice in the next given moment to lean toward one certain way more than the other. Formations therefore are the carriers of kamma, both their effects and their causes. The breaking of this pattern is through the utilization of the eightfold path.

From a neurological perspective, every time a formation arises, activated by the process of contact, feeling, and perception, a synapse is created or fires, to accommodate that formation. In the active sense, formations are the signals that traverse through the synapses that then condition and activate certain types of consciousness during the process of an intention, feeling, and the reaction or response to such a feeling. While in the passive sense, formations are the effects of choices and intentions, and thus are the synapses themselves.

If each formation was a synapse or a signal passing through neurons and synapses, then there are trillions, even hundreds of trillions, of formations that have come to be and cease, as you mature in a lifetime. This is not to say that these trillions of formations remain as they are or continue to grow or decrease indiscriminately. Rather, they are pruned, depending on the amount of energy provided via your choices and activities. The less you react with craving, the less those formations in relation to those reactions, will become active, and will fade away without remainder. While the more you respond with insight, the more the formations in relation to those responses will strengthen.

Each formation has the potential of arising and ceasing at any given second, that then conditions millions of iotas of consciousness based on the type of contact, feeling, and perception that may arise. In either the active or passive case, there can be trillions of occurrences of arising and ceasing, depending on the levels of contact, feeling, perception, and intention, which bring formations to action in any given timeframe.

Where then in any of those occurrences is there the sense of self?

> *If a self were tied to each occurrence, there would be hundreds of trillions of selves within one lifetime.*

Moreover, the process and faculty for intention both undergo change, every time formations arise, and are given to rise, via contact, feeling, and perception. It would be unwise to tie the concept of a permanent, unchanging, singular self to the process or faculty for intention. There cannot be in that case a permanent, unchanging, singular self that is equated or tied to the formations aggregate.

If you understand that formations and the process and faculty for intention are all part of an impersonal process that continually arises and ceases at the level of microseconds, and changes based on the inputs through contact, feeling and perception, and your intentions as a reaction or response to those inputs, you can see that no part of this can pertain to an independent, permanent, singular sense of self. Dropping this notion, clarity sharpens. With such sharp clarity, you will penetrate the dhamma, and insight and release are experienced.

Consciousness

Consciousness is purely cognition.

> For the process of consciousness to be measured, it must be tied to mentality-materiality.

If the faculties for feeling, perception, intention, contact, and attention within the form rooted in materiality, are not present, consciousness is not experienced, let alone at the level of the processes of those faculties. At the same time, it is through consciousness that we experience mentality-materiality. In this, there is interdependence between consciousness and mentality-materiality.

Formations condition consciousness. Whatever formations arise, whether conditioned by ignorance - in which case they are fettered by craving - or established from right view, in both circumstances they come to be through the process of contact. When the formations arise, they activate the consciousness, or type of cognition, through which a certain intention drives it forward to be experienced through one of the six sense bases.

Using some contemporary estimates that if there are 11 million bits of data per second arising through the physical sensory input and feeling, then each bit of data is a quantum of consciousness or cognition. In other words, consciousness - that is established and tied up with the experience of the senses, or through any form of contact internally via pain or pleasure -arises and ceases, connected to that experience of feeling, perception, intention, contact, or attention. This indicates that consciousness cannot be singular, permanent, and thus taken to be a continuous sense of self. At the snap of a finger, using the figures of current research, there are up to 1,650,000 occurrences of arisings and cessations of physical sensory consciousness. Where is there a sense of self in any of those individual occurrences of consciousness arising and ceasing, of which hundreds of millions have ceased by the time you finish reading this question?

Consciousness therefore continues to arise and cease, dependent on the experience. As experiences are ever changing, so is consciousness. Even the notion of a consciousness from which everything emerges and that is experienced outside of the scope of the five aggregates or the three symptoms of reality, cannot be sustained without a mental framework. Anything experienced is not only subjective, but it is also always changing. To say there is a substratum of eternal consciousness would indicate that it is a state of existence, or an experience, even if it allows the truth of the impersonal nature of that same consciousness. And how is it experienced? All experience falls within the subjective bounds of mentality-materiality. Therefore, even such an experience of "infinite, eternal, unending, all-encompassing consciousness" would fall within these bounds. And since it is not always present but arises only when attention is put on such an ideated consciousness, then such a consciousness is temporary, subject to change, and dependent on causes and conditions.

Impersonal Kamma

If none of these aggregates arise from/are/produce/pertain to any form of a permanent, singular self, then what is the self through which kamma is produced, felt, and experienced? This is a question that is rooted in ignorance. Kamma itself arises as an impersonal process through formations.

> *Kamma can only be experienced through the modalities of mentality-materiality, and the six sense bases – kamma is dependent on them for it to be experienced in the same way consciousness is – and since it is dependent, it arises and ceases in the same way as the links within dependent origination would, making it impersonal, impermanent, and therefore not worth holding on to, whether it is good, bad or neutral kamma.*

Kamma terminates at the point of the process of contact and feeling. How you perceive that kamma, determines whether that reaction to such kamma will take it as personal - and thus cause craving in the form of identification with it, delighting in it or averting from it - or whether you let go with wisdom rooted in the eightfold path.

In the first case, where you react with taking that kamma personally, so, taking the effects of a choice previously acted upon in the past to be personal and belonging to a self, this causes identification with it. This then leads to the rest of the links of dependent origination, in which suffering is experienced.

However, when kamma is felt at the process of feeling and is perceived as impermanent, unsatisfactory, and therefore not self or pertaining to a sense of self, you immediately let go. This letting go is utilizing the eightfold path through the process of the 6R's. When you let go, that kamma is experienced but does not produce suffering or give rise to a sense of self that experiences that suffering, thus creating new kamma. In doing this, formations continue to be reconditioned until, whatever remnants of previous choices are experienced, are let go a final time, never to be experienced again. This is called the cessation of kamma.

Questions

Consciousness and mentality-materiality

"In dependent origination, consciousness conditions mentality-materiality and vice versa. How do I understand this?"

Answer:

Consciousness can only be reckoned, measured, through the experience of the six sense bases. There is the consciousness that arises from the contact. You have the sensory consciousness of the eye, you have the consciousness of the visual object – that is in the external reality, so to speak – and then you have the consciousness of the seeing itself. So, in each of the six sense bases there is a triad of consciousness, you could say that there are altogether eighteen different types of consciousnesses, depending upon where you put your attention to.

When the suttas talk about that – and Sāriputta talks about that – he says that it's sort of an interlinking between consciousness and mentality-materiality. You cannot really experience the eye without consciousness, for example, but at the same time you are conscious of something through the eye.

On a broader scale, on a macrolevel, through the process of rebirth, it's consciousness that then gets linked with a certain mentality-materiality. It gets linked at conception with the fetus or whatever it might be; mentality or mentality-materiality. As the experience of that mentality-materiality starts to arise, there is a consciousness which links through it and experiences that feeling. There is a consciousness before mentality-materiality, and there is a consciousness that arises after it links with that mentality-materiality. However, it's the same consciousness in the flow of that consciousness. And when I say that, in the mentality-materiality, when you have the experience of the eye, that same consciousness arises, or is conditioned by formations. Formations in this regard, unless you become an arahant, are conditioned by ignorance. But how does the formation arise? It arises through contact, through feeling, and perception. Primarily through contact and feeling when you have contact with the outside world. Let's say you have the visual sensation, you have the visual object; upon having that contact, the formations related to seeing that arise, then activate the consciousness and that consciousness links with the six sense bases. Particularly with the eye, and that same consciousness experiences the triad of the eye consciousness, the visual object consciousness, and the feeling or the sensation of seeing consciousness.

It always begins with formations, and you have to see that it happens so fast. At the level of the base of infinite consciousness, you experience about up to two million per second of consciousnesses arising and passing away. The actual links of dependent origination are several, several times faster. As soon as you make contact with light, as soon as the photons hit the receptors, you have already activated formations, which activate consciousness and through attention you experience, whether it's the eye, whether it's the photons or whether it's the seeing of whatever is being shown. So, it's one and the same thing; they are interdependent.

Sāriputta talks about ignorance and the defilements, or the taints. He says those two are interdependent; ignorance is conditioned and caused by the taints, but at the same time the taints arise because of ignorance. There is always an interdependency.

The formations arise, based on contact. This means that the flow of dependent origination, while on a broader scale might seem linear, is actually cyclical. But within that cycle of DO are smaller cycles, from contact to formations and so on. And within that is embedded the cycle of the five aggregates, which are then embedded within the mentality-materiality, so it's circles within circles within circles; it's a spiral thing.

"Can you explain some more about vedanā/feeling?"

Answer:

When I talk about sensory experiences, these are the five physical senses, and the mind.

But there are also sensations in relation to contact, internal and external contact of the body. That can also relate to the mind, particularly in the five aggregates.

In either case, the sensory experiences are still part of the mental faculties, because all of this ultimately is experienced through the process of mind.

Meditator Experiences

Third Jhāna

There is a lot of goodness flowing. Mind is getting quieter. But all this radiating Mettā is actually hard work, and I know there is more to relax into. I simply just let go of any effort and allow the glow of vitality to seep into my entire body. There is a feeling of the warmth seeping out of my chest into my arms and legs and this delicious feeling of contentment.

Not doing anything, not trying to do anything, not even trying to relax. The best way I can describe it is the body is making a sigh as it lets go of all tension and truly relaxes. At this point moving, or any desire to change anything is such a chore, I am just so content. Mind is stiller, and breathing is getting slower and deeper and more effortless. Breath is much finer. One just feels like one could not be more satisfied. Totally content and tranquil.

- Meditator from California, USA

A feeling of happiness arose and the body feeling somewhat more relaxed, noticing some thoughts as distractions and letting go if a noise was noticed not drawn into it.

- Meditator from Australia

Continuing to use mettā as the object of meditation, the feeling is that of a continuation of cooling and calming. Similar to the second, the third jhāna feels as if things are continuing to cool down, to a point where you gain depth, clarity, and expansiveness. Gone are the strong vibrations felt in the first jhāna. There is the feeling of being in a calm, cool, lake, but the lake does not run deep. Verbal formations can arise, but the mind is tranquil enough at this point that it feels like there is now a "Teflon coating" on the mind and as mental formations arise, they simply don't have anything to stick to. Mind becomes quieter at this stage, and there is a deep sense of contentment. There is the beginning of a feeling of vastness.

- Meditator from Missouri, USA

Fourth Jhāna

Mind is still, thoughts are coming up, but they are wispy and not really moving mind. Now in the background for sure. The energy of the third jhāna is passing, and my body is starting to feel hollow, and transparent even. The energy is seeping out and strangely this feels even better.

If a thought arises, it just flows through mind and doesn't attach. Mind is hollow, frictionless, like a glass tube, the thoughts are not that interesting. Breathing at this stage starts to become very light, it's almost like I am not breathing at all, or if I am I can't feel it. So, there is this feeling of hollowness, almost emptiness. Like a glass tube, with light flowing through it. There is not a super pleasant feeling, just a feeling that things are balanced and as they should be. Everything is as it should be.

- Meditator from California, USA

The feeling of Mettā was moving from the chest area and I can't not exactly feel it moving through my neck, rather it is feeling of fulness and a tingling sensation in my head. It just appears up there with a feeling of happiness. The body felt like it disappeared.

- Meditator from Australia

Here the last of feelings of motion or vibration are brought to an almost standstill. The sense of being in a cool deep lake in the third jhāna gives way to an expansiveness that is soft and vast. It initially felt like an energy field of very soft material. Mental activity in the background has fallen away, and there is a sense of expansiveness that just keeps going out from my head in all directions. It is a very subtle sensation. The lower half of my body "disappeared" as the sense of touch or tactile feedback went away. The upper half of my body seemed to be dialed down to about 50% of its normal sensory input. There is sense of clarity that arises here not present in the other jhānas.

- Meditator from Missouri, USA

Day 6:

Consciousness and Rebirth

Suttas

Majjhima Nikāya 106 The Way to the Imperturbable
Translation by bhikkhu Bodhi.

1. THUS HAVE I HEARD. On one occasion the Blessed One was living in the Kuru country at a town of the Kurus named Kammasadhamma. There the Blessed One addressed the bhikkhus thus: "Bhikkhus." - "Venerable sir," they replied. The Blessed One said this:

2. "Bhikkhus, sensual pleasures are impermanent, hollow, false, deceptive; they are illusory, the prattle of fools. Sensual pleasures here and now and sensual pleasures in lives to come, sensual perceptions here and now and sensual perceptions in lives to come - both alike are Mara's realm, Mara's domain, Mara's bait, Mara's hunting ground. On account of them, these evil unwholesome mental states such as covetousness, ill will, and presumption arise, and they constitute an obstruction to a noble disciple in training here.

(THE IMPERTURBABLE)

3. Therein, bhikkhus, a noble disciple considers thus: *Sensual pleasures here and now and sensual pleasures in lives to come...constitute an obstruction to a noble disciple in training here. Suppose I were to abide with a mind abundant and exalted, having transcended the world and made a firm resolution with the mind. When I do so, there will be no more evil unwholesome mental states such as covetousness, ill will, and presumption in me, and with the abandoning of them my mind will be unlimited, immeasurable, and well developed.* When he practices in this way and frequently abides thus, his mind acquires confidence in this base. Once there is full confidence, he either attains to the imperturbable now or else he decides upon [perfecting] wisdom. On the dissolution of the body, after death, it is possible that this consciousness of his, leading [to rebirth], may pass on [to rebirth] in the imperturbable. This, bhikkhus, is declared to be the first way directed to the imperturbable.

4. "Again, bhikkhus, a noble disciple considers thus: '[There are] sensual pleasures here and now and sensual pleasures in lives to come, sensual

perceptions here and now and sensual perceptions in lives to come; whatever material form [there is], all material form is the four great elements and the material form derived from the four great elements.' When he practices in this way and frequently abides thus, his mind acquires confidence in this base. Once there is full confidence, he either attains to the imperturbable now or else he decides upon [perfecting] wisdom. On the dissolution of the body, after death, it is possible that this consciousness of his, leading [to rebirth], may pass on [to rebirth] in the imperturbable. This, bhikkhus, is declared to be the second way directed to the imperturbable.

5. "Again, bhikkhus, a noble disciple considers thus:

Sensual pleasures here and now and sensual pleasures in lives to come, sensual perceptions here and now and sensual perceptions in lives to come, material forms here and now and material forms in lives to come, perceptions of forms here and now and perceptions of forms in lives to come - both alike are impermanent. What is impermanent is not worth delighting in, not worth welcoming, not worth holding to. When he practices in this way and frequently abides thus, his mind acquires confidence in this base. Once there is full confidence, he either attains to the imperturbable now or else he decides upon [perfecting] wisdom. On the dissolution of the body, after death, it is possible that this consciousness of his, leading [to rebirth], may pass on [to rebirth] in the imperturbable. This, bhikkhus, is declared to be the third way directed to the imperturbable.

(THE BASE OF NOTHINGNESS)

6. "Again, bhikkhus, a noble disciple considers thus: *Sensual pleasures here and now and sensual pleasures in lives to come, sensual perceptions here and now and sensual perceptions in lives to come, material forms here and now and material forms in lives to come, perceptions of forms here and now and perceptions of forms in lives to come, and perceptions of the imperturbable - all are perceptions. Where these perceptions cease without remainder, that is the peaceful, that is the sublime, namely, the base of nothingness.* When he practices in this way and frequently abides thus, his mind acquires confidence in this base. Once there is full confidence, he either attains to the base of nothingness now or else he decides upon [perfecting] wisdom. On the dissolution of the body, after

death, it is possible that this consciousness of his, leading [to rebirth], may pass on [to rebirth] in the base of nothingness. This, bhikkhus, is declared to be the first way directed to the base of nothingness.

7. "Again, bhikkhus, a noble disciple, gone to the forest or to the root of a tree or to an empty hut, considers thus: *This is void of a self or of what belongs to a self.* When he practices in this way and frequently abides thus, his mind acquires confidence in this base. Once there is full confidence, he either attains to the base of nothingness now or else he decides upon [perfecting] wisdom. On the dissolution of the body, after death, it is possible that this consciousness of his, leading [to rebirth], may pass on [to rebirth] in the base of nothingness. This, bhikkhus, is declared to be the second way directed to the base of nothingness.

8. "Again, bhikkhus, a noble disciple considers thus: *I am not anything belonging to anyone anywhere, nor is there anything belonging to me in anyone anywhere.* When he practices in this way and frequently abides thus, his mind acquires confidence in this base. Once there is full confidence, he either attains to the base of nothingness now or else he decides upon [perfecting] wisdom. On the dissolution of the body, after death, it is possible that this consciousness of his, leading [to rebirth], may pass on [to rebirth] in the base of nothingness. This, bhikkhus, is declared to be the third way directed to the base of nothingness.

(THE BASE OF NEITHER-PERCEPTION-NOR-NON-PERCEPTION)

9. "Again, bhikkhus, a noble disciple considers thus: *Sensual pleasures here and now and sensual pleasures in lives to come, sensual perceptions here and now and sensual perceptions in lives to come, material forms here and now and material forms in lives to come, perceptions of forms here and now and perceptions of forms in lives to come, perceptions of the imperturbable, and perceptions of the base of nothingness - all are perceptions. Where these perceptions cease without remainder, that is the peaceful, that is the sublime, namely, the base of neither perception-nor-non-perception.* When he practices in this way and frequently abides thus, his mind acquires confidence in this base. Once there is full confidence, he either attains to the base of neither-perception-nor-non-perception now or else he decides upon [perfecting] wisdom. On the dissolution of the

215

body, after death, it is possible that this consciousness of his, leading [to rebirth], may pass on [to rebirth] in the base of neither-perception-nor-non-perception. This, bhikkhus, is declared to be the way directed to the base of neither-perception-nor-non-perception."

(NIBBANA)

10. When this was said, the venerable Ananda said to the Blessed One: "Venerable sir, here a bhikkhu is practicing thus: *If it were not, it would not be mine; it will not be and it will not be mine. What exists, what has come to be, that I am abandoning.* Thus he obtains equanimity. Venerable sir, does such a bhikkhu attain Nibbana?"

"One bhikkhu here, Ananda, might attain Nibbana, another bhikkhu here might not attain Nibbana."

"What is the cause and reason, venerable sir, why one bhikkhu here might attain Nibbana, while another bhikkhu here might not attain Nibbana?"

"Here, Ananda, a bhikkhu is practicing thus: *If it were not, it would not be mine; it will not be and it will not be mine. What exists, what has come to be, that I am abandoning.* Thus he obtains equanimity. He delights in that equanimity, welcomes it, and remains holding to it. As he does so, his consciousness becomes dependent on it and clings to it. A bhikkhu, Ananda, who is affected by clinging does not attain Nibbana."

11. "But, venerable sir, when that bhikkhu clings, what does he cling to?"

"To the base of neither-perception-nor-non-perception, Ananda."

"When that bhikkhu clings, venerable sir, it seems he clings to the best [object of] clinging."

"When that bhikkhu clings, Ananda, he clings to the best [object of] clinging; for this is the best [object of] clinging, namely, the base of neither-perception-nor-non-perception.

12. "Here, Ananda, a bhikkhu is practicing thus: *If it were not, it would not be mine; it will not be and it will not be mine. What exists, what has come to be, that I am abandoning.* Thus he obtains equanimity. He does not delight

216

in that equanimity, welcome it, or remain holding to it. Since he does not do so, his consciousness does not become dependent on it and does not cling to it. A bhikkhu, Ananda, who is without clinging attains Nibbana."

13. "It is wonderful, venerable sir, it is marvelous! The Blessed One, indeed, has explained to us the crossing of the flood in dependence upon one support or another. But, venerable sir, what is noble liberation?"

"Here, Ananda, a noble disciple considers thus: *Sensual pleasures here and now and sensual pleasures in lives to come, sensual perceptions here and now and sensual perceptions in lives to come, material forms here and now and material forms in lives to come, perceptions of forms here and now and perceptions of forms in lives to come, perceptions of the imperturbable, perceptions of the base of nothingness, and perceptions of the base of neither-perception-nor-non-perception - this is personality as far as personality extends. This is the Deathless, namely, the liberation of the mind through not clinging.*

14. "Thus, Ananda, I have taught the way directed to the imperturbable, I have taught the way directed to the base of nothingness, I have taught the way directed to the base of neither-perception-nor-non-perception, I have taught the crossing of the flood in dependence upon one support or another, I have taught noble liberation.

15. "What should be done for his disciples out of compassion by a teacher who seeks their welfare and has compassion for them, that I have done for you, Ananda. There are these roots of trees, these empty huts. Meditate, Ananda, do not delay, or else you will regret it later. This is our instruction to you."

That is what the Blessed One said. The venerable Ananda was satisfied and delighted in the Blessed One's words.

Dhamma Talk

The Buddha explains ways of attending the mind toward various jhānas and talks about three ways to the *imperturbable*, as it is translated. This is in relation to the fourth jhāna, in which one develops deep equanimity and there is a deep state of mind in which there is neither pain nor pleasure. Nor attending to any form of thought, sensual pleasures, or sensual perceptions. In the fourth jhāna the mind is deeply rooted in equanimity.

The second way toward the imperturbable is through understanding infinite space and the third way is through infinite consciousness.

Infinite Space and beyond

With infinite space the Buddha refers to expanding your awareness beyond the body, expanding it with the brahmavihāra of compassion, as you know it through the TWIM practice. Through infinite space you understand that space is infinite. In other words, mind expands to the outer limits of space, to the point that it reaches the limits of conscious perception, or sense perceptions. In this process you start to see infinite consciousnesses arise and pass away through one or more of the sense doors.

When meditating, if you are inclined toward the visual forms, the sense of the eyes, you might see a ring of light in the periphery of your inner vision. Or flickers of light going on and off, each flicker being an arising and passing away. Likewise with relation to the ears, where you might hear auditory consciousnesses arise and pass away, like flickers or certain sounds coming in and out, turning on and off. With the nose consciousness, you might experience various fragrances, likewise for the tongue in experiencing certain sensations there. And with the skin, you could notice certain jolts of electricity, or any other form of tangibles on the skin, turning on and off. Each turning on and off, of any of these five physical senses, is an arising and passing away of consciousness.

In the case of the mind sense, you might start to see that the mind sinks deeper and does not attend to any of the background thoughts, it does not become distracted. The wisps of thoughts become even lighter and become frames of thoughts, coming in and out of the periphery of the mind. These are mind-objects that arise and pass away, without attending to them, not being distracted by them. They are the arising and passing away of the mind consciousness. What happens is that you understand that *this is not me, this is not mine,* because there is no controller in any of this arising and passing away. You realize that there is impermanence to this arising and passing away of consciousnesses, that occur in every second.

Then, the mind dives deeper, into what is known as the base of nothingness, with the perception that there is nothing. But there is still a *perception* of nothingness and awareness of this nothingness. In other words, by having this awareness, there is a sense that there is a *being* experiencing this nothingness.

Let go of even this perception and move beyond that. In some sense, *ignore* the perceptions that might arise, including the perception of nothingness. The way to do that is to understand that even this perception is dependent on various factors, causes, and conditions. Let go of that, and the mind further sinks deeper, into a state of clarity, a clear, tranquil, bright mind.

Surpassing the base of nothingness, you will see even subtler formations in the depths of mind. You begin to see various forms of perceptions from these formations. In that, there is a lucidity of being aware. At the same time, there is no thing, no perception that is fully being formed. In the way of being completely conscious of it and grasping onto it, as soon as it arises in the vision of this tranquil mind, so to speak. It is let go of through the automatic 6R process. Gradually, the mind silences even further into tranquil mind. Not paying attention to any perceptions or any formations that are arising. You reach that still point of signless collectedness, signless *samadhi.* You experience that no formations are worth holding on to, and you let go of it. But there is still an idea, a concept, a consciousness, of that form of samadhi or collectedness, a form of awareness. When you see through this as well, you let go of even the Formations that have fabricated that state of perception and consciousness. Letting this go, the mind switches off into cessation of perception and feeling.

Emerging from this, the mind experiences the links of dependent origination, and nibbāna, without involving any personal sense of self as the links arise. Through that experience, one or a set of different fetters gets destroyed, depending on where the mind is, having attained nibbāna. It depends on how you grasp or not grasp the relief that is experienced after the contact that arises from the nibbāna element.

This determines the mind's state thereafter. You then understand through your own experiences which level of awakening was attained. But the ultimate is non-identification with any of these states, even post-nibbāna. By doing so, you destroy all fetters, all taints, defilements/projections. Then, you attain the ultimate; Arahantship.

Death and Rebirth

The Buddha talks about the evolving consciousness. A mind can remain rooted in any of these states, identifying with them and attaching a personalized sense of self because of having achieved these states. If you have not gone further, there is the possibility that you have developed these states to such a level that the Formations have been reconditioned.

From contact with these states, upon dissolution of the body, when death approaches, these formations will start to appear. Medically or biologically speaking, the body would seem completely dead. There is no more heartbeat, and the brain – if it would be scanned - would no longer have any indication that it is functioning. But within the depths of the mind, there is still activity arising; the formations that are strongly rooted through having been well developed in your life.

For example, if you have developed no further than the realm of neither-perception-nor-non-perception, and developed the formations from that meditation practice, it may very well be that those formations will arise and create and activate a consciousness. Through grasping and taking it personal, your mind will then grasp onto those formations with a certain intention. That consciousness will carry forth those formations, rooted in that intention, and then establish itself into another mentality. Through the establishment of that mentality, the formations related to neither-perception-nor-non-perception, are then further experienced in the realm of neither-perception-nor-non-perception. Here, the mentality continues to experience it for so many countless years and countless eons, that eventually the formations wear out, having been fully experienced. The mindfulness or the attention to that realm of neither-perception-nor-non-perception starts to erode. Then, upon dissolving from that realm, that being will then re-appear through the process of rebirth. This means that, since the formations of the neither-perception-nor-non-perception have been eroded, have been experienced, other formations start to arise that were in relation to the experiences of one's life, whether it was in the human realm, the deva realm, the animal realm, or in the hell realms, depending upon which formations are strongest at the point of dissolution. They will then activate a certain consciousness, which will then take root through, again, intention. By grasping onto those formations, through either craving, having taken it personal, or not wanting that. Those formations will be established through that consciousness, which establishes itself into a new mentality-materiality.

Let us take a human birth, in which that consciousness establishes itself at conception into the new mentality-materiality, that has just been conceived. After establishing itself and experiencing that establishment, that consciousness dissipates. But those formations that are rooted, will now activate another consciousness altogether. These consciousnesses dissipate, appear, dissipate, appear, based on the experiences of the being that develops in the womb. So, the formations that take root through the experiences of that fetus as it develops, establish and activate through more arising and passing away of consciousnesses. This arising and passing away of consciousnesses continues, all through physical birth, growth, and maturation. Depending on the experiences of that new being, new formations take root, and all formations may be reconditioned, or other formations from previous lives will activate. These therefore cause the arising and passing away of other consciousnesses, through which experiences of those formations are then understood in that body, in that being. This all arises through the mechanics of Kamma.

Therefore, holding onto neither-perception-nor-non-perception or even the signless *samadhi*, is not the ultimate, because it is dependent on various causes and conditions. It is still rooted in formations, in taking those states personal. You would continue to take rebirth through various evolving consciousnesses, at the dissolution of mentality, when in the higher realms, the jhāna and arūpa-jhāna realms, or the mentality-materiality of the deva realms and lower, among which are the human, animal, or even the hell realms.

The realm of neither-perception-nor-non-perception is not the ultimate, because there is still a level of clinging that is associated with the formations that arise from that state, through the perception of that state, through taking that state to be personal, in which there is the sense of a self that is experiencing it. This means that one has the understanding that *I am experiencing this right now.*

When you attach that sense of self and clinging onto it, there is no further development. If you can continue to consistently let go, however, you will experience nibbāna. Then, at the very end of your life, in that lifetime, depending upon the attainment, certain formations - which could have caused rebirth in the lower realms, lower than the human realm - will have been utterly destroyed.

The levels of attainment

When you attain stream-entry, you close off entrance into the lower realms, lower than the human state, because you destroy the fetters and the formations rooted in those fetters, or the fetters rooted in those formations. There is no longer any doubt about the practice; you no longer consider any other practice to be the way to nibbāna; and you will not have a notion anymore that there is some form of a soul or permanent self. You eradicate these layers of wrong views. Because of the destruction of these wrong views, there is no way for you to take birth again in the lower realms.

Likewise, you can extrapolate that for the sakadāgāmī, who has weakened the fetters of sensual craving and ill will.

The anāgāmi has completely eradicated the first five fetters, will take one more rebirth in the Pure Abodes and attain final nibbāna there.

Finally, the arahant. They, upon the Parinibbāna – the destruction of this final mentality-materiality – do not attach any sense of self to anything. All throughout that existence, after attaining Arahantship, there is no more holding on to things, no more holding on to any of the links of dependent origination. They understand with wisdom, and they realized complete right View of the four noble truths. They understand that all things that arise are temporary, impermanent. Therefore, they are not worth holding on to, and hence cannot considered to be self. With that understanding, when there are formations that arise at the point of dissolution of the body, there is no grasping onto anything and because of that, and the correct understanding of the perfected right view, there is no new consciousness that develops and activates through taking the arising formations as personal, craving for them, attaching a sense of self to them, or not wanting them. That is why, upon dissolution, the final consciousness that had arisen, extinguishes with that parinibbāna, just like these final five aggregates. Therefore, there is no more rebirth.

On the micro level, there will be no rebirth at the level of the links of the dependent origination. Nothing is being taken personal; therefore, craving cannot arise, clinging cannot arise, being cannot arise, birth cannot arise. So, there is no rebirth into a new level of suffering.

What's important to understand now, in the context of meditation, is that when you attain these higher states of meditation, including cessation of perception and feeling, you should not grasp onto them with a sense of *I*, with a sense of being, with a sense of delight that is rooted in a personalized self. Because this creates and conditions craving and continues through the links of dependent origination that subsequently follow. That is why, when you emerge from that cessation, you should continue to be uninvolved in experiencing the links. Don't even take the experienced relief to be personal or affecting a sense of self. If you let go completely, you can attain Arahantship.

So, in the meditation, it is all about continually letting go of the idea that there are states that are being attained by a sense of self, that are being clung to through a sense of self. When you start to detach from that through the 6R's, letting go of even the subtlest formations that might create desire, delight, or the attachment of the idea and the conceit that *I am the one who has attained neither-perception-nor-non-perception* or *I am experiencing neither-perception-nor- non*-perception. Let go of that conceit and you get closer and closer to nibbāna. All that is left to be done is to continually let go of every notion, idea, concept, and expectation. Even the expectation of nibbāna, which is just a created *concept* of nibbāna. Letting go of all of this is the way to nibbāna.

Daily Reflection Day 6

Additional Suttas to read

SN12.39 – Dutiyacetanasutta (intention and rebirth)

AN3.76 and AN3.77 – Pathambhava Sutta and Dutiyabhava Sutta (fuel for existence)

Evolving Consciousness

Evolving consciousness is not permanent. It is not a soul. It is not a being, in so far as being is conceptualized in most minds. Evolving consciousness is what is activated through formations. That consciousness links with the mentality-materiality and is understood, i.e., experienced, through the modalities of mentality-materiality. But once that is experienced, it dissipates, and the cycle of a new consciousness arising and ceasing repeats, based on the choices and views you have built up for a sense of self. Those choices and views either continue to fetter the next set of formations with craving, conceit, and ignorance, or they grind away at them, reducing the burden further and further with the arising of the next consciousness, after the previous one ceased.

When you continue to 6R at the point of the process of contact, feeling and perception, and you understand that there is nothing in any of the links of dependent origination, and nothing in any of the five aggregates worth holding on to, you will completely let go. At the time of the breaking up of the body, no craving arises that grasps on to the intentions, conditioned by the formations. And thus, the evolving consciousness is not present, since no fettered intentions carry it forward. In this way, consciousness dissipates and is unestablished, making rebirth impossible.

Rebirth and Cessation of Rebirth

Within one lifetime, as you have seen, there are multiple rebirths occurring in every microsecond, based on kammic impulses. If the formations are tainted by the projections of craving, being, and ignorance, they will continue to bring suffering through a state of new being, in every flow of dependent origination.

On a macro level, when the body breaks apart and vitality is no longer present in the body and the heart has stopped pumping blood, there is still activity within the mind, though for microseconds at most. Just as your heart rate, blood pressure, and breathing become diminished in higher jhānas but the mind is still active, so too at the point of what is conventionally called death, there is an active mind. Although in the latter case, the other vitality factors have ceased at the body's termination. Some cellular metabolism will continue as effects of bodily formations, but the signs of life otherwise are not present. People who have reported NDE's, Near Death Experiences, sometimes say they experienced their lives flash before them, or a light, or otherworldly beings – these experiences are the mental perceptions that were brought on by the formations in the active mind.

In the active mind of a dead corpse, when there is craving, being, and ignorance still rooted in the formations, these formations are grasped with craving through intention. That means whatever mental feeling may arise in the form of their life flashing before their eyes, or whatever thoughts were predominantly influenced by certain formations, are taken to be self or pertaining to a self. This allows for a new consciousness to arise, through an intention fettered by craving and hindered by ignorance.

This consciousness then spontaneously establishes into a new mentality-materiality at the point of conception, for a new rebirth to occur. Let us assume for example that it is a human rebirth that occurs. As the fetus grows and based on the experiences within the womb, new iterations of consciousness arise and cease, through the formations that were carried via the consciousness first established at the point of conception. These iterations arise, based on the way the fetus responds to various inputs from outside the womb, the mother's emotional, physical, and hormonal states, as well as the food it receives, creating new formations to arise and cease within the fetus. Nowhere in this process is there a continuous, singular self, only the illusion of it. Instead, the sense of self arises and ceases with every passing consciousness, and every response of the fetus within the womb.

> *This entire process, therefore, has been brought about by the causes and conditions most conducive for such a rebirth to occur.*

As the formations of previous lives, and of the new fetus, continue to iterate through a new consciousness in every passing microsecond, they also build up the faculties of the fetus, through which it experiences contact, feeling, perception, intention, and attention in the womb. The sense of self continues to develop through these iterations during the formative months, prior to the birth of the new being. After their physical birth, both sets of old formations from previous lives, and the formations built up in the womb, continue to arise and cease, cultivate and take root through the synapses and signals of neurons, that then continue to grow in clusters in the first few years of infancy. As the life matures, the formations are strengthened or pruned away, based on choices made – whether to hold on to feeling as personal, or to let feeling go with wisdom rooted in right view, which is using the 6R's or right effort, with right mindfulness. And thus, the whole cycle repeats until it is broken, through right knowledge and right liberation.

If formations and the intentions in a being, prior to mind shutting down in the corpse, were rooted in certain mindsets, then that being's formations will activate a consciousness that will spontaneously arise in a mentality, or a mentality-materiality, that is best suited for those formations and intentions to come to fruition. Using a human birth as an example, such a mentality-materiality would match, based on many factors, including but not limited to the genetic makeup, contributed by the mother and father of the incoming life form.

In broad terms, if such a being was ethical, moral, and of an unrealized right view, the formations and intentions of such a being may activate a consciousness that propels them into a mentality-materiality of better circumstances, i.e., in a higher realm, a better human birth, etc. Likewise, you can extrapolate the sort of births and planes of existence a being would incur, based on formations and intentions that were predominantly leaning toward unethical, depraved, animalistic, or evil actions and processes.

This is not to say that the formations and intentions rooted from ethical actions won't come to fruition in a negative birth, or that those formations and intentions rooted from unethical actions won't come to fruition in a positive birth.

> *Such fruition of kamma is interwoven with components of biological, societal, psychological, and ecological scenarios and circumstances, and their interaction with the faculties for mentality-materiality.*

Some fruition of formations will immediately arise in the next life, based on their strength, including the projection of a new consciousness that gets established into a new mentality-materiality. Other fruition of formations arises much later, even lifetimes later, unless one stops the flow of the projections of craving, being and ignorance altogether. In that case, there is no more grasping onto any formations, and no intentions would arise that could activate a new consciousness whatsoever. Thus, no new kamma would be produced to be experienced later. Then, there is the cessation of craving, the cessation of being, the cessation of ignorance, and cessation of rebirth. There is nibbāna.

Be in the Jhāna, Don't Become the Jhāna

In whatever jhāna you are practicing, it is important to remain detached.

> *Identifying with any of the factors of the jhāna, the process of going into jhāna, or the process of coming out of jhāna, causes clinging through taking any of that personal and relating it to a self.*

Especially when you enter the higher levels of perception, it is crucial to see what arises, in terms of whether you are becoming addicted to that level. In other words, do you attach a sense of self to the jhāna or its factors, thereby not only becoming distracted from your object, but also feeding craving? Or do you see through the factors, understanding nothing is worth holding on to? This happens when you understand that if the factors of jhāna arose based on causes and conditions, then there is no permanent and abiding self in those factors, and those factors would cease when the causes and conditions for them cease as well.

> *Whenever you recognize that you are starting to enjoy the feeling that arises from any of the jhānas, know that you have strayed from your object of meditation.*

With attention rooted in reality, you notice that your mind's attention is now on the equanimity of the fourth jhāna more than it is on your original object of meditation. Or it has started to observe the spaciousness of the dimension of infinite space more than it observes the compassion that is the object, in this sphere of existence. With attention, you then 6R to return to your original object.

As long as you continue to remain open with attention rooted in reality, and you do not utilize one-pointed focus, you will continue to stay in a jhāna without becoming distracted. For example, you know that in infinite consciousness, there is the experience of seeing consciousness arising and passing away through one of the sense doors. But as long as your attention and observation remain around the feeling of empathetic joy, your mind will not stray from it and get caught up in the experience of consciousness arising and passing away, and thus crave and cling to it, and identify with it.

Suppose the formations that get created from the attainment of infinite consciousness, are strongly fettered by craving and hindered by ignorance, through taking the effects and factors within that dimension to pertain to a sense of self. Then, if one develops the notion that there is no state higher than this, at the dissolution of the body, such formations could propel a new consciousness to take rebirth in a mentality in the higher realm of infinite consciousness. Likewise for one who craves, or identifies with, the dimensions of nothingness and neither-perception-nor-non-perception.

Don't Mistake Exquisite Peace for Boredom

When you experience infinite consciousness, your mind will start to tire of the constant arising and passing away of the consciousness. You will see through the impermanence of consciousness, penetrate that this tiresomeness is indeed unsatisfactory, and see that the arising and passing away do not have any self in them – they occur based on causes and conditions.

Eventually, as you stay in infinite consciousness, all the while using the 6R's to continue to stay with the empathetic joy, your attention deepens further, the arisings and cessations slow down, fade away, and there is a sense of the mind entering a deeper state where there is quietness. You have traversed through the frames of consciousness and entered the perception of nothingness. It is 'nothingness' because you have seen there is nothing worth holding to in terms of a self. In other words, the sense of self has started to erode. There is still some minute sense of self in that as you perceive this nothingness, you are observing it and therefore there is still the sense of an "observer" there.

In this nothingness, the empathetic joy turns into a deep equanimity. You have no thoughts of the outside world because contact and feeling with the physical senses have diminished greatly on their own, without force or suppression. Here, you start to access the territory of formations, but not quite yet – in order to stay here with a sharp, alert mind, you require an object, and that object is the radiating of equanimity. But very little movement of mind is required. Softer, gentler, more minute and miniscule movements – you nudge the intention to radiate equanimity. Like a pebble dropped into a smooth, unmoved lake, the intention drops the pebble of equanimity and lets the waves of intention move on their own. You just observe. It may happen that the waves dissipate, and you then intend for the equanimity again.

At a certain point, mind unravels itself to such a point that even that slightest effort of intention becomes unnecessary. At first, the intention of sending out mettā activated the first jhāna. Then, that activation through verbal intention was dropped at the second jhāna. In the third jhāna, that intention of mettā is observed and its changes are observed, at which point the mettā moves from the heart to the head. After some intermediate meditation exercises, you learn to radiate mettā in all directions from the head, and this softens into *karuna* (compassion). The radiation is attended to with your observation and attention rooted in reality and is much coarser compared to the radiating of equanimity. At this point you are in infinite space. Naturally, the compassion in this dimension softens even further into *muditā* (empathetic joy) – it is the type of joy a parent has for their child when they are in a playful mood, the type of joy a sibling has when they see their fellow siblings excel and succeed at something. It is quiet and mature – not the coarser joy you feel in the first and second jhānas.

Then, once mind quiets down even further, that empathetic joy softens to *upekkhā* (equanimity). It is likened to when a grandparent watches their grandchild in a playful mood of mischief. Whereas a parent is concerned or restless and wants to do something about it, the wise grandparent understands that the child is just being a child. They've seen it before in their own children and know nothing bad would come of it. It is only fun, and the grandchild will be all right. They observe with quiet equanimity.

Now, when the intention of radiating equanimity feels coarse as well, then you stop. Mind has unraveled into itself. It is like the reflection of a mirror in another mirror – pure, peaceful, pristine, and unblemished. Reflections upon reflections – these are the formations you may then become acquainted with, through disconnected thoughts, scenes from past lives, or imagery that is foreign to the present life memory. Regardless, as you navigate through these, staying with tranquil, bright, exquisite mind as the object, these are let go of, released, and you relax into that mind. Here, the 6R's are barely used, and if at all, they are done so automatically, without effort, without intention. At this point, the mind wants no more objects because they are all too coarse for the mind. And mind is resting upon mind, knowing it as only mind, intent, fully conscious and present, letting go of tension and distractions.

> *Here is where the clinging needs to be let go of – if you identify with this mind, taking it easy and crave for it to go on, you will not go any further.*

Likewise, if "boredom" sets in, you let it go and return to tranquil mind. This boredom is a reaction of the faculties in mentality-materiality, receiving no stimulation. For countless rebirths, mentality-materiality has been used to receiving stimulation. At this point, mind becomes restless or lethargic out of this boredom. These are formations being created almost in real-time and need to be 6R'd, as and when they arise, along with activating the appropriate factors of awakening.

The Seven Factors Revisited

At this point, ill will, doubt, and sensual craving will not arise in this dimension, but restlessness and sloth and torpor may arise. Now, mind is ultra-sensitive to even the tiniest amount of input. Therefore, the input of activating the seven factors is just as miniscule to keep mind balanced. If mind slips into lethargy, or what is the hindrance of sloth and torpor, then you very gently intend the factors of silent joy, investigation and right effort – at this point, your mind will know what is required through observation. The only effort, if at all, is the intention. Similarly, if mind slips into restlessness, you intend the factors of relaxation, collectedness, and equanimity. Continue on in this tranquil mind until the final formations are let go of and all stops. Then, there is cessation.

Questions

"When we are dying, is it best to be in jhāna, or do we need to let go of the formations as much as possible?"

Answer:

Yes, if you have already practiced, it would be advisable to continue to practice at the highest level that you have attained. Let's say you attained the level of nothingness. Allow mind to incline toward that nothingness. Once you have established that consciousness in nothingness, the work there is to continually let go from there on. It is possible that, before the dissolution, you may still attain nibbāna. It is a matter of continually practicing, developing, and strengthening those formations, and ultimately letting go of any attachments to those formations. The more you develop your jhāna practice, the more you are inclined toward one of the realms associated with the rūpa or the arūpa jhānas. But in the end, it is still important to try to let go of them.

"Is it advisable to leave a dead body undisturbed for a couple of days?

You explained that when the heart stops beating and no activity is measured in the brain, there are still things happening in the deeper mind, and there are still formations."

Answer:

At that level of mind, there is no connection to the body anymore. It is like being in the cessation of perception and feeling; if someone touches the body, there does not arise any feeling from it, because the mind has completely disconnected from that body. The formations are not purely physical, in the form of materiality. Even if they are physical formations that are attributed to the breathing, they are rooted in the mentality. The formations start on the mental level. So, there is a subtle level beyond the material form, where this activity happens.

Some traditions talk about leaving a body for one or two days, or even longer, but it is not connected to anything related to the formations. That process will still occur, where the mind, beyond the level of the brain, will continue to either attach or detach itself from the formations. This determines whether a new consciousness arises, which immediately, spontaneously takes rebirth, through conception, into a new mentality or mentality-materiality. It depends on what formations that consciousness clung to with the intention.

"When emerge from cessation, do you see the links of dependent origination and touch the nibbāna element.

Right afterward, there is a feeling of relief. Is this relief and joy a form of craving, attaching this relief to the sense of a self?"

Answer:

Yes.

"Where does that relief come from?

I know that if you attain a higher stage, like anāgāmi, there would be no identification with that relief. When people talk about the first level of attainment, the sotāpanna, it's like the Buddha's description of giving up an ocean of suffering. Does this relief originate from having experienced nibbāna? Or from the fact that you have let go of three lower fetters and the search has ended, because you know the Path and there is no doubt anymore? (Doubt can generate a lot of suffering in the mind.)"

Answer:

Yes, that ocean of suffering would have still been experienced with the presence of these three fetters. This has the potential of taking rebirth in lower realms. The removal of that ocean of suffering is because the first three fetters have been destroyed. You experience the links of dependent origination and then enter the stream. You understand that this is the path that leads to your welfare and to ultimate liberation.

The relief is the happiness and bliss that arises from having contacted nibbāna at the level of contact, but there is still attachment to that relief. There is still some more work to be done. But it does not mean that there is no cause for celebration, because the destruction of the first three fetters is a huge step into entering the path. You are assured full awakening at some point. Whether in the same or another lifetime.

"When you start on the path and see the Buddha's teaching, you conceptually start to understand dependent origination and the states of higher mind. There is an intention, craving if you will, to start on the path, to do a meditation retreat, to attain nibbāna, to do all these great things. And when you progress on the path, you let go more and more. Is that the lifetime of a meditator?"

Answer:

I would not say it would be craving because, although it is a response to a feeling which directs you toward wanting to better yourself, or wanting to enter the path, it is, what is known in Pali as *chanda*. This is a positive, wholesome desire, or as I translate it, a cultivated intention. It is an intention that gets cultivated by first understanding through analysis. You see for yourself that there is a potential to attain nibbāna, to attain happiness. Rooted in this wholesome desire, you then go on toward the path. You develop the meditation practice, and so on.

The interesting thing here to note is that, from one who has *not* entered the path, all the way up to one who has attained the level of anāgāmi, the links of dependent origination run through to the link of suffering. Because even at the level of an anāgāmi, there is still conceit which takes something as personal, although there is no sensual craving or ill will. At the level of feeling there is still a personalizing of that, which then clings to an idea of *I, me,* or *mine.* There is some level of suffering, though it is very subtle compared to the suffering of someone who has never entered the path, or a stream-enterer, or a sakadāgāmī.

A thing to point out here is that suffering is the beginning. You have understood and analyzed that nothing so far has helped you out of the suffering. Through seeing that you are suffering and wanting a way out, this cultivated intention gets developed. This is known as the *transcendent dependent origination,* which leads from suffering to investigation, to faith and conviction. This leads on to joy and bliss through the jhānas, equanimity, tranquility and to development of all the path factors. Ultimately, this leads to nibbāna.

It is important to see whether someone wants to continue to be in suffering, or whether they want a way out. The start is always seeing that so far, what you have been doing is not working. You need a way out. Then, you start to investigate for yourself. If it works for you, you will further develop it.

Meditator Experiences

Infinite Space Jhāna

After the meditation, I had my breakfast and then as I quietly sat down to have my coffee, a couple of things happened. There was a recognition in the mind that the observation/ attention was very much focused on the front and sides of the body. Then it started to wrap around the attention to the back of the body on its own. Soon after, everything started to feel balanced and almost like the body was emitting energy (as well as surrounded) evenly in all directions.

- Meditator from England

At this stage, mind is very still. What I do is focus on the space between my eyes and kind of expand it. I do that relaxing my eyes and it feels like the space between them is growing. I do that for a few minutes, then radiate compassion 360 degrees around me, gently visualizing this green healing color going out in all directions, then back to the expanding of mind by relaxing the eyes. When I am looking with mind's eye, there seems to be a black screen in front of my eyes with nothing on it.

- Meditator from California, USA

Spacious as its name. I believe that everyone, even non-meditators felt this experience many times in life: it happens when falling asleep we get feeling that we are falling to some abyss - this is one of the experiences of Infinite Space. In meditational mode it feels calm and quiet as the space around. As if I forgot about the physical space around the body. But suddenly remembered about it and it started to be felt. In common life and during walking meditations this state feels like when I start "seeing" space between objects and feeling expansion around the head.

- Meditator from Kyrgyzstan

After sitting for over 1.5 hours radiating Mettā, I rose to walk and felt some expansion in my head and there was the feeling of Compassion and Infinite Space. I took that feeling straight back into sitting in a continuous thread.

- Meditator from Australia

Began meditating using compassion as the object of meditation. Mind quickly became clearer, and there was a sense of expansion as the feeling of compassion radiated out in all directions from my head. There was a lightness, a sense of calm that came into mind almost immediately. The compassion then became somewhat of a mental radar. I got a very clear message and information about my mother-in-law, and how much she was suffering at night, alone, with the passing of her companion. It was clear to me that she suffers greatly but keeps this to herself and does not speak of it to anyone, making the situation worse. Mind then returned to the feeling of compassion going out in waves until an image of a cow somewhere on the East Coast of the United States. There was a vivid image of this cow, which was thin, wasting away and had something like a large leather collar around its neck. The cow knew that its life force was fading, and I felt a lot of compassion for this being. I told it that I was perceptive of its situation, wished it well and there was a subtle acknowledgment back to me.

- Meditator from Missouri, USA

Infinite Consciousness Jhāna

Sometimes it feels as if I'm connected to the Universe, to every act and moment of existence because I start to feel very brightly all sounds, thoughts, tangibles, and visual objects. Everything is very clear and vivid. But sometimes when mind gets tired of the infinite consciousness it becomes even painful that the six spheres are always present and active. As if I have no way to run from the constant activity of senses. That's the eternal humming of the fridge, endless thoughts and everchanging bodily sensations.

- Meditator from Kyrgyzstan

Following from that lasting a couple of hours, the mind has been seeing rapid firing of thoughts preceding any physical movements which never used to get registered before. The mind right now feels deeply exhausted. It's not mental tiredness but it's tired of seeing sheer amount of mind activities and relentless nature of arising and passing away of phenomena.

- Meditator from England

Now it's time to let go even more, whatever is holding me back from relaxing I let it go, through the 6R's, whatever it is, I want to let go of it. And you realize that there is nothing fixed or permanent or stable in your experience. It is all being created in the moment and passing in the moment. Everything is ultimately empty, there is no single objective reality we all agree on. We all are watching our own movies, and all experiences are being fabricated by mind moment by moment. There is an immense feeling of relief. You start to see insights about the Four Noble Truths and how suffering is a mental creation of your own.

- Meditator from California, USA

Radiating out Compassion, I realized quickly just let it do its own thing without controlling, just let go. Saw circles or suns arise then disappear one after the other quickly for about thirty seconds, then they disappeared completely. I was in this state for a long time and then it changed to a feeling like I was happy for everyone and everything. I felt it increase my smile a little bit more, then after a while went into some darkness and saw things come up and drop.

- Meditator from Australia

Taking joy as the object of meditation, my energy level picked up, and then there was an expansiveness going out from my head. The feeling is like an energetic field instead of waves. There is happiness, but not the kind of happiness that is loud and boisterous like from laughing. Mind is quiet and experiencing an uplifted state. This then morphed from a field into waves radiation out in all directions from my head. Coming out of the meditation, there was a large amount of gratitude that was felt. There is a loosening of the sense of self. The experience is more like observing things occurring with a "me" tied up in the feeling.

- Meditator from Missouri, USA

Nothingness Jhāna

The best way I could describe was, something came over like a wisp of breeze and it happened very quickly. It's really hard to articulate what it was but on reflection, here are the qualities the mind could comprehend of that 'something' - It was independent of me (her stories/ her experiences). I want to go as far as saying, it's independent of awareness/ consciousness itself (it felt totally independent to anything one can conceive). It has no identifiable qualities (soft/ hard, love/ hate, feminine/ masculine…, nothing I can associate to anything I know of). It was here and not here at the same time, and yet it's all pervading. Those would be the words I would use to describe the experience. When it was gone, it left a deep sense of grounded-ness and clarity in the mind.

- Meditator from England

It feels very restful and quiet in this state. Sometimes as if I'm in a swimming pool of warm silence. Six spheres are dimmed and seem to be far away. Sound and voices of thoughts are like whispers and visions are very pale. Sometimes I see complete darkness, sometimes pure light that fills all the "space" of consciousness, without body. Sometimes boredom appears because nothing happens. The aftertaste is stillness, silence, equanimity.

- Meditator from Kyrgyzstan

Then the black screen in front of eyes kind of open up, it's like looking into a dark room knowing there is something there but not being able to see it, and mind moves off into this space. It feels like everywhere you look up, down, right left, is just dark. And then when you look back at mind's eye you feel like you are hovering on a point in the middle of nowhere.

- Meditator from California, USA

Radiating joy to each direction and all around. Seeing flickering at ears, eyes, tongue, nose, thoughts, I 6R straight away. I saw myself breathing, then everything stopped. Went into darkness for a while, then a feeling of fear arose as if I was losing my life. I 6R it. Deep feeling of relaxation and neutral feeling. Then went into some dreamy state, seeing things not of this world. Then came out and very deep relaxation followed. No cares for anything.

- Meditator from Australia

Taking equanimity as the object of meditation, there was an immediate sensation of diving down, of slowing down, into a deep quietness. This was a space that I was very familiar with, and very comfortable in. Any concerns or worries quickly dissipated, and mind was stable, calm, present. There was less a sense of radiating, and more of just being in that state. I observed mind in equanimity closely and could see that there were almost no mental or verbal formations, mind was whole, unified, and simply present. There is great clarity in this state, like the lake feeling experienced earlier now has very clear water. Everything feels very even and balanced out.

- Meditator from Missouri, USA

Day 7:

Kamma and Cessation

Suttas

AN6.63 – Nibbhedika Sutta - Penetrating the Four Noble Truths
Translation by Bhante Sujato.

"Mendicants, I will teach you a penetrative exposition of the teaching. Listen and pay close attention, I will speak."

"Yes, sir," they replied. The Buddha said this:

"Mendicants, what is the penetrative exposition of the teaching? Sensual pleasures should be known. And their source, diversity, result, cessation, and the practice that leads to their cessation should be known.

Feelings should be known. And their source, diversity, result, cessation, and the practice that leads to their cessation should be known.

Perceptions should be known. And their source, diversity, result, cessation, and the practice that leads to their cessation should be known.

Defilements should be known. And their source, diversity, result, cessation, and the practice that leads to their cessation should be known.

Deeds should be known. And their source, diversity, result, cessation, and the practice that leads to their cessation should be known.

Suffering should be known. And its source, diversity, result, cessation, and the practice that leads to its cessation should be known.

"Sensual pleasures should be known. And their source, diversity, result, cessation, and the practice that leads to their cessation should be known." That's what I said, but why did I say it? There are these five kinds of sensual stimulation. Sights known by the eye that are likable, desirable, agreeable, pleasant, sensual, and arousing. Sounds known by the ear … Smells known by the nose … Tastes known by the tongue … Touches known by the body that are likable, desirable, agreeable, pleasant, sensual, and arousing. However, these are not sensual pleasures. In the training of the Noble One they're called *kinds of sensual stimulation.*

Greedy intention is a person's sensual pleasure.
The world's pretty things aren't sensual pleasures.
Greedy intention is a person's sensual pleasure.
The world's pretty things stay just as they are,
but a wise one removes desire for them.

And what is the source of sensual pleasures? Contact is their source.

And what is the diversity of sensual pleasures? The sensual desire for sights, sounds, smells, tastes, and touches are all different. This is called the diversity of sensual pleasures.

And what is the result of sensual pleasures? When one who desires sensual pleasures creates a corresponding life-form, with the attributes of either good or bad deeds—this is called the result of sensual pleasures.

And what is the cessation of sensual pleasures? When contact ceases, sensual pleasures cease. The practice that leads to the cessation of sensual pleasures is simply this noble eightfold path, that is: right view, right thought, right speech, right action, right livelihood, right effort, right mindfulness, and right immersion.

When a noble disciple understands sensual pleasures in this way—and understands their source, diversity, result, cessation, and the practice that leads to their cessation—they understand that this penetrative spiritual life is the cessation of sensual pleasures. "Sensual pleasures should be known. And their source, diversity, result, cessation, and the practice that leads to their cessation should be known." That's what I said, and this is why I said it.

"Feelings should be known. And their source, diversity, result, cessation, and the practice that leads to their cessation should be known." That's what I said, but why did I say it? There are these three feelings: pleasant, painful, and neutral.

And what is the source of feelings? Contact is their source.

And what is the diversity of feelings? There are material pleasant feelings, spiritual pleasant feelings, material painful feelings, spiritual painful feelings, material neutral feelings, and spiritual neutral feelings. This is called the diversity of feelings.

And what is the result of feelings? When one who feels creates a corresponding life-form, with the attributes of either good or bad deeds—this is called the result of feelings.

And what is the cessation of feelings? When contact ceases, feelings cease. The practice that leads to the cessation of feelings is simply this noble eightfold path, that is: right view, right thought, right speech, right action, right livelihood, right effort, right mindfulness, and right immersion.

When a noble disciple understands feelings in this way ... they understand that this penetrative spiritual life is the cessation of feelings. "Feelings should be known. And their source, diversity, result, cessation, and the practice that leads to their cessation should be known." That's what I said, and this is why I said it.

"Perceptions should be known. And their source, diversity, result, cessation, and the practice that leads to their cessation should be known." That's what I said, but why did I say it? There are these six perceptions: perceptions of sights, sounds, smells, tastes, touches, and thoughts.

And what is the source of perceptions? Contact is their source.

And what is the diversity of perceptions? The perceptions of sights, sounds, smells, tastes, touches, and thoughts are all different. This is called the diversity of perceptions.

And what is the result of perceptions? Communication is the result of perception, I say. You communicate something in whatever manner you perceive it, saying 'That's what I perceived.' This is called the result of perceptions.

And what is the cessation of perception? When contact ceases, perception ceases. The practice that leads to the cessation of perceptions is simply this noble eightfold path, that is: right view, right thought, right speech, right action, right livelihood, right effort, right mindfulness, and right immersion.

When a noble disciple understands perception in this way ... they understand that this penetrative spiritual life is the cessation of perception. "Perceptions should be known. And their source, diversity, result, cessation, and the practice that leads to their cessation should be known." That's what I said, and this is why I said it.

"Defilements should be known. And their source, diversity, result, cessation, and the practice that leads to their cessation should be known." That's what I said, but why did I say it? There are these three defilements: the defilements of sensuality, desire to be reborn, and ignorance.

And what is the source of defilements? Ignorance is the source of defilements.

And what is the diversity of defilements? There are defilements that lead to rebirth in hell, the animal realm, the ghost realm, the human world, and the world of the gods. This is called the diversity of defilements.

And what is the result of defilements? When one who is ignorant creates a corresponding life-form, with the attributes of either good or bad deeds—this is called the result of defilements.

And what is the cessation of defilements? When ignorance ceases, defilements cease. The practice that leads to the cessation of defilements is simply this noble eightfold path, that is: right view, right thought, right speech, right action, right livelihood, right effort, right mindfulness, and right immersion.

When a noble disciple understands defilements in this way ... they understand that this penetrative spiritual life is the cessation of defilements. "Defilements should be known. And their source, diversity, result, cessation, and the practice that leads to their cessation should be known." That's what I said, and this is why I said it.

"Deeds should be known. And their source, diversity, result, cessation, and the practice that leads to their cessation should be known." That's what I said, but why did I say it? It is intention that I call deeds. For after making a choice one acts by way of body, speech, and mind.

And what is the source of deeds? Contact is their source.

And what is the diversity of deeds? There are deeds that lead to rebirth in hell, the animal realm, the ghost realm, the human world, and the world of the gods. This is called the diversity of deeds.

And what is the result of deeds? The result of deeds is threefold, I say: in this very life, on rebirth in the next life, or at some later time. This is called the result of deeds.

And what is the cessation of deeds? When contact ceases, deeds cease. The practice that leads to the cessation of deeds is simply this noble eightfold path, that is: right view, right thought, right speech, right action, right livelihood, right effort, right mindfulness, and right immersion.

When a noble disciple understands deeds in this way ... they understand that this penetrative spiritual life is the cessation of deeds. "Deeds should be known. And their source, diversity, result, cessation, and the practice that leads to their cessation should be known." That's what I said, and this is why I said it.

"Suffering should be known. And its source, diversity, result, cessation, and the practice that leads to its cessation should be known." That's what I said, but why did I say it? Rebirth is suffering; old age is suffering; illness is suffering; death is suffering; sorrow, lamentation, pain, sadness, and distress are suffering; not getting what you wish for is suffering. In brief, the five grasping aggregates are suffering.

And what is the source of suffering? Craving is the source of suffering.

And what is the diversity of suffering? There is suffering that is severe, mild, slow to fade, and quick to fade. This is called the diversity of suffering.

And what is the result of suffering? It is when someone who is overcome and overwhelmed by suffering sorrows and wails and laments, beating their breast and falling into confusion. Or else, overcome by that suffering, they begin an external search, wondering: 'Who knows one or two phrases to stop this suffering?' The result of suffering is either confusion or a search, I say. This is called the result of suffering.

And what is the cessation of suffering? When craving ceases, suffering ceases. The practice that leads to the cessation of suffering is simply this noble eightfold path, that is: right view, right thought, right speech, right action, right livelihood, right effort, right mindfulness, and right immersion.

When a noble disciple understands suffering in this way … they understand that this penetrative spiritual life is the cessation of suffering. "Suffering should be known. And its source, diversity, result, cessation, and the practice that leads to its cessation should be known." That's what I said, and this is why I said it.

This is the penetrative exposition of the teaching."

SN35.146 – Kammanirodha Sutta - Cessation of Kamma
Translation by bhikkhu Bodhi.

"Bhikkhus, I will teach you new and old kamma, the cessation of kamma, and the way leading to the cessation of kamma. Listen to that and attend closely, I will speak….

"And what, bhikkhus, is old kamma? The eye is old kamma, to be seen as generated and fashioned by volition, as something to be felt. The ear is old kamma … The mind is old kamma, to be seen as generated and fashioned by volition, as something to be felt. This is called old kamma.

"And what, bhikkhus is new kamma? Whatever action one does now by body, speech, or mind. This is called new kamma.

"And what, bhikkhus, is the cessation of kamma? When one reaches liberation through the cessation of bodily action, verbal action, and mental action, this is called the cessation of kamma.

"And what, bhikkhus, is the way leading to the cessation of kamma? It is this Noble Eightfold Path; that is, right view, right intention, right speech, right action, right livelihood, right effort, right mindfulness, right concentration.

"Thus, bhikkhus, I have taught old kamma, I have taught new kamma, I have taught the cessation of kamma, I have taught the way leading to the cessation of kamma. Whatever should be done, bhikkhus, by a compassionate teacher out of compassion for his disciples, desiring their welfare, that I have done for you. These are the feet of trees, bhikkhus, these are empty huts. Meditate, bhikkhus, do not be negligent, lest you regret it later. This is our instruction to you."

AN3.74 – Nigantha Sutta - Cessation of Kamma
Translation by Bhante Sujato.

At one time Venerable Ānanda was staying near Vesālī, at the Great Wood, in the hall with the peaked roof. Then the Licchavis Abhaya and Paṇḍitakumāra went up to Venerable Ānanda, bowed, sat down to one side, and said to him:

"Sir, the Jain leader Nāṭaputta claims to be all-knowing and all-seeing, to know and see everything without exception, thus: 'Knowledge and vision are constantly and continually present to me, while walking, standing, sleeping, and waking.' He advocates the elimination of past karma by mortification and breaking the bridge by not making new karma. So, with the ending of karma, suffering ends; with the ending of suffering, feeling ends; and with the ending of feeling, all suffering will have been worn away. This is how to go beyond suffering by means of this purification by wearing away in this very life. What, sir, does the Buddha say about this?"

"Abhaya, these three kinds of purification by wearing away have been rightly explained by the Blessed One, who knows and sees, the perfected one, the fully awakened Buddha. They are in order to purify sentient beings, to get past sorrow and crying, to make an end of pain and sadness, to end the cycle of suffering, and to realize extinguishment. What three?

It is when, Abhaya, a mendicant is ethical, restrained in the code of conduct, with good behavior and supporters. Seeing danger in the slightest fault, they keep the rules they've undertaken. They don't perform any new deeds, and old deeds are eliminated by experiencing their results little by little. This wearing away is visible in this very life, immediately effective, inviting inspection, relevant, so that sensible people can know it for themselves.

Then a mendicant accomplished in ethics, quite secluded from sensual pleasures, secluded from unskillful qualities, enters and remains in the first absorption ... second absorption ... third absorption ... fourth absorption. They don't perform any new deeds, and old deeds are eliminated by experiencing their results little by little. This wearing away is visible in this very life, immediately effective, inviting inspection, relevant, so that sensible people can know it for themselves.

Then a mendicant accomplished in immersion realizes the undefiled freedom of heart and freedom by wisdom in this very life. And they live having realized it with their own insight due to the ending of defilements. They don't perform any new deeds, and old deeds are eliminated by experiencing their results little by little. This wearing away is visible in this very life, immediately effective, inviting inspection, relevant, so that sensible people can know it for themselves.

These are the three kinds of purification by wearing away that have been rightly explained by the Buddha ... in order to realize extinguishment."

When he said this, Paṇḍitakumāra said to Abhaya, "Dear Abhaya, is there anything in what Ānanda has said so well that you would disagree with?"

"How could I not agree with what was said so well by Ānanda? If anyone didn't agree with him, their head would explode!"

SN 41.6 – Kāmabhū Sutta - Formations and Cessation
Translation by Bhante Sujato.

At one time Venerable Kāmabhū was staying near Macchikāsaṇḍa in the Wild Mango Grove. Then Citta the householder went up to Venerable Kāmabhū, sat down to one side, and said to him:

"Sir, how many processes are there?"

"Householder, there are three processes. Physical, verbal, and mental processes."

Saying "Good, sir," Citta approved and agreed with what Kāmabhū said. Then he asked another question:

"But sir, what is the physical process? What's the verbal process? What's the mental process?"

"Breathing is a physical process. Placing the mind and keeping it connected are verbal processes. Perception and feeling are mental processes."

Saying "Good, sir," he asked another question:

"But sir, why is breathing a physical process? Why are placing the mind and keeping it connected verbal processes? Why are perception and feeling mental processes?"

"Breathing is physical. It is tied up with the body, that's why breathing is a physical process. First you place the mind and keep it connected, then you break into speech. That's why placing the mind and keeping it connected are verbal processes. Perception and feeling are mental. They're tied up with the mind, that's why perception and feeling are mental processes."

Saying "Good, sir," he asked another question:

"But sir, how does someone attain the cessation of perception and feeling?"

"A mendicant who is entering such an attainment does not think: 'I will enter the cessation of perception and feeling' or 'I am entering the cessation of perception and feeling' or 'I have entered the cessation of perception and feeling.' Rather, their mind has been previously developed so as to lead to such a state."

Saying "Good, sir," he asked another question:

"But sir, which cease first for a mendicant who is entering the cessation of perception and feeling: physical, verbal, or mental processes?"

"Verbal processes cease first, then physical, then mental."

Saying "Good, sir," he asked another question:

"What's the difference between someone who has passed away and a mendicant who has attained the cessation of perception and feeling?"

"When someone dies, their physical, verbal, and mental processes have ceased and stilled; their vitality is spent; their warmth is dissipated; and their faculties have disintegrated. When a mendicant has attained the cessation of perception and feeling, their physical, verbal, and mental processes have ceased and stilled. But their vitality is not spent; their warmth is not dissipated; and their faculties are very clear. That's the difference between someone who has passed away and a mendicant who has attained the cessation of perception and feeling."

Saying "Good, sir," he asked another question:

"But sir, how does someone emerge from the cessation of perception and feeling?"

"A mendicant who is emerging from such an attainment does not think: 'I will emerge from the cessation of perception and feeling' or 'I am emerging from the cessation of perception and feeling' or 'I have emerged from the cessation of perception and feeling.' Rather, their mind has been previously developed so as to lead to such a state."

Saying "Good, sir," he asked another question:

"But sir, which arise first for a mendicant who is emerging from the cessation of perception and feeling: physical, verbal, or mental processes?"

"Mental processes arise first, then physical, then verbal."

Saying "Good, sir," he asked another question:

"But sir, when a mendicant has emerged from the attainment of the cessation of perception and feeling, how many kinds of contact do they experience?"

"They experience three kinds of contact: emptiness, signless, and undirected contacts."

Saying "Good, sir," he asked another question:

"But sir, when a mendicant has emerged from the attainment of the cessation of perception and feeling, what does their mind slant, slope, and incline to?"

"Their mind slants, slopes, and inclines to seclusion."

Saying "Good, sir," Citta approved and agreed with what Kāmabhū said. Then he asked another question:

"But sir, how many things are helpful for attaining the cessation of perception and feeling?"

"Well, householder, you've finally asked what you should have asked first! Nevertheless, I will answer you. Two things are helpful for attaining the cessation of perception and feeling: serenity and discernment."

Dhamma Talk - Kamma

This was quite a lot of reading. But within the framework of this understanding of kamma, and how it relates to meditation, especially the attainment of cessation of perception and feeling and what happens afterwards, it is important to have all this information.

Let's unwind all of this. First, it is important to understand that kamma is not deterministic. There is no predetermination in the Buddha's dispensation. It all arises through kamma that occurs in every present moment in which choices are provided to us.

There is one more sutta, which I will only refer to, so you understand. It is called: To **Sivaka [SN 36.21]**. In it, the Buddha basically says that kamma is not all. Kamma is not everything that determines the actions or the present state of a person. In other words, it is not just kamma in the sense of a predetermined kamma that decides the fate of an individual being. Kamma is interwoven through the various factors, causes and conditions. Also, primarily, the components of things, related to where a being is born in terms of the geography and climate, the sort of imbalances that might be there in the body of that individual, and the influences of climate, the body, genetics, and so on and so forth. All interact with one another, and this is felt at the level of contact, feeling and perception.

Choices

How we choose to act, is determined by how we perceive what is experienced or felt in every given moment. That is why our choices condition whether we do or do not produce new kamma, at the level of contact. Kamma gets created by, number one, personalizing what is felt and therefore wanting either more or less of it. Secondly, through the taints of ignorance, being and sensual craving. This determines choices when we tend toward things that we believe will provide us lasting happiness and are permanent, therefore things that satisfy a sense of self.

Or we can choose to understand with right mindfulness and right effort. That what arises, though it might be unwholesome or pleasing to the senses, is not the cause of the craving. The cause is *how* we take it. We can experience what is felt and leave it alone, let it be. Then, there won't be any personalization that will cause the arising of craving, clinging and being, and further down the lines of dependent origination.

It is important to know that whatever is experienced, is experienced through the previous choices that were made. These choices create the next set of the links of dependent origination. They either strengthen certain formations that are fettered and hindered by the defilements of ignorance, craving and conceit, or they condition and weaken those formations. You gradually wear away the fetters through choices you make that are rooted in wholesomeness, in the eightfold path. This is why it is said that the eightfold path is the cessation of suffering, contact, feeling, perception, and of kamma. Whenever you act in alignment with the eightfold path, you act in accordance with that. This conditions the formations in a way that roots out the fetters in them. This, bit by bit, destroys the ignorance, and therefore the conceit and the craving. Whenever you act in line with the eightfold path, you use, altogether, the tools within that path. Namely, you understand through right view - first on an intellectual level - that there is kamma, there is rebirth, there are the four noble truths. Then, you apply that by making choices that are rooted in right intention, namely, to let go of things - the choice of renunciation -; to cultivate harmlessness; or to cultivate the brahmavihārās. From that standpoint you act, speak, behave, or think in a way that produces no harm to anyone, including yourself. By doing that, you experience the kamma or the effects of previous choices.

You understand the process of letting go. In the case of right effort, when something unwholesome arises - which can be the root of craving, taking something as personal - you know that craving is arising. You abandon it or even prevent it from arising, and then you bring up a wholesome state of mind, a wholesome quality of mind. You do this through right mindfulness, the mindfulness to be present in every choice that will be made. You know that one choice leads to suffering, and another choice invariably, in some way or another, leads to nibbāna.

How is this done? If this choice leads to nibbāna, how is that the case? It is because every time you act in accordance with the eightfold path, you further develop the mind through mindfulness and collectedness. Additionally, you develop the foundations by following the precepts. These help to prevent certain hindrances from arising and to purify the mind. They basically allow mind to come into the meditation already to some extent, clarified and purified. And you can quickly generate the factors of jhāna by effectively observing your object or vehicle of meditation, which in this case is one of the brahmavihāras. It all works in sync, in alignment, to then develop right collectedness and go through each of the jhānas. Whenever you are in alignment with the eightfold path, which culminates in the jhāna practice, you are effectively experiencing the hindrances and letting go of them. Thereby you experience old kamma and let that go. Then you return to your object of meditation and the jhāna factors, getting back into that jhāna. By doing that, you produce no new kamma, and you generate, condition, and strengthen certain formations while weakening the formations that are rooted in craving, conceit, and ignorance. Weakening these formations and strengthening the others helps you to create better choices in daily living while practicing right effort within the meditation process. This influences daily living and vice versa. You continually produce choices that are rooted in right view, and you understand that choosing out of craving will produce suffering. Then, you apply the four noble truths to let go of that craving and you return to a peaceful mind, mindfulness, and collectedness. This way, the formations that are hindered and fettered by the defilements, by the projections, keep deteriorating.

Formations

As you get deeper into the jhāna practice, there comes a point - as was mentioned in the last sutta - where various formations subside and cease. These are:

- the verbal formations, because thinking and applying thought are let go of in the second jhāna. While certain thoughts may arise, they are not verbal thoughts. See if you can notice this when you are in jhāna.

If certain distractions arise, they may be primarily image-based thoughts. And there may be background wisps of verbal formations, but they are not attended to. They do not dominate the mind but will slowly, bit by bit, completely fade away. What can remain in the way of distractions are certain imageries which come from the

- mental formations of feeling and perception. That is the contact of mind and mind-objects.
- physical formations. As you enter the fourth jhāna and beyond, the body calms down. You start to lose some sense of awareness with the body, or there is a sense of expansion of the body. The breathing, for certain periods of time, may even stop, but usually will slow down to a great extent. The breaths get shorter, but the pauses in between each exhalation and inhalation get elongated. The oxygen consumption is affected in that regard. So, from the fourth jhāna onwards, the bodily formations start to cease. They completely cease at cessation of perception and feeling, but while they may still be there in higher jhānas, they are nearly imperceptible unless you pay attention to it. When you would pay attention, you should use the 6R's to come back to your object.

Finally, as you get higher into the jhānas, up to the level of nothingness, you begin to see that you are working with formations themselves. The infinite consciousnesses subside and you now pay attention to the gaps in between the consciousnesses to enter nothingness.

Let go of the concept of being in nothingness, let go of the idea that 'you'- as a sense of self - are in nothingness, and you will sink into the level of neither-perception-nor-non-perception. Here, you deal with the formations as close to as when they arise. You automatically let go of them, using the automated 6R's. Then you come to mind where it rests within itself. The mind continues to unravel and lets go of these subtle formations. In neither-perception-nor-non-perception, you let go of the perceptions - the proto-perceptions, if you will - as soon as they arise. They will have no chance to develop into full-fledged perceptions. So, you let go of all these things and stay with that tranquil mind. This is the point where you play around with the balancing factors, the seven factors of awakening. When there is sloth & torpor, you can use them to bring up a more energetic state of mind. In this case, you use the factors of mindfulness, energy and interest, investigation, and joy. When you notice, through mindfulness, that mind slopes toward restlessness, you can use equanimity, tranquility, and collectedness. You do that by a subtle intention, just as soon as you notice that the mind is inclining one way. You intend the balancing factors, allow that intention to unravel and then see that the mind returns to itself in a balanced, collected manner. Then, you continue with that bright, radiant, luminous, tranquil mind, the quiet mind. The longer you stay here and sit with this, and the more you allow the mind to disentangle and let go of those subtle formations, the higher the chance that you will enter the cessation of perception and feeling. At that point, having let go of the subtlest formations, the mental formations of perception and feeling completely cease. And then the breathing ceases altogether for a certain length of time, while cessation is happening.

Cessation of Perception and Feeling

When you emerge from cessation of perception and feeling, what happens next is important. Make sure that your mind remains unattached, depending on which level you are at, in terms of the awakening path and fruition. If you are in the beginning stage, you will notice the relief, which ultimately arises at the level of contact.

Here is how this process happens in detail; the mind emerges from cessation of perception and feeling. Next, the links of dependent origination arise. The formations arise and give way to a certain consciousness, that then gets established through the six sense bases. Primarily, at the level of mind, there is the contact with the nibbāna element, there is the emptiness contact, the signless contact, and the contact that is undirected.

- The signless contact, through the understanding of impermanence.
- The emptiness, or void, contact, arising through the understanding of not self.
- The undirected contact, through the understanding of suffering, by not holding on to anything.

This all happens without any involvement from a sense of self. But invariably, there is the feeling of having let go to a great extent and then experiencing nibbāna at the level of contact. A feeling of great, vast relief. When that relief arises, depending on the level of awakening, there is either the attachment to a sense of self - in which case the rest of the links follow, from craving onwards -, or the understanding that this feeling of relief is not self, and the letting go of that feeling, seeing through it, and destroying craving altogether. In that case one has fully penetrated the four noble truths and understood that craving is the root cause of suffering, and therefore one will no longer personalize any contact, feeling, consciousness, perception, any aspect of mentality and materiality, and any formations. In essence, one will no longer have the clinging aspect of the five aggregates, no longer personalize the five aggregates, no longer identify with them. The relief will be understood as it is, merely a feeling, merely a sensation.

So, how you perceive it and how you take it, determines whether craving will arise or not. It is the *intention* of taking that personally, by delighting in it with a personal sense of self, that creates craving. Therefore, it will continue to create new kamma.

If, on the other hand, both conceit and ignorance are destroyed - by penetrating the four noble truths and by having understood and penetrated what and how craving arises -, one lets completely go of the relief, sees through it, understands it as it is, and does not delight in it, does not personalize it, does not take it to be self. Through that experience, all fetters, all the taints, are destroyed, because one no longer grasps. By not grasping one has therefore destroyed the taints and attained Arahantship.

Once that happens, the – now elevated - right view replaces ignorance. Therefore, any formations that then arise, arise from contact with the outside world, through the various six sense bases internally, and the external forms, sounds, odors, taste, tangibles, and of course the mental objects within the mind. Contact with these gives rise to formations. It is at the level of contact that old kamma is experienced. But since the arahant no longer personalizes or identifies with that old kamma - at the level of contact, feeling and perception -, it is right there and then that this old kamma is worn away, terminated.

It might require more wearing away, in the sense of allowing it to be felt over and over, but because there is no reaction that is based in craving, personalizing, identifying, no new kamma will arise. It is old kamma, the effects of choices that were created prior to full awakening, which continue to be seen through, to be experienced, and then finally let go of and understood to be not self, that this is not to be taken personally. Therefore, it is worn away. This is also applied in the meditation practice. Within the meditation, there is no sense of *I*, *me*, or *mine* in relation to the factors of the jhānas, or in relation to experiencing the meditation and entering or coming out of it.

In the case of your jhāna practice, whenever a hindrance arises, you should consider that to be old kamma. Consider it to be Kamma that needs to be let go of. Instead of reacting in a way that personalizes it, by trying to push it away or by feeding it with your attention, let it go so that you produce no new kamma. More importantly, once you come back to your vehicle of meditation, do not push the mind to be with that object of meditation. This would create new kamma, which would give rise to further hindrances.

So, it is within the meditation practice that you understand how to let go of old kamma and how not to produce new kamma, using mindfulness, right effort and coming into right collectedness. And when you do this, it is important not to identify with it. Don't push the object, don't force the mind to be with that object, and don't push down the hindrances. Let go and observe. These are the two things that need to be done. In letting go, you practice insight, because you understand that this is not me, this is not mine, this is not myself. You allow the mind to let go of it and return to the observation of the object. By doing so, you practice serenity. This is *samatha vipassanā*, serenity and insight. Observing is serenity. Letting go with understanding is insight. When you have these two and you continue to do this for as long as you can, and stretch that out toward higher levels of meditation, through the jhāna practice, you inevitably come to the cessation of perception and feeling and will attain, understand, and experience nibbāna.

Daily Reflection Day 7

Kamma and Fruition of Kamma

> *In plain terms, kamma is an action via thought, speech, or physical deed. Kamma arises, based out of intentions. You choose, based on an intention which is conditioned by formations. Formations arise from contact. These formations condition a particular consciousness to arise, which will take root in mentality-materiality. Intention in mentality carries that consciousness forward through the experience of the six sense bases. Moreover, that intention, conditioned by formations, will then condition a choice that leans more toward one way than the other when you are faced with a choice, due to conditioning of the formations. This is the so-called cycle of kamma.*

You produce an action, either based out of choice rooted in craving, conceit, and ignorance, or rooted in right view. Those choices then will either bring suffering through the flow of dependent origination, or the effect of whatever fruition of kamma arises in feeling is taken to be impermanent, impersonal, and unsatisfactory at the level of perception, guided by attention rooted in the three symptoms of reality. And no new suffering for a new perception, or sense of self arises in that moment. In essence, while action is kamma, your conditioning as effects from those choices is the fruition of kamma.

As choices change, so too do the formations. Every choice made in each given present moment, will either strengthen the projections' fetters within the formations, or will unravel them and bit by bit wear them down. If you continue to take every contact, feeling and perception to be self or pertaining to a self, to be permanent, and take delight or avert from it with the perspective of it affecting a sense of self, then you continue to dig deeper the formations. They will continue to condition the choices you make, through the process of dependent origination. At some point, however, you understand, through practicing the eightfold path, that you can decide to not take anything at all personal. It may seem difficult at first, but as your practice, both in daily living and in meditation, deepens, using the 6R's, your choices change. And as your choices change, you recondition the formations.

Old Kamma and New Kamma

In every given present moment, there is the delineation between old kamma and new kamma. That delineation point is the process of contact. In every microsecond, there is a different set of formations that arise, based on the choices you make in each present moment. These formations then activate to produce a consciousness, which is driven forward by an intention that conditions your next set of choices. The more you choose one side over the other, the further certain formations become more active and stronger. Moreover, everything that led to the moment in which a choice is provided, is old kamma.

What you do with that choice is new kamma. In other words, old kamma is the fruition of kamma, produced through a previous set of choices. New kamma is the current choice you make that will then come to fruition in a new set of old kamma, i.e., a new set of formations, consciousness, mentality-materiality, and six sense bases, The changes in these will be minute or noticeable, based on the strength of your choice. For example, if you act (new kamma) in a way that causes damage to one of the senses or the body, the next set of old kamma will be the damaged sense receptor, or a scar on the body. More subtly, if you continue to strain your eyes on a computer with bad posture (new kamma), eventually you may have a bad back or your vision may deteriorate – this is the old kamma.

Contact is the Key – Contact with the Unconditioned

> *The process of contact is where choices are made – how you decide to act in mind, body, and speech in relation to the process of feeling and perception, will decide the next set of old kamma that you inherit, as it were.*

The cycle is broken when you start to understand right view intellectually and determine to practice the eightfold path, until it comes to fruition in a post-cessation event.

Even during a post-cessation event, the process of contact, and what happens thereafter, is crucial. The links of dependent origination arise, and there is contact with the nibbāna element because of having seen the links. This contact is considered to be empty or void, signless, and undirected or desireless. In other words, it is empty or void because such a mind has understood that there is no controller in any aspect of reality, and all is impersonal and thus it is empty of self. It is signless because, with every passing second, there are millions of rebirths, so there can be no permanent sign of reality to hold on to. And it is undirected, or desireless, because you understand that since everything arises and passes away, and nothing remains the same ever, there is no point in expecting satisfaction in anything completely. These insights come about as a result of infinite consciousness, but their fruition of that experience comes through nibbāna, where there is the unconditioned. After that experience with the unconditioned, great relief arises at the level of feeling.

> *The experience of seeing the links is itself nibbāna because there is no holding onto any of them – just pure seeing, completely unconditioned.*

After you let go, nibbāna is experienced. After you have let go of all formations, nibbāna occurs after cessation. Not only after cessation of perception, feeling and consciousness, but also after the cessation of a link from, and prior to, craving. It does not occur through the process of formations, or through the arising of the links. Rather, unraveling of the links has led to nibbāna. Nibbāna is not just the unconditioned, it is the *un-conditioning* of the links. It is seeing through each link as it arises with wisdom – and the mind naturally gravitates toward the ceasing of the links, not the arising, when it touches nibbāna.

*It is the unformed and **the un-forming (or deconstructing)*** – without formations and the letting go of formations. It is the cessation of being because until the point of contact, no links have arisen to create a being through craving. Since at this point the links are pure, there is no conditioning arising – only the seeing with wisdom. This seeing with wisdom without identifying, without craving, is nibbāna. It is the process of contact that is empty or void, signless, and desireless. It has touched nibbāna. Each link up to contact has been unconditioned. What occurs next, will determine the attainment of a path and its fruition.

Post-Cessation Attainment

Through right collectedness, you will reach a point where you come face to face, as it were, with formations, and as you 6R them, you are rooting out the fetters in those formations on a deeper level. As you continue the practice, deepening it to the point of cessation of perception, feeling and consciousness, you then bring all formations to rest, and weaken the fetters. And then you reduce the infection of the projections through those fetters.

Upon emerging from cessation, you will experience nibbāna. Here, all is pure, unaffected, and there is the seeing of the links of dependent origination arising – mind has turned into itself and sees the links from a retrospective lens, only microseconds after they have arisen. This is how you become aware of formations in almost real-time post-cessation because mind has become so pristinely sharp that it can attend to them without interference or resistance from other active aspects of itself.

When contact arises at this point, it is contact with the nibbāna element. It is here that the breaking of the fetters occurs, although they do not always break at once but sometimes in batches, based on the response you have at the point of feeling that arises after contact with the nibbāna element.

Sotāpanna

In the entrance of the path of a sotāpanna, when contact with the nibbāna element occurs, the feeling that arises is immense relief, caused by the shattering of the fetters of belief in a permanent soul, doubt in the practice, and attachment to rituals and techniques with the belief they will lead you to nibbāna. This feeling, however, is so peaceful and serene, that great joy arises, and you identify with it. Thus, there is still craving in that form, along with conceit, due to the identification with it. And ignorance, by not fully understanding the four noble truths, as you have just begun to lay down the foundations for the four noble truths, to be established into the mind.

If you do not experience the fruition of sotāpanna before the dissolution of the body, you will experience it at that point. Now, because the first three fetters have been broken, there is no more identifying with any practices outside of the eightfold path. In other words, your mind has practiced and is becoming more and more rooted in right view. While this right view is still unrealized, it is nonetheless present in the form of understanding the importance of maintaining your precepts. As well as seeing the process of rebirth firsthand in infinite consciousness and having an experience of the third noble truth of cessation. As a sotāpanna, you are less inclined to break the precepts, or to cause intentional harm and immoral acts. If you do commit them, or break a precept, you immediately take them again and the mind is easily purified. Due to the inaction, and more importantly inattention, to choices rooted in in right view, the formations tied to such choices weaken and do not experience further fruition.

Therefore, if you have not experienced the fruition before death in that life, the formations that arise, are from those that are rooted in the unrealized right view. This means that your inclinations or intentions will be conditioned by such formations, which then will activate a consciousness that leads it to spontaneously link with a mentality-materiality best suited for those formations to continue to activate. This could be in the human realm in better circumstances, or a higher realm. Since the formations rooted in in right view - that cause choices that are unwholesome - are no longer active, the possibility of rebirth in a lower realm has been cut off.

Sakadāgāmī

If, after that point, whether in the same life or in another life, you have another in-depth look at the links of dependent origination that arise, the formations that are fettered with craving will have weakened even further. At the point of contact with the nibbāna element, the relief that you experience is lessened to a much larger degree, and you still identify with the relief. You have entered the path of a sakadāgāmī. Here, the craving rooted in the formations has reduced to such a degree that in daily living, any delight or aversion from a feeling will be greatly diminished and easily 6R'd.

When such delight or aversion is diminished, the link of craving loses momentum, and the rest of the links likewise have less of an effect on formations, fettered by craving. Since there is such little delight or aversion, or taking personal any feeling that arises, the choice to 6R and let the delight go, becomes stronger. In this way, craving does not arise. As craving does not arise, your mind further roots itself into right view. Having done this, the formations fettered by craving, are now unstable, ready to break. Another in-depth look at dependent origination will cause you to establish this mind further into the fruition of a sakadāgāmī. If this does not arise in your lifetime, the fruition will occur at the dissolution of the body, at which point most craving has been let go of. Any formations that arise, are nearly pure, with hints of craving. There still remain the fetters of ignorance and conceit. With them, the establishment of the four noble truths has not yet been concretized, and you still identify with the consciousness that activates with the nearly pure formations. That consciousness will then link with a mentality-materiality that has formations that are now mostly hindered by ignorance, and barely fettered by feeble craving.

Anāgāmi

Whether in the next life or in the same, you continue the practice of the eightfold path even further. This time, there is very little relief in the feeling that arises from contact with the nibbāna element. You have seen the links of dependent origination once again, in a much clearer manner, with the retrospective mind. While the relief is there, you do not take delight in it, seeing through with wisdom and not identifying with it. However, there is still identification with the process. There is still the notion of *I am* in the links, and in the five aggregates. At this point, there is only conceit and ignorance present, and you have fully destroyed craving, having attained the path of the anāgāmi.

Here, the link of craving is fully destroyed. But there is clinging to the five aggregates, and there is still an incomplete understanding of the four noble truths. You understand suffering and the cause of it. And if you develop the mind, you can experience cessation of perception and feeling, as it were, if you intended. But there is clinging to the eightfold path. An anāgāmi clings to the dhamma, the raft, and is just not yet willing to step off the raft to get to the other shore of full liberation. As an anāgāmi, you identify with the process. Despite this, you will have destroyed the fetters of craving and ill will forever, as well as eradicated the projection of craving. Now, those formations, fettered by this projection, are destroyed. However, the formations that take the process personally - through conceit and the projections of being and ignorance - activate the consciousness that causes you to consider the five aggregates intrinsically as a self. The fetters of conceit and ignorance are so deeply ingrained into the formations, for so many lifetimes, that effort is required to truly unravel them and break them apart.

If you then experience the fruition attainment, whether in the same life or when the body breaks apart, and you have not gone any further, the formations that are present continue to be fettered by conceit and ignorance, which will activate a consciousness carried forward by an intention hindered by ignorance, into a mentality-materiality that spontaneously takes rebirth in the Pure Abodes. Because the fetter of craving (that is sensuous craving) has been destroyed and does not exist in such a mind, the formations you identify with do not lead you to a realm of sensuous experiences. Therefore, an anāgāmi will never return to earth, nor to any of the realms bound by sensuous experiences. However, from the Pure Abodes, work is further to be done to de-identify with all the higher fetters, which are the craving for existence, the craving for non-existence, restlessness, conceit, and ignorance.

Caveat – Your Experience is Your Best Guide

While an attempt has been made to clarify the various attainments, do not consider the process to be set in stone in one way or another. There are notable instances, in the suttas, of individuals attaining Arahantship just upon listening to the dhamma – in such experiences as well, the being's mind looked deeply into the process of dependent origination and by not holding onto anything, experienced Arahantship. The most important thing to understand and see is, where you are in this process – no one is going to tell you or confirm it. You must confirm it for yourself, using the wisdom of the suttas. But remember, even in the suttas, the demarcation of path and fruition and the attainments are not always so clear-cut, especially in the case of a sakadāgāmī. Usually, in the case of confirming one's level of awakening, such a task is left to a Buddha. Since such a being is not present, we must be our own true reflections of where we are on the journey. For example, if you have the idea that you have become a sakadāgāmī, the truth of the matter of craving and aversion significantly having been reduced, can only be truly judged by yourself. In all cases, see for yourself in the days, weeks, even months after a deep experience whether the fetters are broken, and which fetters remain. This will help you know what work is yet left to be done. No matter what anyone tells you, your own experience and your own understanding are your best guide.

Questions

Old Kamma before an attainment

"In the jhānas, even if you don't attain cessation and don't remove any of the fetters, do you still nullify old Kamma and hence clarify and develop your mind in a wholesome way?"

Answer:

That is correct, that is exactly it. The nullifying of kamma always happens at the level of contact and feeling. When you take it personal, in the context of the meditation, you choose to take that hindrance - which is the old kamma that arises - and try to push it, fight with it, or ignore it. From that level of taking it personally, you let it continue by taking it personal, by trying to ignore it.

Or, instead, you face it, allow it to be there as it is, and then let go of it, and relax the tension, which is the result of the craving that may arise from it. When you do the latter, you do not produce any new kamma. You recondition the formations in such a way that will almost automatically continue to let go of those hindrances, both in the meditation and in daily living.

"What determines the time it takes to attain a stage of nibbāna?

Is the time it takes both determined by the way you practice Right Effort/6R's, and by the amount and severity of old kamma? If someone has a wholesome past, with good kamma created, will they, with the right level of effort, be able to attain any attainment quicker than someone with a lot of unwholesome Kamma created in the past?"

Answer:

Yes, that is correct. The five hindrances are inversely related to the five precepts. And the five precepts are rooted in the eightfold path. It is all about committing to right action, right speech, and right livelihood. When you continue to keep your precepts, you will notice that the mind becomes calmer much quicker. Whereas, if you break a precept, you will notice that there are disturbances in the mind through the hindrances.

So, it is right to say that, when continuing to maintain the precepts, you will have a better meditation practice in that regard. You will have the ability to achieve higher states much quicker. And finally, attain nibbāna much quicker. If you continue to keep the precepts, you will notice this in your practice.

That is not to say that, if you decide to maintain your precepts, results of having broken the precepts in a previous choice will not take effect within the meditation. It is not like you confess and now you maintain the precepts, and you are absolved. The effects of the kamma of having broken a precept will be experienced. This may be in daily life, through the mental plane, in which you may be disturbed, and in how you respond or react to situations. Or they may take effect in the meditation itself. In both cases, you should let go of them. Understand that they are there, they have arisen, and then let go of them. Let go of the craving of trying to deal with them. Then, return to a wholesome state which, in the meditation, would be one of the brahmavihāras, or the tranquil mind. Or in the case of daily living, have the intention of being in a wholesome state. Or the intention to project and radiate one of the brahmavihāras, or to be in a state of clarity, whatever it might be.

"Does the mind of an anāgāmi or arahant generate new formations?

In case of a mind which has released most of the fetters, there is still contact, perception, and feeling. Will the sense input that they receive, like somebody speaking or doing a bodily action, generate new formations, even though there will not be a sense of self attached to it? Even though those formations will be rooted in right view? "

Answer:

Yes, the formations themselves will arise through the level of contact. Contact determines what formations arise. An anāgāmi is still capable of taking it personally through the fetter of conceit. It will not necessarily produce new formations, but new kamma. This then produces new formations.

At the level of an arahant, because he or she destroyed all sense of personal being, the formations that arise will be rooted in Right View. They are always acting from the noble eightfold path. Right view conditions the formations.

It is a matter of taking the contact itself as impersonal, as suffering, and therefore not worth holding on to, and taking it as impermanent. So, whenever a contact arises, the mind of an arahant takes it to be impersonal, impermanent, and suffering. They will not even need to let go, because they have understood with wisdom that there is nothing worth holding on to. The mind will not abide in it, so the formations that arise will be in response to it, rather than creating new formations which are created through the fetters and the defilements of craving, being, and ignorance.

At the level of a released mind, right view is installed, so to speak. Before awakening, they continuously strengthened the formations that were conditioned by right view. They kept weakening the fettered and hindered formations, which were conditioned by the taints/projections. And finally, they were rooted out completely.

Suppose a negative situation arises. An arahant will respond from right view and from right intention. They will respond in a way that will not produce new kamma, and therefore it will not produce new formations. Ultimately, It is a matter of letting go of the old formations.

Meditator Experiences

Neither Perception nor Non-Perception Jhāna

Now is the time to really let go. There is nothing to do but let go. I notice that my sense of self is really a reflection of my senses. The world is incredibly silent, the little voice of thought feels far away and distant, and you know the thing that is speaking, and listening are different mental modules.

There is an alert sleeping that is kind of interesting in that in normal mode it feels like thoughts are on a screen in front of you, but here it feels like they snuck up behind you and you were in them before you realized you had thought them. Kind of like visualizations are arriving on the screen in front of you, but they are coming from behind you, and you already almost know what they look like before you see them. If thoughts are bubbles, it's like sticking our head into the bubble. So, the order and sense of time is a little disrupted. Hard to describe and I am not sure I am describing it. But it's very dreamlike and fragile.

- Meditator from California, USA

It's truly state of "anatta for anyone." When I get out of this space, I always get some taste of the impersonal. It's a "place" where control and controller dissolved and relaxed and when active consciousness comes back, I can recall that creation of thoughts/mind phenomena/dhammas is automatic experience where I am unable to 6R. Usually these words come to mind: "As if I'm dreaming being awake, as if I was falling asleep but I'm energized instead of being sleepy after. It's very pleasant and very calm and calming."

- Meditator from Kyrgyzstan

Radiated a relaxed balanced state, then it stopped. In a very relaxed state. 6R anything mental and physical, not many. Saw bars of light popping up. For a long time, there were no thoughts. Just got out of the way with dispassion.

- Meditator from Australia

Taking Quiet Mind as the object of meditation, almost immediately any thoughts or mental images disappeared. There is a deep sense of quiet, peace, and non-movement of mind's attention. There is much less to 6R in this state, as mind-objects don't arise as often as in the lower jhānas. There is a wide expansiveness in all directions. There is not much activity in this state, and the body's external sense doors are turned off. There is only vast, open, but un-moving space. Mind is very still, quiet and present, there is a deep satisfaction of just observing, of there being awareness, without mind grasping onto an object. The sense of "me" and the sense of "out there" dim considerably and mind eventually drifts towards a state of only perception occurring. There is the idea that one is watching the process of perception occurring.

- Meditator from Missouri, USA

Signless Collectedness of Mind

When the mind reached the level of the Quiet Mind, mind's attention was staying with a feeling very subtle by its nature. However, here the mind has still a distinctive base where it is resting upon. After some time observing in this state and letting go of any distraction, the mind naturally tends to let go of the Quietness itself. By now the quality of the mind has changed significantly; the mind doesn't have a clear base to rest upon anymore. Just an absolute form of stillness remains. Every attempt from the mind to hold on to some-thing, will cause tension. Every sense of self, every dichotomy the mind fabricates in this state, has to let go of.

- Meditator from the Netherlands

Prelude to a 'signless state of awareness' is very pleasant abiding, with the intent to remain in a quiet space and the mind adhering to it with ease for however long in the dimension of neither perception nor non-perception. Before the mind becomes subtler and devoid of an object, there is still the mind having this 'object of the quietude', the mind resting on itself with intent. When the mind considers this with aptitude that even this 'object' can be relinquished, then there is an open awareness where the mind does not grasp at any sensory inputs and stays afloat with connectedness and takes no part in the details of perception. A slippery slope without the fire of clinging, and I presume beyond this mode of perception lies the other shore, i.e., Nibbana. I am also inclined to think that the signless state of awareness is the default mode of perception of fully awakened ones, where kamma does not take place.

- Meditator from India

Taking Quiet Mind as the object of meditation, I injected a small amount of dispassion into the center of attention, so that attention would not be focused on the Quiet Mind itself. Almost immediately, there was a sense of falling, falling endlessly into nothingness. The space was pitch black, with zero barriers. This continued and I became concerned. My heart rate picked up and my hands started sweating as I continued to fall. I recognized this and continued breathing calmly, knowing that it would eventually pass. The sensation of falling decreased until I felt like I was just awareness floating in a black void. There was no sense of space, direction, or dimensions. Dimensions of up, down, sideways, simply did not exist. I rested in this state trying to "balance" my awareness so that there was no motion. Eventually, everything got very, very quiet and there was just awareness. It was not mind aware of mind; it was just pure awareness. There were no objects for awareness to make contact with. This continued for what felt like several minutes. Eventually I "reached out" with my mind to try to get a sense of where "I" was, to determine if "I" was vertical, horizontal, or otherwise. As my awareness reached out, I made contact with a sensation of some kind.

It was at that exact moment that I had an enormous "A-HA!" It was when mind made contact on an object that I realized "of COURSE mind would think this contact is mine." I could see very, very clearly the chain of causality that contact gives rise to feeling, feeling to perception, and perception to incorrectly labeling that as "my feeling." It is this moment of contact, with the incorrect identification of it being "mine" that gives rise to the sense of self. There is no "me" in that moment before or after, it is only a process that occurs very, very rapidly – so fast that normal awareness does not process the experience correctly.

Once contact had been made, and mind-objects began to arise, I got the sense of these (not a direct mental image) of being like a comet, and that there was a lot more activity in the area just past the head and leading into the tail of the comet. I noticed that attention is normally focused on where all of the action is – where the energy in a thought is – at its source or most forward point. I continued to put my attention on the space between the starts and ends of thoughts and was fascinated to see how much activity was occurring there, albeit much more subtle. I could not see the details, but I know they are there and it's an area I will continue to investigate in my meditation practice.

This experience of the Signless State has deepened my understanding of Dependent Origination. Direct experience always supersedes intellectual understanding. I feel as if I am getting closer to understanding where the end of the path takes a being.

- Meditator from Missouri, USA

Day 8:
The Eightfold Path of the
Noble Ones

Suttas

Majjhima Nikāya 149 The Great Sixfold Base
Translation by Bhikkhu Bodhi.

Thus, have I heard. On one occasion, the Blessed One was living at Sāvatthī in Jeta's Grove, Anāthapiṇḍika's Park. There he addressed the bhikkhus thus: "Bhikkhus."—"Venerable sir," they replied. The Blessed One said this:

"Bhikkhus, I shall teach you a discourse on the great sixfold base. Listen and attend closely to what I shall say."—"Yes, venerable sir," the bhikkhus replied. The Blessed One said this:

"Bhikkhus, when one does not know and see the eye as it actually is, when one does not know and see forms as they actually are, when one does not know and see eye-consciousness as it actually is, when one does not know and see eye-contact as it actually is, when one does not know and see as it actually is the feeling felt as pleasant or painful or neither-painful-nor-pleasant that arises with eye-contact as condition, then one is inflamed by lust for the eye, for forms, for eye-consciousness, for eye-contact, for the feeling felt as pleasant or painful or neither-painful-nor-pleasant that arises with eye-contact as condition.

"When one abides inflamed by lust, fettered, infatuated, contemplating gratification, then the five aggregates affected by clinging are built up for oneself in the future; and one's craving—which brings renewal of being, is accompanied by delight and lust, and delights in this and that— increases. One's bodily and mental troubles increase, one's bodily and mental torments increase, one's bodily and mental fevers increase, and one experiences bodily and mental suffering.

"When one does not know and see the ear as it actually is…When one does not know and see the nose as it actually is…When one does not know and see the tongue as it actually is…When one does not know and see the body as it actually is… When one does not know and see the mind as it actually is…one experiences bodily and mental suffering.

"Bhikkhus, when one knows and sees the eye as it actually is, when one knows and sees forms as they actually are, when one knows and sees eye-consciousness as it actually is, when one knows and sees eye-contact as it actually is, when one knows and sees as it actually is the feeling felt as pleasant or painful or neither-painful-nor-pleasant that arises with eye-contact as condition, then one is not inflamed by lust for the eye, for forms, for eye-consciousness, for eye-contact, for the feeling felt as pleasant or painful or neither-painful-nor-pleasant that arises with eye-contact as condition.

"When one abides uninflamed by lust, unfettered, uninfatuated, contemplating danger, then the five aggregates affected by clinging are diminished for oneself in the future; and one's craving—which brings renewal of being, is accompanied by delight and lust, and delights in this or that—is abandoned. One's bodily and mental troubles are abandoned, one's bodily and mental torments are abandoned, one's bodily and mental fevers are abandoned, and one experiences bodily and mental pleasure.

"The view of a person such as this is right view. His intention is right intention, his effort is right effort, his mindfulness is right mindfulness, his concentration is right concentration. But his bodily action, his verbal action, and his livelihood have already been well purified earlier. Thus, this Noble Eightfold Path comes to fulfilment in him by development. When he develops this Noble Eightfold Path, the four foundations of mindfulness also come to fulfilment in him by development; the four right kinds of striving also come to fulfilment in him by development; the four bases for spiritual power also come to fulfilment in him by development; the five faculties also come to fulfilment in him by development; the five powers also come to fulfilment in him by development; the seven enlightenment factors also come to fulfilment in him by development. These two things—serenity and insight—occur in him yoked evenly together. He fully understands by direct knowledge those things that should be fully understood by direct knowledge. He abandons by direct knowledge those things that should be abandoned by direct knowledge. He develops by direct knowledge those things that should be developed by direct knowledge. He realises by direct knowledge those things that should be realised by direct knowledge.

"And what things should be fully understood by direct knowledge? The answer to that is: the five aggregates affected by clinging, that is, the material form aggregate affected by clinging, the feeling aggregate affected by clinging, the perception aggregate affected by clinging, the formations aggregate affected by clinging, the consciousness aggregate affected by clinging. These are the things that should be fully understood by direct knowledge.

"And what things should be abandoned by direct knowledge? Ignorance and craving for being. These are the things that should be abandoned by direct knowledge.

"And what things should be developed by direct knowledge? Serenity and insight. These are the things that should be developed by direct knowledge.

"And what things should be realised by direct knowledge? True knowledge and deliverance. These are the things that should be realised by direct knowledge.

"When one knows and sees the ear as it actually is... These are the things that should be realised by direct knowledge.

"When one knows and sees the nose as it actually is... These are the things that should be realised by direct knowledge.

"When one knows and sees the tongue as it actually is...These are the things that should be realised by direct knowledge.

"When one knows and sees the body as it actually is... These are the things that should be realised by direct knowledge.

When one knows and sees the mind as it actually is... These are the things that should be realised by direct knowledge."

That is what the Blessed One said. The bhikkhus were satisfied and delighted in the Blessed One's words.

Dhamma talk

The Buddha talks about the six sense bases, and he begins with an individual who is not yet on the path, or who has not developed the path. They take the experience of the six sense bases to be personal, with craving, becoming inflamed by delight and lust as the Buddha said. They take this into every experience, and identify with it by feeding it with craving, by wanting more of the experience, or by wanting less of it. It negatively affects a sense of self. Or in a neutral sense, they still take it personal and attach that sense of self.

The Three Characteristics of Existence

But when you cultivate the understanding on starting the noble eightfold path, you begin to exercise your wisdom and cultivate collectedness and mindfulness. As you become mindful, as you continually observe, you begin to see the sensory experiences that are felt in every present moment. Having cultivated some level of insight and knowledge, you are able to understand that the experiences of visual forms through the eye, auditory sounds through the ears, odors and fragrances through the nose, tastes on the tongue, tangibles with the skin and the body, and the experience of mental objects, thoughts within the mind, are not worth holding on to, because they are impermanent. And they can cause suffering by identifying with it, and therefore are not to be considered a sense of self that is satisfying, unchanging, and independent of causes and conditions.

If you watch and observe without involvement, without looking for it, without trying to control the present moment, merely observing, using the four foundations of mindfulness, using right mindfulness, you can see that in the arising and passing away of each iota, of each quantum of sensory experience, there is no controller there. It happens all on its own, through a series of causes and conditions and different factors, both inside and outside the body. As you see this, you will understand that in the arising and passing away - since there is no controller, and it is not self-caused in that sense - it must be seen as something that will not be satisfactory. Each arising and passing away happens so rapidly, that it appears to be one flowing motion of sensory experience. The mind considers it to be permanent and flowing. However, you start to see that each arising and passing away is a frame of sensory experience and therefore it is impermanent. As soon as it arises, it passes away. There is no abiding in that.

You see this primarily through the meditation, at the level of infinite consciousness, the sixth jhāna. After seeing infinite space, it gradually shows you this. Don't focus, push, or try to create it, don't try to intellectualize or analyze it. Just allow the mind to unravel naturally and rest in the mind's clarity of observation, and these phenomena will present themselves. In this way the sensory phenomena will slow down and will begin to appear as frames of a film. When you see this, just continue to observe. Since the mind is not so focused that it suppresses and pushes down the mind, insights can arise. These insights will be into the three characteristics of all phenomena. It will confirm that these sensory experiences indeed arise and pass away and are impermanent because of this. It is not worth it to hold on to anything in this arising and passing away. You cannot abide in any of this arising and passing away. Therefore, it becomes tiresome to watch and this can be extrapolated toward all of saṃsāra.

This continually arising and passing away of sensory experiences - linking one iota of consciousness per one iota of sensory experience -, also happens on the macro level, on the larger scale of the macrocosm, if you will. The experience of rebirth, which arises from one life, from one mentality-materiality to another, is also tiresome. It is not self-caused, we did not choose, so to speak, through a sense of permanent self, a divine soul or spirit, to take birth in this. It was 'chosen' through previous actions, which were enacted by the given choices that each present moment provided. This created or activated certain formations and strengthened or weakened whichever formations in relation to that choice. When, at the dissolution of the body, the mind - with intention - held on to those formations, it activated a certain consciousness through that intention. Then it took birth, or conception, in a particular mentality or mentality-materiality.

Whether it is on the level of the microsecond or the level of the eon, this rebirth is always impermanent, always transient. And it does not have a controller that is overarching and all-encompassing, in the sense of a permanent, unchanging, everlasting self. It is built up through the choices that one takes personal. And this microcosmic and macrocosmic rebirth is suffering because it becomes tiresome.

Purifying the mind

Once you penetrate, with wisdom and understanding, this impermanent nature of arising and passing away, you will see that it is suffering. Then you can decide, based on that foundation of suffering, to make an end to the suffering. This leads you on a path to inquiry, a path to find out the answers. At a certain point, you will encounter the noble eightfold path in the dispensation of the Buddha, and you will intellectually see and understand right view. Initially, you will understand things through the theoretical knowledge of kamma and rebirth, and the beings that inhabit the different realms of existence. You will understand and build up faith and conviction, that this is indeed the right path to follow, and realize that the fruit of kamma is through action. Eventually, you will make an intention, a right intention, to always try to keep the precepts and act, speak, and think from a sense of harmony, loving-kindness, collectedness, and through mindfulness. When someone negatively affects you, it is not required to respond or react in the same way. Instead, such a being needs understanding and compassion, or empathetic joy, equanimity, tranquility, or silence.

So, you get to understand the value of acting from right action, speaking from right speech, and having right livelihood. When you act, speak, think, and live like this, rooted in the eightfold path, the formations begin to purify. Through each action, each thought, through the level of contact, you will make choices that condition and strengthen formations that enable a mind that is clear and collected for the purposes of entering jhāna. Formations that are fettered by craving and ignorance start to weaken. Those fettered formations were strengthened at a previous time, through acting in a certain way - breaking the precepts, through unawareness and not using mindfulness

-, that causes the hindrances. The way to weaken them, acting through the eightfold path, is through right effort.

When making a choice, you understand that if you act in a negative manner, you should *abandon* it. You *stop* any more of that outflow of negativity. You abandon the craving, the ignorance, and the conceit that caused the flow of that negativity, when you acted in a way that was not rooted in the eightfold path. Then, you cultivate and *bring up* a wholesome quality of mind. A mind that is cool, calm, and collected. A natural sense of clarity arises from bringing up that wholesome state of mind, and you *maintain* that.

On a larger scale, continue to make the effort to maintain a wholesome state of mind. And maintain the sort of mind that is ready and capable to see reality as it is without any kind of filters. Understand how the body is in the present moment, and how the senses are arising right now. Where is mind, what sort of a mindset has been developed for that present moment, what sort of emotional moods are arising right now and what kind of mental states are present within such a mindset.

When you do this, you become aware and start to develop collectedness by using and applying right mindfulness. Then, the mind will naturally tend toward seclusion, toward a wholesome state. You will practice precepts in daily living and make an intention, a choice, to act out of harmlessness, to act from the brahmavihāras. To speak, act and live in accordance with that. You'll develop an attitude of letting go of the unwholesome, letting go of the craving, and the personalizing through conceit, by being aware of the present choices that are given in every moment.

This translates into collectedness, which makes it easier for the mind to enter jhāna. As you meditate and enter jhāna, you cultivate the ability to continue to have clarity of mind by using the four right efforts, or the 6R's, whenever a hindrance distracts you from your object of meditation.

As spoken about before, as higher levels of understanding develop, you begin to see the sixth jhāna of infinite consciousness. This will allow your mind to sink deeper into nothingness, the seventh jhāna. Then you enter the eighth jhāna of neither-perception-nor-non-perception. And as you next enter cessation, come out of it, and have that nibbāna experience, you will see for yourself how the quality of your thoughts might have changed. How the perspective might have shifted for you, how the quality of the words that you speak, the actions you take, and the perceptions that you have of reality, shift, and change. You must be your own judge in that regard and understand whether there has been a transformation through this process.

After a nibbāna experience

At first, you will experience great relief and there will be quite a lot of joy and energy in the mind. Allow this joy and energy to be seen as impermanent, as impersonal. It is not worth holding on to, because it *is* impermanent and impersonal. From that mindset, come back to your chair and try to sit again. Do not expect anything. Watch what happens, allow the mind to further unravel itself. Don't expect that the cessation experience will arise again, because if you do, you create a conception that it is going to happen again. You are going to look for it. And by trying to look for it, you activate the fetters within the formations again, that create that craving, conceit, and ignorance.

So, just return and continue to observe. 6R the expectation that was built up through the experience of cessation and nibbāna. 6R that concept of how it needs to be experienced, or *'what should I be looking for'*, or *'what are the signposts that are leading to it'*. Just watch and 6R all these things that might come up. It may take some time and that's okay. Just know if you see in your own mind that there has indeed been a perspective shift, and therefore you have cultivated, entered, and walked the eightfold path. That cessation and nibbāna experience has given you a preview of what is to come. Now, you must deepen the practice by further letting go of any concepts that arise from those experiences.

When you go back into your daily life, continue to see the choices that are presented to you, and watch where your mind tends to. Your mind will inevitably incline toward choices that are wholesome. By continually doing this and constantly letting go, the need to control the outcome of choices - both in the sitting practice and in daily living – weakens and the attitude of letting go gets cultivated. As you let go, you release the personalizing aspect of the mind and the craving - which would create suffering through the rest of the links of dependent origination - that could otherwise take root.

Right View

Both before and after this experience, develop the attitude and intention to let go of anything that arises from the sensory experiences. Good, bad, indifferent, neutral, whatever they may be. If you need to, first understand from an intellectual perspective that *this is not me, this is not mine, this is not myself, and therefore I should not crave for it*. Together with mindfulness in letting go of that perspective and that wrong view, you cultivate right view. You continue to develop this in your daily choices and whenever you 6R in the meditation. And you will know for yourself what the four noble truths, within action, are. Bit by bit, the experiential understanding of the four noble truths develops, and you keep whittling away at the ignorance, which continues to condition the formations. The fetters of ignorance, conceit, and craving get worn down and replaced with this continual practice of right view, of applying the four noble truths from that perspective.

Ultimately, right view completely takes over the place of ignorance and any actions will be from that perfected right view. An actualized, realized, and experientially understood right view. From then on, every choice you make will automatically be rooted in right view. Because of that, you will speak, act, and have a livelihood that is rooted in this. Your mind will be in a state of automatically not abiding in anything from a sense of self, not in any arising of activity or phenomenon that appears through the senses.

Due to experiencing the three characteristics of existence, first at the level of infinite consciousness and then on the deeper level, as you observe the sensory experiences, you can no longer take them to be permanent. You know they are impermanent. You no longer depend upon them as a source of happiness, so you let go of them. You know that there is no controller, and they are impersonal, so you do not attach a sense of self. Every time you do that, you close off the ability to create further new kamma, and the potential for suffering, to arise. Each time you have a feeling or a sensory experience, you will know it is old kamma and you let it go at the level of contact, feeling, and perception. So, you know how to apply right view at this level; by not holding on to the unwholesome or that which could cause further ignorance, craving, or being. As you keep doing this before attaining full awakening, it will translate in the meditation.

Once right view replaces ignorance, the taints, the defilements, the projections of craving, being, and ignorance are fully destroyed. When you have achieved and understood it, the right effort that you 'do' will only be to continue to see the emptiness of self in each phenomenon, the impermanence of it, and the understanding that it is not worth holding on to. You naturally are mindful. It is a natural, uncontrived, unfabricated clarity of mind which automatically observes and is mindful of every moment, in relation to the four foundations. So, in relation to where the body is; what the sensory experiences of the mind and body are; the mindsets and moods; and the mental contents within those mindsets and moods.

When you enter jhānas, there is no sense of self there. You just automatically enter and abide in the jhānas for that time being, without the sense of self. And eventually, you will be able to cultivate the ability to get into cessation at will. You can get into the signless *samadhi* at will, as well as into the other levels of meditation. You understand the three characteristics of existence and let go of any sense of self in the aggregates for that time being. The practice gets deeper and deeper.

Ultimately, you need to understand the five aggregates. The clinging aspect of the five aggregates needs to be understood, penetrated, and let go of with correct understanding, with right view. Just see that these aggregates in and of themselves are impermanent, impersonal, and not worth holding on to. By applying this understanding to the aggregates and to the six sense bases, you are naturally at ease, and in a state of mind that inclines toward seclusion and nibbāna.

The released mind

Just upon reflecting the aggregates in this way, after having established right view and destroyed the fetters, a released mind enters and takes the third noble truth of cessation as its vehicle of meditation. The mind naturally attends to the cessation of being, the cessation of suffering, and cessation in of itself. By attending in that manner, it enters and contacts the nibbāna element, takes that as the object, so to speak, and finds bliss and peace from that nibbāna. That mind does not apply a sense of self to any of that process, because it cannot anymore. It has made such a mind void of the ability to crave, void of the ability to take anything personal, and it no longer misperceives reality. It will always automatically understand the reality of the situation as it arises. And because of such a mind, it can enter and exit various stages of meditation, practice various levels of meditation at will.

Requisites for Awakening

In this sutta, the Buddha also talks about the seven enlightenment factors - which we have gone through and somewhat understood through the process of this retreat.

He also refers to the four right efforts, the four foundations of mindfulness, the five faculties, the five powers, the four bases of psychic abilities, and the eightfold path itself. All of these make up the requisites for awakening. By developing the eightfold path, you automatically develop the four foundations of mindfulness, and develop and understand how to balance the seven factors of awakening. You energize the mind with the four bases for psychic abilities, which are the cultivated intention, the energy or the effort, the mindfulness, and the investigation or understanding aspect of the mind. You also further develop the five faculties, and the five powers of those five faculties.

In the same way that contact, feeling, and perception are *faculties* through which the *processes* of contact, feeling, and perception occur, the five faculties are from which the five powers occur. And this is also developed. These five faculties and five powers are the mindfulness, or the mind; the energy and effort; the conviction and the faith; collectedness; wisdom or understanding. You cultivate and develop these whenever you walk the eightfold path. So, everything revolves around cultivating the eightfold path. All these aspects are part and parcel of practicing the eightfold path.

When you have developed these, you could further develop the four bases if you want. Through jhāna practice, you could develop psychic powers if the inclination were there. There are formations that might have been built up through previous rebirths, where there was a cultivated intention to be able to develop such powers. They are brought about when you experience the jhānas, cessation, and nibbāna. And so, the formations that were cultivated, start to bear fruit through the four bases to actualize the psychic abilities that the mind was inclined toward.

To simplify everything, what needs to be understood for the purposes of liberation, is to see with understanding. To see with a collected mind, with mindfulness, and with wisdom the destruction of the taints, the destruction of the fetters. That is the ultimate psychic power, so to speak, which provides one with complete peace, complete liberation. One gets off the wheel of saṃsāra.

Daily Reflection Day 8

Unrealized and Realized Eightfold Path

You can see these two versions of the path, namely as the path and as the fruition of having practiced each step of the eightfold path. The unrealized path is the entry into the path, while the realized path is the fruition of that same path. In other words, while you are yet to be fully realized, you are still on the path. When you attain Arahantship, the factors of the eightfold path have been fully developed, and you then access the ten factors of the realized path.

When you are training to the end, the path is still being developed, suffering is still being understood, the cause is still being recognized, and cessation is being exercised. In this way, the four noble truths are being discovered as you continue to study, contemplate, and practice right intention, right speech, right action, right livelihood, right effort, and right mindfulness in daily living, thereby getting in touch with reality as it is, attention rooted in reality. In doing so, the mind becomes less distracted, more collected, and naturally tends toward right collectedness, the final fruit of which is the complete knowledge of the four noble truths, namely the realized right view. Let's unpack each step of the path from development to fulfillment.

Right View

Ultimately, right view is the experiential knowledge and insight into each of the four noble truths. If you start on the path, you must make an effort to understand how suffering arises. It is through the link of craving, which is to take the link of feeling as personal, and to take delight in it, or avert it through a false sense of self. Whenever you practice the 6R process - both during meditation to free the mind of hindrances, and during daily living where feeling arises constantly - and you continue to release and relax any craving that may arise, you effectively begin to realize that the way out of suffering is through cessation of that craving.

This practice of cessation is systematically understood and exercised through the rest of the factors of the eightfold path. In this way, as you continue to understand suffering, and release craving, with the realization of cessation through the development of the eightfold path, you are living the four noble truths every time these are done. Thus, reconditioning formations, breaking away at the fetters which are rooted in the projections. At a certain point, you have a complete breakthrough and fulfill the work needed to cease birth, end suffering, and know in every way the four noble truths. When this is done, right view is realized. This includes not only the insight into the four noble truths, but also into the three symptoms of reality, the mechanics of kamma, and therefore the knowledge of ending rebirth.

Right Intention

Right Intention is the cornerstone of the practice. It is the choice you practice in every given moment to give up, abandon, to let go and release and relax craving, and to replace it with a wholesome quality of mind. Right intention is what conditions your next set of old kamma. Right intention is the new kamma when you apply it, but such a choice does not create good, bad, or neutral kamma, because in such a choice, you are choosing to see every arising and ceasing of contact, feeling, and perception as impermanent, and therefore not to be considered worth holding onto, and therefore not considered to be self or pertaining to self. In doing so, you effectively stop the arising of craving, and therefore the rest of the links of dependent origination thereafter. Moreover, you respond instead of reacting. You do not take anything personal, and you naturally choose to behave in accordance with the brahmavihārās.

In the realized right intention, the choice is automatic. There is no exercise or practice involved. Right Intention has been made so many times, that it roots out the projections and weakens and ultimately breaks apart the fetters in the formations. Then, every choice you make is an effective and right choice. You always see through the lens of the three symptoms of reality. You understand it and do not need to think about it. It is reality as it is. There is no study or thinking involved. You intuitively, without hesitation, continue to make right intentions – that is, always staying free and unconditioned by the links, and you always stay non-abiding in any link in whatever way, shape or form. No formations or the links thereafter are ever held on to, because in the holding on to something, craving arises. There is no choice to release because all that needed to be released was done so and sustained in that way, at the final realization of Arahantship

Right Speech, Action and Livelihood

> *Whenever you practice right intention, you always respond, and never react.*

Initially, there is effort involved through the 6R's, to pause and release and relax craving that has already arisen. And as you do so, the mind is pure and responds intuitively to what is required in every situation, and for every being, that you interact with, through speech, action, and your daily living. You make choices in harmony with the principles of the dhamma – you act and speak rooted in the brahmavihārās, without ill will, and with a view to let go of craving in general, not taking anything personal, and acting with observation in every given present moment.

Once the formations have become unfettered and unhindered – that is, the projections have been removed – there is no influence that creates intentions rooted in in right view. In other words, with the destruction of the projections, you can no longer, even at the subtlest level, identify with any of the processes that arise or cease. And since nothing is ever taken personal, even when you receive negative reactions from other beings, the response that is aroused still comes from right view and right intention. Therefore, in the realized right speech, right action, and right living, you always choose that which causes no harm and is void of any sense of self-interest.

Right Effort

You aim to continue to activate the seven awakening factors, while effectively recognizing and releasing your attention from the hindrances during meditation. In daily living, you aim to apply the same principles, by continuing to remain in a wholesome mindset, and releasing any craving and other hindrances that may arise in your mind, by using attention rooted in reality.

As your mind becomes purer and purer through the attainments, when it is fully released, there is the realized right effort, which is simply to enter jhāna without any identification; or cessation of perception, feeling and consciousness if you have developed the mind for it; and to enter conscious cessation by merely attending to the nibbāna element. In the fully released mind, the seven factors are naturally present and remain balanced, and you are in a state of mundane nibbāna, always attending to the cessation of the links instead of their arising, or in between the arising and cessation. In this way, your mind is naturally quiet, in equanimity, and automatically collected in every given moment.

Right Mindfulness

In the unrealized factor of right mindfulness, you use attention rooted in reality to see with wisdom how the four aspects of conditioned existence arise and cease, namely the body, feeling, mindsets and moods, and phenomena. You begin to know the three symptoms of reality of each aspect, and in doing so, the fetters of craving, conceit, and ignorance are loosened. As you continue this practice, both in daily living and in meditation, the formations continue to recondition, until you finally experience right knowledge and right liberation.

Then, the realized right mindfulness is the automatic way of functioning for a fully released mind. It is how the mind continues to operate – being observant of every aspect of reality, and of every situation that arises in each moment. When this is the natural way of your perspective, right intention and therefore right speech, behavior and living are always the default setting for the mind.

Right Collectedness

When developing the path, you are training the mind, making it softer, more sensitive, and easier to work with, in terms of reconditioning formations. Through the process of traversing the jhānas and higher dimensions of perception, you unravel deeper and deeper layers of the mind. In doing so, you surgically dull the sharpness of craving, making it less prone to occur, and more importantly, you develop the ability to recognize when craving arises, so you can release and relax it, and rouse up the wholesome qualities of the mind. As the work of right collectedness is fulfilled, the projections are deactivated and destroyed, unable to fetter the formations ever again. This creates a mind that is prone to nibbāna. In other words, the mind naturally tends toward the cessation of the links. Mind is collected without effort and thus can enter jhāna, cessation of perception, feeling and consciousness, and be in a state of conscious cessation.

Right Knowledge

When the fetters are destroyed, when the projections are destroyed, ignorance can no longer be the influencer of the links of dependent origination, nor can craving arise ever again. And, having destroyed conceit, you can no longer identify with anything as permanent or self. Right knowledge is the knowledge of the destruction of the projections, and the wisdom that arises from fulfilling the eightfold path. It is the irreversible establishment of the knowledge of the four noble truths in the mind.

Right Liberation

Right Liberation closely follows right knowledge. When there is right knowledge, there is right liberation, which is the untainted, pure mind, the luminous mind void of fetters, defilements, or any conditions. It is nibbāna, pure and simple. Release of the mind that can never be shaken or reversed. These last two, right knowledge and right liberation, are not factors to be developed – they are the fulfillment of the path, the fruition of the path.

Fulfillment of the Thirty-Seven Qualities Required for Awakening

When you follow the eightfold path, you fulfill through development the thirty-seven qualities required for awakening. These are divided into seven sets, which include the observation of the four aspects of conditioned existence, the four right efforts, the seven factors of awakening, and the eightfold path, as you have already seen and understood through the course of the retreat. The remaining three sets include the five faculties and five energies, and the four bases for psychic development.

Five Faculties and Five Energies

The five faculties are the faculties from which the five energies arise. In the same way that there is the faculty for contact within mentality, and the process of contact which functions through the faculty for contact, the five energies are the output of the five faculties. Therefore, the faculties and energies both include conviction, application, observation, collectedness, and intelligence. Conviction is cultivated through right view via right effort, mindfulness through right mindfulness, collectedness through right collectedness, and intelligence through right knowledge.

Four Bases for Psychic Development

The four bases for psychic development are cultivated intention (*chanda*), application, mindset (*citta*), and reflection (*vimamsa*). Cultivated intention is rooted in right intention, application in right effort, and mindset and reflection in right mindfulness, and right collectedness through attention that is rooted in reality. While these four bases are the launch pads for so-called psychic abilities – including, but not limited to, telepathy, remote viewing, recollecting past lives, and knowing the rebirth and destinations of other beings - they are also utilized in collectedness, in order to attain the supreme of all psychic abilities – the destruction of the projections.

Restful Clarity

Samatha (restfulness) and Vipassana (clarity) are joined together.

It is through the development of the eightfold path that you gain a mind that is prone to be in a restful, tranquil, and undisturbed state. When the mind does not utilize one-pointed focus but uses the tools provided by the dhamma, it is naturally restful. And in this restfulness, clarity of the dhamma arises. You understand in a way that flows, rather than through mere analysis and being entranced through just noting what arises. Restfulness and clarity are interdependent – without restfulness, true clarity will not emerge. If you do not have clarity that is at ease, mind will not flower into restfulness. These two go hand-in-hand. Through developing right view, clarity emerges. When that clarity matures, there is the realized right view. Restfulness is the natural way that develops and is then fulfilled through realized right collectedness.

Interconnectedness of the Realized Eightfold Path and its Fruition

When right view replaces ignorance in dependent origination - and therefore directs formations - formations code mind, body, and speech activities with right intention. From these formations, cognition and mentality-materiality are rooted in right view and right intention. The six sense bases, contact, and feeling are all understood and seen with wisdom through right mindfulness, with attention rooted in reality. When old kamma terminates at feeling, then perception rooted in right view nullifies any ability for it to create more kamma, with right mindfulness conditioning new action that arises. Through right mindfulness, you act in sync with right action, right speech, and right living, according to what any given situation requires.

Right effort (the 6rs) has perfected the tranquilizing of pure formations for the purpose of either conscious cessation - where you attend to the nibbāna element by attending to the cessation aspect of each link starting from formations - or stopping the formations, for the purpose of cessation of perception, feeling, and consciousness. Right view determines right collectedness. Right collectedness has developed right view. Right knowledge has informed right view. Right liberation has perfected and established right view.

Instead of the projections influencing ignorance, now right collectedness, right knowledge, and right liberation influence right view.

In essence, the wheel of dhamma has replaced the wheel of saṃsāra.

Questions

Right Effort and three characteristics of existence

"Do the 6rs need to be practiced all the time, both in meditation and in daily life? When we do this, over time, will we see more clearly the three characteristics of existence?"

Answer:

Yes, right effort (6rs) should always be exercised. That happens through developing mindfulness of the present moment. The ability for the mind to be aware and conscious of what is happening right now, and then applying right effort to see that whatever arises is not permanent, is suffering, and is impersonal. By cultivating that attitude, you recondition the mind to do it automatically.

First you do this in a conscious manner, with the intention to be able to see it in that way. Eventually, you automate that process by having conditioned the mind.

"You talked about Kamma, rebirth and the fact that certain formations might bear fruit in one's life. It is almost like a hard drive of kammic fruits that will be handed over to a new rebirth and the rebirth-consciousness. Is it correct to assume that the fruits come up and move all the way to contact, based on the circumstances?"

Answer:

That is a good analogy to use, but understand that, if you say that the hard drive is a repository of all these formations, that the repository itself is also impermanent. Therefore, the Buddha's last words in the suttas is that all formations are impermanent. At the most minute level of the mechanics of kamma and rebirth, are formations. But the formations themselves can be changed, depending upon the choices that we make.

The way to destroy rebirth forever is to not take those formations as personal, not to take the repository of formations as a person or as permanent. That is why rebirth is impossible for a released mind, because at parinibbāna such a mind does not grasp onto anything, let alone life itself. Even in death, the dissolution of the five aggregates, such a mind does not allow for the ability of the formations to create a new consciousness that could cause rebirth, as there is no intention of personalizing what is arising in the mind. It is a complete letting go, instead of holding on to.

Yes, the kamma and rebirth arise because of formations, but there is a way out of it, by not holding on to those formations and letting them go.

Cessation and relief

When there is a cessation experience and relief is felt afterwards, the recommendation is to go back and sit, letting go of any expectations. Two things that can happen are:

The level of energy and joy is so high that meditating again is almost impossible. You just want to experience the senses, because they are so open and receptive to reality.

The second one might be that, if one continues to sit and mind is so pristine that it experiences nibbāna for a second time, the release experience is significantly less than the first time.

Answer:

The entry into sotāpanna, and the fruition of sotāpanna, is the destruction of these fetters:

1. the fetter of doubt
2. the fetter of taking things to be a permanent self
3. the fetter of depending on rites and rituals, thinking that they are the way toward liberation

Stream-entry destroys the potential for rebirth in lower realms, lower than the human realm. This is a great relief for the mind, and of course the bliss that arises from having contacted the nibbāna element is another aspect. But after more Nibbana experiences, the relief is not necessarily as profound as the first time. There are two aspects to this. One is that the mind compares this to the previous experience and does not see that it was the same. It is like - and this might sound ironic - taking an intoxicant for the first time and seeing *wow, what an amazing experience*. And the next time, you may need a double dose to experience it in the same manner.

The second aspect is that, in the case of a sakadāgāmī, you only *weaken* the fetters of sensual craving and of hatred, or ill will. You do not break these fetters.

At the level of an anāgāmi, once you break these fetters, there too the relief is not necessarily as profound. This is because the mind has let go of so much mental, emotional, and psychic debris of all the suffering that it has inherited - through countless lifetimes, countless rebirths -, that it will not be the same as when a sotāpanna released all of this (which in essence are the formations), that could have caused lower rebirths. The sotāpanna has shut off the ability to take rebirth in a lower than the human realm.

So, that is the second aspect of it. Of course, at the level of an anāgāmi, there is still the identification process in which there is the *I feel this relief*, and *how amazing is this, that I just felt this*.

At the entry into Arahantship, the five higher fetters are destroyed. That extinguishes the ability to take rebirth in any of the higher realms. It destroys ignorance, the craving for existence or non-existence, and it destroys restlessness. There is some sense of relief, but there is no identification with that relief since the fetter of conceit has also been destroyed. That relief will only be seen as what it is; impermanent, not worth holding on to, and impersonal.

"Is there a difference if my motivation is to get rid of my suffering or my motivation is to achieve awakening – whatever that is?"

Answer:

In either case, you are still cultivating the potential for craving to arise. One is the desire for awakening, even though it is *chanda*, a cultivated intention for awakening, having entered the path. But wanting this removal of suffering is identifying with that. *I* want to remove that suffering.

You must recognize and let go of the desire for awakening. You cultivate a noble intention by letting go of all things, by letting go of the potential for craving, but you also need to let go of the idea that *I no longer want this suffering to continue*, since this creates agitation in the mind. You need to find a middle way here, a way in which you understand the mechanics, the tools of the path. All you do is from an objective, impersonal mindset say: *Now I understand this, and I have entered the path.* In the case of one who has entered the stream; *I have become a sotāpanna.* Check your reactions and responses to see whether they are in alignment with the destruction of the fetters, or not. Then you can return to the meditation with the intention of wanting to liberate the mind, but then let go of that intention and these expectations. Because attaching toward the intention of either awakening or the removal of suffering, you will not achieve either.

So, it is important to let go of the intention, after returning to the sit. Just have the attitude of *let's see what happens.* Just pretend it is a new season of a tv show of the mind. There are other things that will arise then, and other things that might start to unravel, whatever they may be.

Also, do not compare an experience with a previous one. Do not expect it to be the same.

Student's Attainment Experiences

Stream-Entry

It was quite an extraordinary event for me. I was in Neither Perception nor non-Perception for quite some time, like close to two hours. I felt some strong pull. It is like I got sucked into a powerful vacuum. First, I noticed myself resisting it, kept going back to Equanimity and then to Neither Perception nor non-Perception a few times.

At last, I just let go entirely and then blackout. And then I noticed very faintly but distinctive light first appeared, and some "flickers" followed. After my session, then I noticed the magical part. First thing, all colors of the trees are very vibrant, crisp, and sharp. The ordinary gravels on the road were almost like floating. I had to keep adjusting my glasses when I saw things I never noticed before. And I experienced the joy and relief that I never felt before. It was an incredible experience.

My second time was similar, but I felt "the pull" is even stronger. I felt like I was pulled apart from both ends. Before that "pull" moment, I noticed I lost my senses starting from my feet and hands towards my heart. (You don't feel the body while in arūpa jhānas. However, this was a different sensation.) And I lost my hearing too and blacked out for a brief moment. Once I came out of this very short cessation moment, I noticed that my hearing changed. I remember sitting and watching some butterflies from ten to fifteen feet away and hearing their wings. I was just there to witness it. Truly amazing!

- Meditator from Toronto, Canada

This sense of alert sleeping starts to blip a little, one feels like everything is slowing down and the voices stop talking. It's like going down an elevator and having the elevator slow down and then stop, very briefly, and you are asleep but know that you are asleep. Like awake sleeping. Then you open your eyes, and you are not sure if you are awake or sleeping, or how long it's being gone for, are you dreaming, is this real, the world looks different, then you realize, I was dreaming, this is what it feels like to be awake! Oh, now I get it, this is what the awakening part is all about. To see the world as it is, without commentary and the blah blah blah of our emotional pressures and tensions. Not creating concepts and adding to experience, just sitting in the flow of phenomena as they arise and pass away. Just this immense feeling of absolute relief, that everything is going to be okay. Like a dam breaking and all this suffering flowing out of you, all these foolish worries and regrets and remorse just flowing away.

- Meditator from California, USA

Observed whatever came up. 6R'd a couple of things that came up. Relaxed and observed, then knowledges/insights started to come – some reassurance of a no self. Formations were observed, then a big buildup of energy. Body felt like it was undergoing some sort of huge change, then a blackout. Came out with a feeling of increased clarity and a lack of caring about anything, having no desire at all. Observing again, just letting go. Another blackout, not as deep, then clarity and a lack of caring about anything, having no desire at all. Finished and got off the chair with energy and clarity. Hard to get to sleep. Woke up and had no craving for coffee at all. Couldn't care if I had one or not.

- Meditator from Australia

I had been meditating all winter and probably trying too hard and not really getting how to just smile and relax. It was like the Dhamma came and said you are hopeless, but we are going to just give it to you anyway!

Jan 13, 2013, I got up at midnight to go to the bathroom and then came back and lay back down to sleep. I just relaxed, and with no real effort just noticed the mind arising and passing away. A few minutes later, I experienced a dramatic shift in consciousness. This kind of luminous mind arose; energetic yet balanced. I had this profound insight into Dependent Origination. It was like when Ananda experienced seeing

Dependent origination and went to the Buddha and says it is so easy to see and understand! I virtually could see how everything was just causes and conditions. One thing at a time. In a moment it was clear. Then a few minutes later another rush of understanding how the word "sutta" meant threads and how it was all tied together. It all made sense and I understood DO clearly. There was a shift of mind but no apparent blackout. But immediately, Joy arose and lots of energy and I lept out of my bed to just contemplate it all. I felt great.

- Meditator from Missouri, USA

It was August 2013. I just returned from walking my dogs. I made tea and sat down. I didn't meditate, I didn't even think about meditating. Suddenly – as I reached for my cup – from one second to the next everything dropped away inside. I became unbelievably calm. All emotions were gone. No thoughts at all. 'I' wasn't (my name) anymore. I didn't have 'my' stories, memories anymore, no history of 'me'. There was only perception of sense contacts. This had happened before, but only a second or maybe two. It felt exactly as if I had walked through life with my head permanently stuck in a beehive; everything buzzing and screaming inside my mind. Now that beehive was gone. Or a crackling bag of paper that was ripped from the mind.

But this went on and on. I looked at the dogs; no stories. Not my beautiful old, big dogs who I loved so very much. They were just beings. We weren't in the living room, it just was a space with things that enclosed the space (walls, roof, and floor).

All people, including me, were just beings. I felt completely empty, there was no attachment to anything, not to people, animals, 'me'. After 10 minutes one thought popped up: the only thing that is missing is mettā. After that again no thought, not even anything on the verge of popping up. I decided - without thinking - to do a guided meditation, 40 minutes, and there was incredible focus and collectedness, but after that I noticed (without any thoughts) that this 'condition' was still there.

I emptied the dishwasher. There was uninterrupted mindfulness. There was a decision, but no thoughts. No stories, no aversion to doing this. No, just emptying it. Anything could have happened, and there wouldn't have been any aversion or desire. The best I can do to describe that state is as if I was a recorder with the possibility of noticing all the sense contacts. No concepts, just stuff.

After two hours slowly, slowly, things went back to normal. This period took another 2 to 3 hours, where thoughts slowly returned, some very, very light emotions. After all of this I realized that I wasn't a 'self' during that time, I was just one of many creatures that roam the earth, no more important than a cockroach. The difference between a rock and a being was that a being had awareness, while a rock has not.

Also, I now understood what the Buddha meant when he said something like: "Don't compare yourself to anyone. Don't feel you are less worthy, more important, or equal." Because there was nothing to compare. It is not important. Do I compare one piece of dust to another, no. Why would I?

The next day things were still a bit different. I was often spontaneously mindful. And there was no desire to talk about 'my' problems whatsoever and I could focus on someone who had a difficult time, for the full 100% This sounds not that strange, but that feeling of 'my' own unimportance was very strong. Also, thoughts, feelings and emotions were still diminished, compared to 'normal'. During this day I suddenly felt as if I was somehow flushed from the inside. Something had been cleaned.

The doubts about the Buddha, Dhamma and Sangha were completely gone, and they never returned. Rites and rituals were not important, don't lead to nibbāna. I felt I still had to understand the impersonal nature of everything completely, but the foundation had been laid. I can still bring up this sensation at will, experiencing reality with mindfulness, based on anatta and there is this deep-rooted knowledge that to add a sense of self to anything at all is just misperceiving reality.

- Meditator from the Netherlands

It's like the volume of the world gets turned down. The world is much less threatening, more peaceful and wondrous. And one can see how everything is made of the same stuff, subject to the same physical laws, there is no difference, all part of the same moment in time. All connected. Everything is a minor miracle, given this vast web of phenomena that lead to this moment. One now realizes that much of what we worry about and concern ourselves with is petty, is beyond our control and not worth worrying about and there is simply less stress and attachment. Thoughts arise but they don't stick, they kind of flow through you. Craving does arise but it's less forceful.

There is the feeling that colors and details are much brighter, and you can see much more clearly because mind is not wasting cycles worrying about stuff it can't change or influence, and its only job is to fully enjoy the moment, because this is all there is, or ever will be, and it's perfect, can't be changed, and is to be loved.

- Meditator from California, USA

From sitting in dispassion at the limit of awareness, a natural surrender occurred. The mind needed no more coaxing, no more subtle intentions, no more watching, no more effort whatsoever, just letting go. Then I missed something. Then flooded with bliss, just being. Eventually a flurry of formations came along like a group of butterflies just fluttering through, passing in and out of my awareness. There was no need to let them go as there was no sense of any relation to them, no sense of a me. After a few minutes the bliss died down and the mind was very clear.

- Meditator from British Columbia, Canada

All of a sudden, I felt like large fan blades were falling beside me and I could see all the objects in my room moving in space from some past location to their present location in the room. They were making a click click click sound (although not really a sound) while falling into place, and each one was pushing (or mechanically locking) the present object/link into place. I could see everything from the past had put them here to the current moment. It was a big wow and a big relief because I saw had no control. I felt more fan blades and next I could see all the objects of the landscape of Dhammasukha falling into place. The whole layout of Dhammasukha cabins and paths twisting and turning and falling and locking into place. I could see all the objects moving from past locations into current locations. In that moment I could see everything moves in a mechanical and precise way, there is nothing "willy nilly" about this process. Things are locked into place based on past. I could see that nothing is random- everything is exactly where it is from past conditions. Exact and precise. I realized I had no control over this process and the relief was immense and indescribable. I don't know how to explain this next thing except to say, I felt I was removed from that process, as if I was a phantom (not the ghost phantom but the figment of your imagination phantom). It felt like someone had poured a bucket of water over the thing I had been so upset about over my head, it was totally extinguished and immediately afterwards I was filled with joy - exactly the way Bhante and David describe. Relief and then joy.

- Meditator from Missouri, USA

"LET GO" is the only thing I can say…. No holding back… total surrender. Then and only then is there true Awakening. A snow fake falling onto a snow field. Like a dying candle. Nibbana.

And then… It is seen. That no one can know unless seen. Then you 'zap back in' and everything fades away. I'm back 'here' again; Consensus reality. Then ask the question "what was realized?"

That brings back the inextinguishable memory and all the insights that have led to this Insight. That was Nibbana.

This is entering the Stream. Nobody will ever get this from your consciousness.

One knows like no other what happens at the moment of death. One knows that trip will be undertaken once again. That which was experienced cannot be unseen. Ultimate Reality has been Realized. That is why eventually rebirth is not possible anymore. That is why the illusion has been viewed. No other worldly madness can hold you in.

No 'god' can ever rule you again. The builder of the house has been seen. The inner workings have been revealed.

One understands how previous lives are viewed. The idea Self has been seen through. No rite and rituals can get you here. The Path to It seen and realized. The Mind Stream has been seen.

Compassion abounds. All that suffering because of Unknowing. Hate, Greed, and Lust subsides. The illusionary dream called Life holds less grip. Silence. Stillness. Going nowhere, being nobody, doing nothing, having no worries.

Nibbana exists. The path leading to Nibbana exists. That is the way out of suffering. Because Suffering exists.

May all who suffer be suffering free.

- Meditator from the Netherlands

That experience was a rapid shutdown of the perception and feeling, and it seemed like a blackout then entered a cool area (that's what I can recall afterward). The second day after it happened, another cessation occurred where the perception, feeling, and consciousness seemed to blackout again while I was eating my lunch in the dining hall. I got into a state that nothing nor any condition can be attached to it; it was like the slipping space that slips off everything. Then a third time, there was only the cessation of feeling and perception, but consciousness became the strong awareness factor of just observing – there was no "self" there.

- Meditator from Hong Kong

Day 5 from the 10-day physical retreat. Following a good day of meditation and on and off crying (which I rarely do), mind and body were full of energy. I went to bed at around 11 and there was some sleep at times, and at 3 a.m. I decided to go and sit. There was so much energy and awakeness, and well, what else could I do :-) Within minutes mind abided in Neither Perception nor non-Perception, and at times random and disconnected thoughts or images came up in the background. Perception was too subtle or non-present at all, it was really a state as if awake while sleeping. There was no interest in anything that arose or occurred. All that happened, happened without any involvement or control from my side. There was not enough perception or awareness for 6R. There was just intermittent perception and awareness and mind turned away from it. Dispassion is a good way to describe it. I don't know how long I sat, but the next memory is that of a massive flash of light. Can only compare it to a lighting flash with high energy, though difference was this was happening inside my head. Both a mental and physical feeling and recall later I was wondering if neurons were strong enough to transmit such energy! There simply was a mind black-out (don't know for how long) and it seemed as if the system booted up again. Fresh. And then there came this immense relief. Laying down an ocean of suffering is appropriate expression for the feeling I experienced. This is what I was looking for in my life, now I found it. No doubt about the Dhamma, certainty about the path to follow. I opened my eyes and continued to see these smaller light flashes in front of my eyes.

During morning meditation, a couple of hours later, there was a second black-out experience, though the feeling of relief was less intense than the first time. I recall a thought of "why don't I experience the same kind of massive release?" Seeing links was clearer the second time, although it still happened too quickly for mind to see the individual steps one by one. During the rest of the day, I simply couldn't sit. There was too much energy, too much joy and too much wonder. It was an experience that I can only describe as "seeing in four-dimensions" with vivid colors and it lasted for days. I took my notebook and wrote down a couple of the thoughts including "all that is born, will die" and I recall I had difficulties with using the pronoun "I." Thoughts just arose without my involvement. Driving back from the airport there was music from "Songs from a distant earth" playing from Mike Oldfield, which starts with "and there was light". Yes, there was indeed :-)

- Meditator from the Netherlands

Sakadāgāmī

Going into Cessation was similar for previous times, however coming out of this was a bit different. Firstly, I experienced noticing individual formations of contact, perception and feeling in quite slow motion and details. Secondly, I never felt like the relief that I felt at that time before (even stronger than first time and strong enough for me to remember it in detail). I felt very balanced and satisfied without attachment to any of these.

- Meditator from Toronto, Canada

The meditation began with a very busy experience of the realm of Infinite Consciousness. Consciousnesses were 'coming at me' in a very sustained and almost tiring way. I continued to 6R any disturbances and mind slowly began to give way to nothingness. I have always thought that the mind-objects, seen in the transition between Infinite Consciousness and Nothingness, appear as three-dimensional objects that continually move and change, pulling mind's attention from one place to another in a series of continual mind movements that are felt as unpleasant sensations in mind.

In this meditation, something very profound occurred. These three-dimensional objects suddenly disappeared, and I became aware of what looked like millions of individual points of light coming into and out of existence (these lights are what had been giving the illusion of three-dimensional objects being present in mind). It was as if my mind suddenly came into focus and saw these objects for what they were, which was simply a collection of lights, illuminating and extinguishing in complex patterns.

My attention to these lights became more refined and it was as if mind 'zoomed in' so that I could now see, very close-up, each light individually coming into and out of existence. Mind at this stage had become completely inky black, with now only a few hundred lights at the center of my observation twinkling in and out.

I then had a sudden realization. Whenever one of these lights appeared, it drew my attention to it because I had 'felt' the light appearing: whenever my attention was drawn by one of these lights that came into existence, in that very moment, a sensation arose in mind. I realized that the sensation was the sensation of 'me' – that is, the personality of me. I also realized that each one of these tiny lights coming into existence was craving. I further realized that in the very act of observing these lights of craving, 'I' was being created as a series of individual, discrete sensations in mind.

As this realization arose, all of a sudden, approximately half of the visible lights suddenly switched off, as if somebody flicked a switch. I knew, intuitively, at that moment, that my realization has just caused the cessation of craving. I now knew (by experiencing it) that if craving did not arise, as one of these lights, then 'I' would not exist; the feeling associated with that craving would cease, and 'I' would cease to exist.

In the days that followed, when I tried to sleep at night, I couldn't. Instead, mind wanted to drop into Nothingness for hours at a time (this was natural, and I had no control over it). When in that state, I could see the tiny lights of craving making pictures/images in mind – these were very clear and slightly raised/three dimensional images of incredible detail and clarity. I did not recognize these images, which were of hundreds of different people, events, and places. The lights were just like tiny pixels; creating these pictures/images in the same way that a television picture would be generated. I realized that these were the formations in mind, and the pictures were fragments of thoughts. Whenever I now sit in meditations, or if I am quietly lying in bed at night, these pictures, made of the tiny lights, arise as I transition into Neither Perception nor non-perception or drift into sleep.

Following this experience, I felt extreme levels of joy and ecstasy. I was unable to sleep properly for almost a week, and I noticed my sense of self had receded. When I looked at other people, I intuitively knew and sensed that there was no real person 'in there' and that their actions and thoughts were being shaped by these tiny lights of craving, just as I had been. I also knew, intuitively, that the death of my body is just another moment of these lights of craving extinguishing: I now no longer fear death like I used to, and this has led to a profound sense of peace and tranquility. Other changes began to build in the days and weeks that followed. I no longer felt strong craving for food or drink (I was cured of a long-standing chocolate addiction!), and my mind was very balanced – people began noticing.

The most interesting, lasting effect of this experience is that whenever I go about my daily life, my mind is very quiet, and when thoughts do arise, I now clearly 'see' the feeling that arises with each thought. This means I am able to 6R them automatically. Hence, my meditation is now self-sustaining 'off the cushion' and the depth of the experience is deepening each month, automatically. Reaching the Anāgāmi path stage now feels like an inevitability and any sense of longing I had for Nibbana has vanished – I know it will happen when it is ready – I am not worried any more. I am happier and less tense because of this.

I have also experienced a strengthening of my intuition. If I am feeling very quiet in mind, I can sometimes sense what people are going to say or do, before they do it. My intuition also now *tells me* how to refine my meditation in each sitting. It feels like the Dhamma is now just running its course, and I need to get out of the way and let it happen. I have since gone back to the suttas and I am beginning to spot levels of meaning and detail in them that I simply could not see at the previous stages of noble practice. Because the suttas match my experience of the Dhamma, and my experience is so clear and detailed, my belief in the verity of the Buddha and the Dhamma has been strengthened in completely new and unexpected ways.

Since this experience, I have still felt, on rare occasions, a hint of anger, irritability or craving caused by life situations. However, they are now so obvious when they occur (against the quiet backdrop of mind) that the 6R process manages them quite nicely! I now also feel compelled and determined to reach the end of the path to eliminate all craving.

- Meditator from England

Anāgāmi

Establishing continuous and steady Attention and Observation throughout the day with Equanimity and using the 6R process was the foundation of the practice. As the mind became more collected, discernment of different jhānas during the meditation became clearer. Seeing the three characteristics of existence in everything became more pronounced and dispassion arose. The cessation experience was preceded by an incredible stillness in the mind and the breath slowed down to almost nonexistence, and the mind felt like a black curtain had started to come down. Recalling the experience afterwards, there was no recollection of what happened next (like a temporary blackout) until the awareness of the mind coming back online was noticed. Then there was a seeing of Dependent origination through the ear sense door and the mind experiencing it like a stream flashing light. After the experience, the mind was left with an incredible stillness. Unlike Sotāpanna and Sakadāgāmī attainment experiences, there was no apparent relief or uplifting joy in the mind in the attainment of Anāgāmi. The mind was left still, vast and crystal clear.

In daily living, things that one used to want or desire no longer have the pulling power. Ill-will and judgmental thoughts don't arise. The ability to understand the Dhamma has become much sharper. The mind naturally leans towards compassion for oneself and all beings. Knowing there is still work left to be done for the fully liberated state, there is no pressure or burden on the mind to make it happen. There is just a great sense of freedom and ease in the mind.

When we talk about a sense of self conditioning different parts of D.O (Dependent origination) which then conditions the grasping of five aggregates, in the meditation, similar to the analogy you used, I saw each link of D.O as an individual movie frame. The mind saw specifically the conditioning process as this sense of 'I' very rapidly rushes in and merges and fuses with what arises (almost like a chemical reaction). The further one goes down the link, different aspects of 'I' get added and the chemical formula gets stronger. It's super clear that 'I' is something that gets added but also, it's so difficult for beings to understand that because their living experience is totally infused with 'I.' The fusion makes a lot of sense for the mind as this 'I' is so entangled and integrated that without Wisdom one can't defuse this process.

- Meditator from England

My personality seems to have taken a huge personality shift - away from craving and ego.

Many times, these changes will disappear after some time, but this may stick. I am hoping the final vestiges of hatred and sensual desire are gone for good. I'll be quite happy if I can get to that goal in this life. Maybe you just helped me do it. I spent the whole day in this all-pervading happiness and super high balanced energy. It got more and more and then today now its subsided back but still the balance is there.

When I was listening, I investigated even more the subtle layers to see how consciousness was arising and then 6red right then the moment it arose. I think that new layer of investigation is what did it.

It's interesting that after 20-25 min I fall into a deep silent mind. There is a little restlessness that appears. The feeling of lovingkindness is always there - I just have to bring it up or notice it.

- Meditator from Missouri, USA

Day 9:
The Arahant

Suttas

Majjhima Nikāya 112, the Chabbisodhana Sutta - The Sixfold Purity

Translation by bhikkhu Bodhi.

1. THUS HAVE I HEARD. On one occasion the Blessed One was living at Sāvatthī in Jeta's Grove, Anāthapiṇḍika's Park. There he addressed the bhikkhus thus: "Bhikkhus." - "Venerable sir, "they replied. The Blessed One said this:

2. "Here, bhikkhus, a bhikkhu makes a declaration of final knowledge thus: "I understand: Birth is destroyed, the holy life has been lived, what had to be done has been done, there is no more coming to any state of being."

3. "That bhikkhu's words should neither be approved nor disapproved. Without approving or disapproving, a question should be put thus: "Friend, there are four kinds of expression rightly proclaimed by the Blessed One who knows and sees, accomplished and fully enlightened. What four? Telling the seen as it is seen; telling the heard as it is heard; telling the sensed as it is sensed; telling the cognized as it is cognized. These, friend, are the four kinds of expression rightly proclaimed by the Blessed One who knows and sees, accomplished and fully enlightened. How does the venerable one know, how does he see, regarding these four kinds of expression, so that through not clinging his mind is liberated from the taints?"

4. "Bhikkhus, when a bhikkhu is one with taints destroyed, who has lived the holy life, done what had to be done, laid down the burden, reached the true goal, destroyed the fetters of being, and is completely liberated through final knowledge, this is the nature of his answer:

"Friends, regarding the seen I abide unattracted, unrepelled, independent, detached, free, dissociated, with a mind rid of barriers. Regarding the heard...Regarding the sensed...Regarding the cognized I abide unattracted, unrepelled, independent, detached, free, dissociated, with a mind rid of barriers. It is by knowing thus, seeing thus, regarding these four kinds of expression, that through not clinging my mind is liberated from the taints."

5. "Saying *good*, one may delight and rejoice in that bhikkhu's words. Having done so, a further question may be put thus:

"Friend, there are these five aggregates affected by clinging, rightly proclaimed by the Blessed One who knows and sees, accomplished and fully enlightened. What five? They are the material form aggregate affected by clinging, the feeling aggregate affected by clinging, the perception aggregate affected by clinging, the formations aggregate affected by clinging, and the consciousness aggregate affected by clinging. These, friend, are the five aggregates affected by clinging, rightly proclaimed by the Blessed One who knows and sees, accomplished and fully enlightened. How does the venerable one know, how does he see, regarding these five aggregates affected by clinging, so that through not clinging his mind is liberated from the taints?"

6. "Bhikkhus, when a bhikkhu is one with taints destroyed... and is completely liberated through final knowledge, this is the nature of his answer:

"Friends, having known material form to be feeble, fading away, and comfortless, with the destruction, fading away, cessation, giving up, and relinquishing of attraction and clinging regarding material form, of mental standpoints, adherences, and underlying tendencies regarding material form, I have understood that my mind is liberated.

Friends, having known feeling...Having known perception... Having known formations...Having known consciousness to be feeble, fading away, and comfortless, with the destruction, fading away, cessation, giving up, and relinquishing of attraction and clinging regarding consciousness, of mental standpoints, adherences, and underlying tendencies regarding consciousness, I have understood that my mind is liberated.

It is by knowing thus, seeing thus, regarding these five aggregates affected by clinging, that through not clinging my mind is liberated from the taints."

7. "Saying *good*, one may delight and rejoice in that bhikkhu's words. Having done so, a further question may be put thus:

"Friend, there are these six elements rightly proclaimed by the Blessed One who knows and sees, accomplished and fully enlightened. What six? They are the earth element, the water element, the fire element, the air element, the space element, and the consciousness element. These, friend, are the six elements rightly proclaimed by the Blessed One who knows and sees, accomplished and fully enlightened. How does the venerable one know, how does he see, regarding these six elements, so that through not clinging his mind is liberated from the taints?"

8. "Bhikkhus, when a bhikkhu is one with taints destroyed... and is completely liberated through final knowledge, this is the nature of his answer":

"Friends, I have treated the earth element as not self, with no self based on the earth element. And with the destruction, fading away, cessation, giving up, and relinquishing of attraction and clinging based on the earth element, of mental standpoints, adherences, and underlying tendencies based on the earth element, I have understood that my mind is liberated.

Friends, I have treated the water element...the fire element...the air element...the space element...the consciousness element as not self, with no self based on the consciousness element. And with the destruction, fading away, cessation, giving up, and relinquishing of attraction and clinging based on the consciousness element, of mental standpoints, adherences, and underlying tendencies based on the consciousness element, I have understood that my mind is liberated. It is by knowing thus, seeing thus, regarding these six elements, that through not clinging my mind is liberated from the taints."

9. "Saying *good*, one may delight and rejoice in that bhikkhu's words. Having done so, a further question may be put thus:

But, friend, there are these six internal and external bases rightly proclaimed by the Blessed One who knows and sees, accomplished and fully enlightened. What six? They are the eye and forms, the ear and sounds, the nose and odours, the tongue and flavours, the body and tangibles, the mind and mind-objects. These, friend, are the six internal and external bases rightly proclaimed by the Blessed One who knows and sees, accomplished and fully enlightened. How does the venerable one know, how does he see, regarding these six internal and external bases, so that through not clinging his mind is liberated from the taints?"

10. "Bhikkhus, when a bhikkhu is one with taints destroyed... and is completely liberated through final knowledge, this is the nature of his answer":

"Friends, with the destruction, fading away, cessation, giving up, and relinquishing of desire, lust, delight, craving, attraction, and clinging, and of mental standpoints, adherences, and underlying tendencies regarding the eye, forms, eye-consciousness, and things cognizable [by the mind] through eye-consciousness, I have understood that my mind is liberated.

With the destruction, fading away, cessation, giving up, and relinquishing of desire, lust, delight, craving, attraction, and clinging, and of mental standpoints, adherences, and underlying tendencies regarding the ear, sounds, ear-consciousness, and things cognizable [by the mind] through ear-consciousness... regarding the nose, odours, nose-consciousness, and things cognizable [by the mind] through nose-consciousness...regarding the tongue, flavours, tongue-consciousness, and things cognizable [by the mind] through tongue consciousness...regarding the body, tangibles, body-consciousness, and things cognizable [by the mind] through body-consciousness...regarding the mind, mind-objects, mind-consciousness, and things cognizable [by the mind] through mind-consciousness, I have understood that my mind is liberated.

It is by knowing thus, seeing thus, regarding these six internal and external bases, that through not clinging my mind is liberated from the taints."

11. "Saying *good*, one may delight and rejoice in that bhikkhu's words. Having done so, a further question may be put thus":

"But, friend, how does the venerable one know, how does he see, so that in regard to this body with its consciousness and all external signs, I-

330

making, mine-making, and the underlying tendency to conceit have been eradicated in him?"

12. "Bhikkhus, when a bhikkhu is one with taints destroyed...and is completely liberated through final knowledge, this is the nature of his answer":

"Friends, formerly when I lived the home life I was ignorant. Then the Tathagata or his disciple taught me the Dhamma. On hearing the Dhamma I acquired faith in the Tathagata. Possessing that faith, I considered thus: "Household life is crowded and dusty; life gone forth is wide open. It is not easy while living in a home to lead the holy life utterly perfect and pure as a polished shell. Suppose I shave off my hair and beard, put on the yellow robe, and go forth from the home life into homelessness." On a later occasion, abandoning a small or a large fortune, abandoning a small or a large circle of relations, I shaved off my hair and beard, put on the yellow robe, and went forth from the home life into homelessness.

13-17.Having thus gone forth and possessing the bhikkhus' training and way of life...(as Sutta 51, §§14r-19) [34, 35],..I purified my mind from doubt.

18. Having thus abandoned these five hindrances, imperfections of the mind that weaken wisdom, quite secluded from sensual pleasures, secluded from unwholesome states, I entered upon and abided in the first jhāna, which is accompanied by applied and sustained thought, with rapture and pleasure born of seclusion. With the stilling of applied and sustained thought, I entered upon and abided in the second jhāna.. . With the fading away as well of rapture.. .I entered upon and abided in the third jhāna...With the abandoning of pleasure and pain...I entered upon and abided in the fourth jhāna, which has neither-pain nor-pleasure and purity of mindfulness due to equanimity.

19. When my concentrated mind was thus purified, bright, unblemished, rid of imperfections, malleable, wieldy, steady, and attained to imperturbability, I directed it to knowledge of the destruction of the taints. I directly knew as it actually is:

This is suffering...This is the origin of suffering...This is the cessation of suffering...This is the way leading to the cessation of suffering. I directly knew as it actually is: These are the taints ...This is the origin of the taints... This is the cessation of the taints...This is the way leading to the cessation of the taints.

20. When I knew and saw thus, my mind was liberated from the taint of sensual desire, from the taint of being, and from the taint of ignorance. When it was liberated there came the knowledge: "It is liberated." I directly knew: "Birth is destroyed, the holy life has been lived, what had to be done has been done, there is no more coming to any state of being.

It is by knowing thus, seeing thus, friends, that in regard to this body with its consciousness and all external signs, I-making, mine-making, and the underlying tendency to conceit have been eradicated in me."

21. "Saying *good*, bhikkhus, one may delight and rejoice in that bhikkhu's words. Having done so, one should say to him: "It is a gain for us, friend, it is a great gain for us, friend, that we see such a companion in the holy life as the venerable one.""

That is what the Blessed One said. The bhikkhus were satisfied and delighted in the Blessed One's words.

Ud 1.10 Bāhiya Sutta - The Discourse about Bāhiya
Translation by Bhikkhu Ānandajoti.

Thus, I heard: At one time the Gracious One was dwelling near Sāvatthī, in Jeta's Wood, at Anāthapiṇḍika's monastery. Then at that time Bāhiya of the Bark Robe was living near Suppāraka, on the bank of the ocean, being venerated, respected, revered, honoured, esteemed, in receipt of robes, almsfood, dwellings, and medicinal requisites to help when sick.

Then when Bāhiya of the Bark Robe had gone into hiding, into seclusion, this reflection arose in his mind: *Among those in the world who are Worthy Ones, or have entered the path to Worthiness, I am one of them.*

Then a devatā, who was a former blood-relative of Bāhiya of the Bark Robe, being compassionate and desiring his welfare, knowing with his mind the reflection in the mind of Bāhiya of the Bark Robe, went to Bāhiya of the Bark Robe, and after going, he said this to Bāhiya of the Bark Robe:

"You are certainly not a Worthy One, Bāhiya. Nor have you entered the path to Worthiness. This practice of yours is not one whereby you could be a Worthy One, or one who has entered the path to Worthiness."

"Then who now in this world with its devas are Worthy Ones, or have entered the path to Worthiness?"

"There is, Bāhiya, in the northern countries a city by the name of Sāvatthī. There, the Gracious One dwells at the present time who is a Worthy One, a Perfect Sambuddha. He, Bāhiya, the Gracious One, is certainly a Worthy One, and teaches the Dhamma for attaining Worthiness."

Then Bāhiya of the Bark Robe being greatly moved by that devatā, immediately went away from Suppāraka, and staying for only one night in every place, went to Sāvatthī, Jeta's Wood, and to Anāthapiṇḍika's monastery. Then at that time many monks were walking in meditation in the open air. Then Bāhiya of the Bark Robe went to those monks, and after going, he said this to those monks:

"Where, reverend Sirs, is the Gracious One living at present, the Worthy One, the Perfect Sambuddha? We have a desire to see the Gracious One, the Worthy One, the Perfect Sambuddha."

"The Gracious One, Bāhiya, has entered among the houses for alms."

Then Bāhiya of the Bark Robe having hurriedly left Jeta's Grove and having entered Sāvatthī, saw the Gracious One walking for alms in Sāvatthī, confident, inspiring confidence, with sense faculties at peace, mind at peace, having attained supreme self-control and calm, controlled, guarded, with restrained faculties, a true nāga. After seeing him, he went to the Gracious One, and after going and prostrating himself with his head at the Gracious One's feet, he said this to the Gracious One: "Let the Gracious One preach the Dhamma to me, reverend Sir, let the Fortunate One preach the Dhamma, that will be for my benefit and happiness for a long time."

After that was said, the Gracious One said this to Bāhiya of the Bark Robe: "It is the wrong time for you, Bāhiya, we have entered among the houses for alms."

For a second time Bāhiya of the Bark Robe said this to the Gracious One: "But it is hard to know, reverend Sir, the dangers to the Gracious One's life, or the dangers to my life! Let the Gracious One preach the Dhamma to me, reverend Sir, let the Fortunate One preach the Dhamma, that will be for my benefit and happiness for a long time."

For a second time the Gracious One said this to Bāhiya of the Bark Robe: "It is the wrong time for you, Bāhiya, we have entered among the houses for alms."

For a third time Bāhiya of the Bark Robe said this to the Gracious One: "But it is hard to know, reverend Sir, the dangers to the Gracious One's life, or the dangers to my life! Let the Gracious One preach the Dhamma to me, reverend Sir, let the Fortunate One preach the Dhamma, that will be for my benefit and happiness for a long time."

"In that case, Bāhiya, you should train yourself thus: In what is seen there must be only what is seen, in what is heard there must be only what is heard, in what is sensed there must be only what is sensed, in what is cognized there must be only what is cognized. This is the way, Bāhiya, you should train yourself.

"And since for you, Bāhiya, in what is seen there will be only what is seen, in what is heard there will be only what is heard, in what is sensed there will be only what is sensed, in what is cognized there will be only what is cognized, therefore, Bāhiya, you will not be with that; and since, Bāhiya, you will not be with that, therefore, Bāhiya, you will not be in that; and since, Bāhiya, you will not be in that, therefore, Bāhiya, you will not be here or hereafter or in between the two—just this is the end of suffering."

Then through the Gracious One's brief teaching of this Dhamma Bāhiya of the Bark Robe's mind was immediately freed from the pollutants, without attachment. Then the Gracious One, having advised Bāhiya of the Bark Robe with this brief advice, went away.

Then not long after the Gracious One had gone a cow with a young calf, having attacked Bāhiya of the Bark Robe, deprived him of life.

Then the Gracious One after walking for alms in Sāvatthī, while returning from the alms-round after the meal, after going out from the city with many monks, saw that Bāhiya of the Bark Robe had died. After seeing him, he addressed the monks, saying:

"Monks, take up Bāhiya of the Bark Robe's body, and after putting it on a bier, carrying it away, and burning it, make a memorial mound for him, your fellow in the spiritual life, monks, has died."

"Yes, reverend Sir," said those monks, and after replying to the Gracious One, putting Bāhiya of the Bark Robe's body on a bier, carrying it away, burning it, and making a memorial mound for him, they went to the Gracious One, and after going and worshipping the Gracious One, they sat down on one side.

While sat on one side those monks said this to the Gracious One: "Burnt, reverend Sir, is Bāhiya of the Bark Robe's body, and the memorial mound for him has been made. What is his destination? What is his future state?"

"A wise man, monks, was Bāhiya of the Bark Robe, who practiced Dhamma in accordance with the Dhamma, and did not trouble me on account of the Dhamma. Completely emancipated, monks, is Bāhiya of the Bark Robe." Then the Gracious One, having understood the significance of it, on that occasion uttered this exalted utterance:

"In the place where the water, earth, fire, and wind find no footing,

There the stars do not shine, nor does the sun give light,

There the moon does not glow, there darkness is not found.

And when the sage, the brāhmaṇa, has experienced nibbāna through his own sagacity,

Then from both form and formless, happiness and suffering, he is free."

This exalted utterance was also said by the Gracious One, so I have heard.

Dhamma talk

The mind of an arahant is completely free from all concepts. When he or she experiences reality as it is, through the six sense bases, consciousness, feeling and perception, all these processes are completely empty, completely void. They are empty of any conceit of *I, me,* or *mine.* When an arahant experiences reality, there is no conceptual proliferation that arises from any perception that arises. It is being experienced in that moment, through the senses and the sense faculties. Their consciousness, the awareness, is still functional, but is void of any sense of self. Their perception, while it continues to perceive, is empty of any sense of self. The feeling aspect of their mind, while it continues to feel the experiences felt, is void and empty of any sense of self. There is no projecting onto what is experienced, any bundles of Kamma and activities, or sense of personality – contrary to the underlying tendency of a mind that is *not* fully released.

The mind of an arahant cannot be traced. When they rest the mind within mind, it enters a special state that is conscious cessation. It may be there while the arahant walks, while they sleep, talk, lie down, sit, while they appear to be in sitting meditation, or while they appear to be just vacant and idle, so to speak, not doing anything at all. Their mind always tends toward the perception of cessation. It takes the third noble truth of cessation as its object as it were and enters nibbāna. They experience the bliss that arises from nibbāna, but in that experience itself, there is no sense of experiencer. There is no sense of any personal self that enters these states of mind.

So, when an arahant meditates, or whenever they do anything at all, because there is no longer the fetter of conceit, there is no longer any comparison going on. There is no longer any subject-object duality going on in that sense. There is no sense that *I am eating this food,* or *I am walking,* or *I am entering the first, second jhāna,* and so on and so forth, all the way up to; *I am entering into the signless samadhi; I am entering into Cessation of perception and feeling; I am entering into conscious*

Cessation; I am entering into nibbāna. That *I am* does not arise in the mind of an arahant. It is pure intention, the intention without a personalizing sense of self.

When they experience the links of dependent origination, they always tend toward the cessation of these links. It is the same experience that one has upon emerging from cessation of perception and feeling, in which the links arise. But the arahant's mind is not bothered by the arising, nor is it glued to that arising or abiding in that. Their mind continuously reflects on the cessation aspect of each arising of the links of dependent origination. By doing so, they understand that in the arising, the abiding, the cessation, and in the space between one cessation and the next arising, there is no sense of self. There is no self here or there. There is no abiding in *this* or *that*. All duality of perception and feeling in relation to a sense of self and the outside world, is completely obliterated. The arahant behaves and acts always in accordance with the eightfold noble path.

For conventional purposes, they would use the conventional language of *I, me*, or *mine*, just to be able to communicate with other beings. But in the usage of those words, there are no attachments of sense of self to them. The arahant just sees reality as it is. They understand the elements and the five aggregates just as they are, void of any clinging. Their mind is empty and remains empty because there is no abiding. And because there is no abiding, nothing sticks in the way of craving, or through the fuel of craving and clinging and sense of self. The ignorance that they have destroyed, is the ignorance of the four noble truths. In that sense, they live the four noble truths in every moment. Even while having a conversation, their mind, although it may appear to be fully on the object of conversation or of meditation, or any activity for that matter, does not consider that object to be an object in the conventional sense of the word. There is meditation without an object. He or she does not have the sense of I *am meditating.* There is a process of meditation going on, and even the observation of that process is a series of causes and conditions. Therefore, even that observation is empty of any sense of self. It is pure emptiness, the pure emptiness of self, and of any craving. It is a mind free from craving.

Such a mind has no ability to project any fetters onto anything that appears. So, there is no delusion. A non-awakened mind uses a filtration system through which whatever experience is perceived, one attaches a sense of self to it. The arahant has no filtration system left. Even their memories are completely void of a sense of self. The memories are stored within the mind, insofar as that lifetime is concerned. And even the memories of previous lifetimes if the arahant has the Threefold Knowledge. In that case too, those memories are void and empty of any sense of self. They are memories that are pure, in that they occurred, and they are now in the memory bank as it were. Stored through the formations and the perception that recognizes those memories. But in the recognition of those memories, there is no recognizer. There is no sense of self in that recognition aspect.

The Taints

The arahant becomes an arahant - in the sense of the word *becoming* -, in that they let go of all things, all concepts, fetters, and formations. They let go of all craving, clinging, and being. And through that letting go and that non-grasping, not clinging, not attaching, they destroy what are known as the taints, or the defilements, which can be likened to viruses, or projections. And these are of three categories. Sometimes they are described as four, but they can be categorized into three.

The four categories are:

- the attachment to views. The defilement or projection of views, in relation to a sense of self and other things in this reality. But this can be recategorized as ignorance. In the destruction of all views, you also destroy the ignorance.
- the taint of sensual craving. Craving arises any time there is a mindset that says that *I like this, and I want more of it.* Or *I don't like this and therefore I don't want more of it, I want to avoid it.* Or a neutral sense of a feeling arises, which is being personalized. The arahant can no longer crave because this projection of sensual craving has been

338

destroyed. When they extinguish this, the *link* of craving can never arise again.

- the projection or defilement of being is related to the craving for existence and non-existence. This, as well as the conceit of a *I, me,* or *mine,* or relating a sense of self, internally or externally, gets destroyed. So, they no longer relate to anything from a sense of self.

- Finally, the destruction of the taint or projection of ignorance means that the delusion gets destroyed which beliefs any of this is personal, permanent, long lasting, happiness, self. In other words, the arahant has fully realized and experienced the three characteristics of existence, and they continue to see all of reality in this manner. Such a mind therefore tends toward the cessation of being, craving, clinging, feeling, contact, and the cessation of the six sense bases. This cessation does not only mean the cessation of perception and feeling, but also the cessation of relating a sense of self to any of this. Even while being aware, there is no sense of an aware person in that awareness. While perceiving, there is no sense of a perceiver. While feeling, there is no sense of a person feeling. While acting, there is no sense of a doer and while speaking, there is no sense of a speaker. It is all just an impersonal process, arising from a series of causes and conditions. Therefore, the function of the mind of an arahant is completely empty. That is why it is said in certain suttas, that even the devas cannot trace the consciousness of an arahant.

If you were to hook up an arahant to a brainwave scanner during the cessation of perception and feeling, there would invariably be no, or little, activity, depending upon the function and the ability of that scanner to see in depth the activity arising, or not. Aside from that, if one were to see the arahant's mind, it would appear to be quite normal. There are certain functions that appear in the arahant, which would also appear in the mind and consciousness of a being who is yet to be fully realized.

The difference is that the arahant does not project a sense of self onto any aspect of the mind. Because of the lack of fuel for craving, because of the understanding of this, their consciousness cannot be traced by the devas. Their consciousness cannot be understood or found out when the arahant continues to tend toward conscious cessation. Their mind no longer abides anywhere. There are no concepts that arise. Any concepts that might be utilized for the purposes of conventional conversation - when providing teaching and understanding -, even those concepts are understood and seen to be as they are; empty fragments of consciousness that arise and pass away.

Every aspect of the arahant's mind is purified. The clinging, which is related to the destruction of the taints/projections, has been destroyed and is no longer present within the five aggregates. There is no sense left that these aggregates *belong* to the arahant. They are still a series of processes, causes, and conditions, but while the idea that the clinging has been destroyed from the five aggregates, is there in conventional terms, they do not even relate to the five aggregates in the same way anymore. Everything that arises, is always tended toward ceasing. Therefore, in their mind, they no longer abide in any of the five aggregates, in any of the links of dependent origination, in any aspect of consciousness. In that mind, as it is stated in the Bāhiya sutta, there is no concept of the four elements, or the six elements when one includes space and consciousness. There are no concepts of *this* or *that, here* or *there*, the *positive* or *negative*, or any kind of concepts. If they are present, they are only present for conventional purposes, but the way that they perceive them is that they see through them. They are understood with the wisdom that arises at Arahantship. It is the wisdom and understanding of how the links of dependent origination arise, are impermanent, not worth holding on to, and therefore should not be considered as self. They should not be projected with a sense of self. That wisdom destroyed all fetters, it eradicated and obliterated all the taints.

When an arahant talks and acts, their automatic functioning is rooted in the eightfold path, because now that ignorance has been destroyed, only right view has been established. Right view is the complete understanding of the four noble truths. Any functioning, any thinking as it were, any speaking, any of their behavior is rooted in that right view. So, they will only speak with right speech, act with right action, and think with the right intention, relating to others from a sense of deep compassion and wisdom.

If you were to boil down the fruition of the entire path, and the mind and functioning of an arahant, it is these two; compassion for all beings, and wisdom.

Daily Reflections Day 9

Additional Suttas to read

SN28.1 – 9 – Sāriputta Vagga (How an Arahant Meditates)

The Three Projections

> *When the destruction of the projections occurs, then you know with certitude that you have completed the task and attained final fruition.*

In the process of DO, ignorance is the misperception of existence, not knowing and understanding the four noble truths and the three symptoms of reality. This gives space for the projections to influence and give rise to the formations, which are then chained with these projections, and fettered with craving, conceit, and ignorance.

Conversely these projections also give rise to ignorance by blinding you to the perception and understanding of the four noble truths, the three symptoms of reality, and the eightfold path.

Like the links in dependent origination, which possess the qualities of impermanence, suffering and not-self, and are given rise to and cease by way of the four noble truths, the projections too possess these same qualities and function.

Here is the short form of cessation –

Mass of suffering ceases when Birth ceases

Birth ceases when Being ceases

Being ceases when Clinging ceases

Clinging ceases when Craving ceases

Craving ceases when Feeling ceases

Feeling ceases when Contact ceases

Contact ceases when Six Sense Bases ceases

Six Sense Bases ceases when Mentality-Materiality ceases

Mentality-Materiality ceases when Consciousness ceases

Consciousness ceases when Formations cease

Formations cease when Ignorance ceases

> *So, how do projections arise and cease? Via ignorance. What gives rise to ignorance? The projections. Therefore, the projections and ignorance are interdependent.*

The projections prevent understanding, and this gives rise to ignorance. Because ignorance arises, the projections are given way to influence formations, which give rise to the rest of the links, that are then chained with craving, conceit, and ignorance. That is why, when right knowledge dawns, the projections are seen to be destroyed, which can no longer give rise to ignorance, and which can no longer fetter formations.

> *Ignorance is destroyed when the projections are destroyed. When the projections are destroyed, the formations they have corrupted are also destroyed, unable to produce new kamma for rebirth to arise.*

The projections can be likened to a computer virus in the links, starting from ignorance, becoming stronger in momentum as you go further down the links. The projections are factors for birth. If you follow the map through ignorance down to the rest of the links of DO, you see the false sense of self fully come to be, but if you stop the flow of this programming through the eightfold path, there is a cessation, a seeing, an understanding and the projections are destroyed in the light of wisdom. A complete reformatting has now erased over the corrupted software, which are the formations, so that the computer can now run smoothly.

The projections are like an infection and wisdom is the antibody that eats away at it. There is the recovery marked by intermediary stages - each level of awakening. At the final stage, there is total homeostasis, complete health - the complete seeing of the truth of nibbāna. Now, the infection can no longer take hold and cause harm ever again.

> *The projections determine the factors of kamma, and vice versa.*
> *The projection of craving is activated by the force of reactions (link of craving) to feeling, and vice versa.*
> *The projection of being is activated by the accumulation of tendencies (within the link of being), and vice versa.*
> *The projection of ignorance is activated by seeing self in all that is not-self, permanence in all that is impermanent, and bliss in all that is unsatisfactory, as well as being unaware of the four noble truths, and vice versa.*

Therefore, there is a pendulous reactivity between the projections and the process of the links, in which they feed off each other. It hypnotizes beings to stay in *saṃsāra*. This stops only when an external force (cessation) is applied through the eightfold path.

Arahantship Attainment

The links arise, but when they do so, the mind has become so pristine that it is able to see the space between each link, which is the cessation of each link right after it arises, and before the next link arises. In other words, mind tends towards cessation automatically and because of this, there is no feeling of relief that you identify with. Here, mindfulness is so sharp that mind can see the arising, the middle, the cessation, and the space between each one cessation and the next arising after. It identifies with none of it. It is a special kind of seeing, in which a specific observation of conscious cessation is "unlocked" in the mind.

The mechanics are quite detailed but suffice it to say that there is the observation of the arising, the cessation, and the arising and cessation together, of the links up to feeling, in both directions as well. You understand that conceit has been destroyed and with it the fetters of craving for existence

345

and non-existence, and restlessness, which all depend upon conceit. With the knowledge of the projections destroyed, the fetter of ignorance is destroyed.

Therefore, you understand this is the final life. Rebirth is no more; this life's purpose has been fulfilled and that there is no more being. What had to be done has been done. There is nothing left to do.

Parinibbāna

At the dissolution of the body, an arahant enters Parinibbāna or nibbāna one final time, before disintegration of the body. At the final dissolution of the body, an arahant understands the depth of the Buddha's final advice – "all formations are impermanent." Knowing this, the arahant's mind naturally does not abide anywhere and will not hold onto anything that can create further consciousness, post-dissolution.

> *This is due to the non-arising of any formations within the experience of nibbāna. Instead, that final consciousness that remains unlinked and unconditioned by any formation, and all the rest of the five aggregates, are extinguished. Parinibbāna has occurred.*

Kamma and Fruition of Kamma for an Arahant

For an arahant, realized right view conditions formations. You know formations as purely impersonal. They simply rise as a function to give rise to old kamma down the links to pure thought, pure speech, and pure action - void of the potential to generate new kamma.

Functionally, formations are brought to arising by old kamma, the effect of actions committed prior to full awakening, which manifests through formations down to contact, feeling, and finally to perception. That momentum of old kamma is terminated at feeling, while perception rooted in right intention renders it null and ineffective in producing further seeds.

> *Action is now automatically in accordance with the realized eightfold path, which means no new kamma is produced through craving, conceit, or ignorance. Therefore, an arahant must bear the effects of actions committed prior to full awakening but will not produce seeds for new kamma.*

Conscious Cessation

In the mind of an arahant, there is constant cessation, which means such a mind always tends to the cessation aspect of each link when it arises. This conscious cessation is both what is the natural state of mind for an arahant, and also what refers to a state in which the arahant touches the nibbāna element, taking it as the object of meditation (although nibbāna itself, which is an activity, cannot be considered an object in conventional terms).

> *Mind is conscious but there is no consciousness acting. It senses with no feeling interacting. It is perceptive but no perceptions occur. It is meditation without an object. It is cessation in every moment. With the illusions known, there is no going back to getting caught up in ignorance. Nibbāna occurs when you see the links arise and pass away without involvement. Here you see the constant cessation of the links.*

The mind remains as it is, but you are always awake to the cessation of the links. It is a mind without borders, without stickiness, where you are awake at all times to the cessation aspect of formations, and the links thereafter.

Craving cannot arise because its fuel has burned out. Personality or being cannot arise because the illusion has been seen.

Ignorance is destroyed because the four noble truths are embedded into the mind completely. This is done through –

1. the penetration of suffering,
2. the destruction of craving,
3. the fulfillment of cessation and

4. the ripening of the eightfold path.

> *You are in cessation without effort. It is natural, instant, and effortless cessation that occurs constantly. There is perception but no perceptions take hold. There is feeling but no feeling takes hold. There is consciousness but it takes no hold. It is an active version of cessation. A different quality from the fabricated cessation of perception, feeling, and consciousness.*
>
> *Here, the mind is always in an unconditioned state, in nibbāna, where mind naturally rests. Here, concepts fall away, object and subject are disintegrated. That is why it is likened to effortless meditation without an object.*

The Third Noble Truth of Cessation and the State of Cessation of Perception, Feeling and Consciousness

While there is no activity found in cessation of consciousness, perception, and feeling, and there is no escape beyond it, it is still a state dependent upon factors to enter it, namely the intention and formations related to that intention, when the mind trains to enter such cessation, at the level of an anāgāmi or an arahant. Therefore, it is still a "conditioned" state. The attachment to cessation of perception, feeling, and consciousness is what prevents the "jump" into the final level. The jhānas and cessation of perception, feeling, and consciousness can only take you to a certain level. But it is the continual entrance into these states while seeing a sense of self in them, and identifying with them, that prevents the completion of the path.

> *When even these states are seen through with wisdom and understanding, you will let go of mind's contrivance to enter into them.*

In the conscious cessation – the third noble truth – while there seems to be brain activity there, total rest is to be found. Since consciousness, feeling, and perception are "on", there is activity detected. However, it is referred to as unconditioned because there is the seeing that formations that are conditioned by projections no longer arise. Hence, the mass of suffering does not arise in such a mind. No concepts take hold. It is seeing the painting of the world for what it is. The paints are conditions that arise to form the world, but the empty canvas is seen beyond, where no formations take hold. When you see the painting for what it is, there is no abiding in the world.

The world, as it is called, is perceived through the senses. In conscious cessation, the senses are as they are, and thus the brain seems to show activity. But the total cessation of the world through them, also occurs at the same time. While mind still seems active to the world outside by others, in reality, there is nothing that sticks to it to create the arising of suffering. There is the irreversible knowledge and experience of the unconditioned. Using the analogy of the painting, when you go beyond to see the canvas of the unconditioned, you still see the paints, but you know the truth behind the painting.

The Matrix is a good analogy for this as well. You have seen the coding behind the world, but while the senses experience the world, it is never the same once you have seen the code. Seeing the code is nibbāna. Interacting in the Matrix as it would seem, still occurs, but the wisdom of the code has made it impossible for the mind to ever consider the illusion real again.

The mind of the arahant is this in action — seeing the code and the Matrix at the same time, but the Matrix no longer takes hold.

Questions

Arahant and actions

For an arahant, Dependent origination terminates at Feeling. So, how does an action for an arahant come to be? When not fully awakened, there is, in dependent origination, the link of the birth of action. This is completely personalized in terms of *I am doing this action.*

Answer:

They always respond from right intention. Whatever action they take is first and foremost a response from one of the four brahmavihārās, according to the situation that arises. They are quite pleased to be resting mind within mind without any activity going on. But if there is a request from external reality, a person asking for help, asking for the dhamma, or whatever it might be, even if there are practical considerations, they act from right action without personalizing it.

For example, someone may ask an arahant to give a teaching on the dhamma. The mind of an arahant is already immersed in the brahmavihārās. Their mind has been automated in such a way that it responds from the brahmavihārās.

Let's go back to the links of dependent origination. First, that verbal request, is the *sound.* It enters the auditory processes. This activates the link of formations, which in turn activates a certain type of consciousness. So, at the level of contact of that request on the audible level, it activates the formations, which will go into action and activate the consciousness, rooted in the mentality-materiality. And the intention that is then driven forward, is the intention to teach the dhamma, as that person with wholesome desire, *chanda,* requested.

However, in that intention, there is no relating, or projecting into it, a sense of self. It all arises from what the situation demands, or that someone requests in this case. From there, the other formations in relation to verbalizing – the activity of thought, of mental perception and feeling, and then of verbal thought - come into play. But even in that activity, there is no sense of self. In the entire process, in terms of the voice of the arahant who starts teaching the dhamma, there is no sense of *I am teaching the dhamma*. It is a full flow of the dhamma through the conduit of this mentality-materiality, as it were. In that process too, there is no personalizing with the sense of self. It is purely a response, or reaction, to what is being requested, through a series of causes, conditions, and processes, namely the links of dependent origination. From there, the arahant speaks or acts.

Now, the arahant also has hunger and thirst. For the purposes of maintaining the body, they will seek food. While there may have been preferences that were established prior to full awakening, and those might still be there, they do not project onto reality that these preferences need to be met. There is no sense of needs being met from a sense of self. Just that the body requires sustenance through food, water, and air. And for the purposes of sustenance, they will go seek them. Once they are fulfilled, content, in terms of food and water for the body, they no longer require any more sustenance for that day.

So, when being invited for food, they will accept that invitation, knowing that it provides the individual merit. But there is no projection from their mind that *I enter this person's house, I eat their food, and therefore they get merit*. It is through the compassion and understanding that they want to feed this body and therefore they will allow it, through that process of not projecting a sense of self.

Anything that they do is really done from a standpoint of compassion, though the mind does not relate to that compassion as a sense of self. It is just pure compassion that arises for the sake of relieving the suffering of that being, and for the sake of providing wisdom in that being's mind. Once that is done, the arahant leaves. There is nothing else to be done, and they will go back to their dwelling and sit happily within their mind.

Does an arahant still have a pleasant feeling when drinking a cup of coffee?

Answer:

Yes, there will still be a pleasant feeling, but there will not be a sense of self to that pleasant feeling. For example, the mind or the body has been accustomed to having coffee first thing in the morning. And so, the body may enjoy having coffee. But in that enjoyment, there is no delighting from a personal sense of view, or sense of self. If there is no coffee, they do not get cranky and say, "*where is my coffee?*" They understand that there is no coffee and therefore they move along. There is no personal preference here, no personalizing of any preferences.

If there is food and water, all well and good. If there is no food or water, no problem. Or in this modern day, if there is coffee, all well and good. If there is no coffee, no problem.

In the suttas, there is little reference to lay arahants, can they function in a lay community?

Answer:

Yes, cases of individuals who have become lay arahants might not even be found there at all, but it might be mentioned in the commentaries or later texts. There is the understanding that, if one were to become an arahant while still a lay person, that they must then enter the Sangha within seven days, or they will expire. One should see where that is really coming from, namely from the idea, the concept, which lay arahants will not be able to sustain themselves. Thinking that a lay arahant would not be able to continue to do business, let's say. Or continue to do anything in terms of earning money to sustain themselves. That is why the arahant should enter the Sangha, dependent upon the generosity of other individuals. So, the traditional understanding therefore is that, if such an individual were to become an arahant, they would not be able to function in a lay society, which expects such a person to function within that society. In other words, to have a livelihood to continue to sustain themselves.

However, in the modern day, things have really changed from that perspective. An arahant in modern days, is still able to depend upon the generosity of others. There is, of course, the purity of the sangha of monastics, but in the mind of an arahant the concept of sustaining themselves does not arise.

What usually will happen is, because of their nature of being generous themselves - in terms of teaching, and in whatever other selfless manners there might be -, it is inevitably reciprocated to them. Whether someone knows that this person is an arahant or not, because the arahant is so generous, so kind-hearted - stemming from the Brahmavihārās -, it evokes in the other being the same kind of compassion and generosity. Therefore, whether they know that someone is an arahant or not, the giver, the generous one, from that heart, wants to provide that arahant a sustenance and a way of living in this world.

Giving and merit

When one has a sincere intention to provide for an arahant, or to anyone that has attained any stage of nibbāna, is that the reason giving provides merit to the giver?

Answer:

Yes. If the giver has the inclination, the authentic intention to provide clothing, food, shelter, whatever resources may be required for the daily sustenance of a noble one - a monastic or whoever it might be that is a noble one -, the merit that is produced by the giver arises because of their innate, selfless generosity.

The practice of generosity, without looking for anything in return but for the sake of being generous, whether an arahant or not, cultivates in that person a mindset that is naturally calm and collected. In such a state of mind it is easy for a generous person, to meditate and enter the jhānas quite easily and quickly.

Instant Arahantship

In the suttas, some people listened to a teaching from the Buddha and instantly became an arahant. But there is also the notion that one needs to gradually practice, enter jhānas, and experience cessation several times, to purify the mind and remove the fetters. Are both possible?

Answer:

I will give one more example. In the case of Sāriputta, there are two versions of his full enlightenment. There is the one we know from Majjhima Nikāya 111, **the Anupada sutta**, in which he is going through each of the jhānas and upon emerging from cessation, has wisdom. There is also the sutta in MN 74, **To Dighanakha**, in which Sāriputta is fanning the Buddha. His nephew visits the Buddha for knowledge and wisdom. The Buddha gives him a discourse on feeling. Upon listening to this, Sāriputta, by not grasping and understanding the link of Feeling in relation to the links of dependent origination, - which is the deeper understanding of the sutta - let's go and destroys the fetters and taints.

Aside from that, what one needs to understand is that when you come to a state of mind which is so purified, the whole purpose of jhāna practice is to continue to stay in that collected state of mind. You refine the mind, you clarify the mind all the way to the level of the eighth jhāna, and then finally to cessation of perception and feeling. Upon emerging, there is no abiding of any formations within that mind. When the formations do arise, there is just a pure seeing without a sense of self, as the links of dependent origination flow out. There is a relief, and in the case of some individuals, all the fetters get completely dropped and they attain Arahantship.

It is not always completely divided in this way, as per the suttas. Take for example Kondañña, one of the first five disciples of the Buddha, who upon just listening to the elaboration of the four noble truths [Samyutta Nikāya 56.11 - **Setting in Motion the Wheel of the Dhamma**], and then listening to the concept and understanding of *anatta*, not-self [SN 22.59 - **Anattalakkhana Sutta**, The Characteristic of Nonself], dropped all the fetters, all the taints, or defilements, or projections, and attained Arahantship.

In such a mind, there has been this merit that has been collected through countless lifetimes. Of having refined mind through various meditative attainments, from the first to the eighth jhāna. And then coming to the Buddha's dispensation and discourse, understanding what is the correct jhāna or correct state of mind to be in, to till the soil of the mind so that these seeds of insights can be planted. And then that full wisdom grows. Just upon hearing it, there is the dropping of all fetters. Because even in the case of Sāriputta, Kondañña, and Bahiya - who is the subject of the second sutta -, when they heard this discourse, their mind reflected upon it and had a retrospective looking into mind and seeing the next arising of the links of dependent origination. In seeing that at the level of feeling, letting go, they attained Arahantship.

So, whether it is listening to the dhamma; having had such a purified mind; or going through the jhānas, and therefore purifying and clarifying the mind so that upon seeing the links of dependent origination, the mind just drops the fetters. It is one and the same process in terms of the fruit of that practice.

In the time of the Buddha, many attained Arahantship.

These days, there are very few. If you read some of the commentaries, there are statements about the diminishing number of different stages of attainment after the Buddha's Parinibbāna. We live in a fairly good time, in terms of supporting the Buddha's dispensation, making the teachings available, and using the early Buddhist teachings to reach the same knowledge.

Answer:

Yes, there are certain commentaries which talk about this in relation to whether it is going to be five hundred years after the Buddha's demise, or five thousand, whatever it might be. And that there are certain types of arahants, with the fourfold analytical knowledges - which is in relation to how they can convey the dhamma through language and understanding, and the thinking process-, that will disappear first, and then the arahants that are void of any of the higher, psychic powers.

I just want to take one aside to say this: the entry into Arahantship is first and foremost, and *only*, the destruction of the defilements, the destruction of the taints. The threefold knowledge - which is the knowledge of one's past lives, and then the knowledge of the arising and passing away of beings, and hence the knowledge of how Kamma works, in that regard, through rebirth -, is just the icing on the cake, the cherry on the top.

One should always see that the meaning of entering into Arahantship is the destruction of the taint of sensual craving, the destruction of the taint of being, and the destruction of the taint of ignorance.

So yes, it seems that in today's world there is a growing interest in the Buddha's dispensation. And there is a growing number of individuals who are more and more interested in finding out about the original teachings of the Buddha, through the suttas and other texts of the Pali canon. But the reason that there might not be so many arahants, is because of misinterpretations of the suttas, the texts, in some regard.

Also, when we compare today's world with the time of the Buddha, there is an overstimulation of the senses. To such a high degree that, if an individual from the Buddha's time were to somehow travel forward into today's century, they would go crazy in terms of the amount of stimulation. Sounds, music, the visual forms in the different kinds of media and entertainment, culinary feasts that are available through the fusion of cultures and ingredients, and so on and so forth. It would be overwhelming to their mind. We have come at a point in this planet's evolution as it were, where the senses get overwhelmed. This translates to stress and agitation of the mind.

That is why it is recommended to take a more personal retreat into the forest, with the guidance of one who understands and knows. And to subsist on alms and allow the senses not to be bombarded by activity, so that one can practice without interference and disturbance. In that regard, there are the possibilities of an arahant arising, if such a practice were to be undertaken.

And more than that, it is the ability to continually keep one's precepts. In this global society, alcohol is free flowing wherever you go. And the idea that you do not drink alcohol, for some function, event, or party, is rare. In fact, it is the norm that you drink at a party. And the use of language has become so coarse. The other precepts, which are related to the hindrances, are not always followed through. There is always some level of compromise that occurs, or a disturbance that arises. The idea of maintaining the precepts as well, is a large part of delivering one's mind to Arahantship.

So, if such a being were to arise, they have obviously had a lot of merit through countless lives; have had the inclination toward the Buddha's dispensation; and have developed the meditative attainments, whether in this life or previous lives. And then, they come to the dispensation of the Buddha, in whatever current life they may be in. Then, understanding and being able to see through their intuition what is right and wrong, investigating and understanding, keeping their precepts in this lifetime, and then going into meditative practices as ascribed in the suttas. And through right effort, right mindfulness, and right collectedness, as we understand it through the TWIM process, it is possible to attain Arahantship.

The Threefold Knowledge

MN 51 Kandaraka Sutta - To Kandaraka

24. "When ones concentrated mind is thus purified, bright, unblemished, rid of imperfection, malleable, wieldy, steady, and attained to imperturbability, one directs it **to knowledge of the recollection of past lives.**

One recollects one's manifold past lives, that is, one birth, two births, three births, four births, five births, ten births, twenty births, thirty births, forty births, fifty births, a hundred births, a thousand births, a hundred thousand births, many eons of world-contraction, many eons of world expansion, many eons of world-contraction and expansion:

There I was so named, of such a clan, with such an appearance, such was my nutriment, such my experience of pleasure and pain, such my life-term; and passing away from there, I reappeared elsewhere; and there too I was so named, of such a clan, with such an appearance, such was my nutriment, such my experience of pleasure and pain, such my life-term; and passing away from there, I reappeared here. Thus, with their aspects and particulars one recollects one's manifold past lives.

25. When one's concentrated mind is thus purified, bright, unblemished, rid of imperfection, malleable, wieldy, steady, and attained to imperturbability, one directs it to **knowledge of the passing away and reappearance of beings**. With the **divine eye**, which is purified and surpasses the human, one sees beings passing away and reappearing, inferior and superior, fair and ugly, fortunate and unfortunate. One understands how beings pass on according to their actions thus: *These worthy beings who were ill-conducted in body, speech, and mind, revilers of noble ones, wrong in their views, giving effect to wrong view in their actions, on the dissolution of the body, after death, have reappeared in a state of deprivation, in a bad destination, in perdition, even in hell; but these worthy beings who were well conducted in body, speech, and mind, not revilers of noble ones, right in their views, giving effect to right view in their actions, on the dissolution of the body, after death, have reappeared in a good destination, even in the heavenly world.* Thus, with the divine eye, which is purified and surpasses the human, one sees beings passing away and reappearing, inferior and superior, fair and ugly, fortunate and unfortunate, and one understands how beings pass on according to their actions.

26. When one's concentrated mind is thus purified, bright, unblemished, rid of imperfection, malleable, wieldy, steady, and attained to imperturbability, one directs it to **knowledge of the destruction of the taints**. One understands as it actually is:

This is suffering; one understands as it actually is: *This is the origin of suffering*; one understands as it actually is: *This is the cessation of suffering*; one understands as it actually is: *This is the way leading to the cessation of suffering*. One understands as it actually is: *These are the taints*; one understands as it actually is: *This is the origin of the taints*; one understands as it actually is: *This is the cessation of the taints*; one understands as it actually is: *This is the way leading to the cessation of the taints*.

27. When one knows and sees thus, one's mind is liberated from the taint of sensual desire, from the taint of being, and from the taint of ignorance. When it is liberated there comes the knowledge: *It is liberated*. One understands: *Birth is destroyed, the holy life has been lived, what had to be done has been done, there is no more coming to any state of being*.

MN 51 To Kandaraka/Kandaraka Sutta. Bhīkkhu Ñānamoli *and* Bhīkkhu Bodhī, (2000) *The Middle Length Discourses of the Buddha, A Translation of the Majjhīma Nikāya*, Wisdom Publications. P351-353

An Experience of the Threefold Knowledge

The First Knowledge

[Interviewer]

Is it necessary for the final awakening experience to experience the threefold knowledge? Or is it always included in walking the path if one walks it to the end?

Answer:

Yes, the threefold knowledge is principally the understanding of kamma and rebirth. The first knowledge is related to one's own previous actions. And the way you see it is – how did this action come about. This action came about because of intention. And this intention was created by formations. And these formations are what drives forward rebirth. So, the cause of rebirth is action, the birth of action. Which then causes one to project into a new state of existence, whether it's in this life or – on a macro level – a next life, another lifetime.

You start to use the meditation to be able to go back in your choices, of how one choice was conditioned by certain contact with the outside world. Because every initiated choice comes through intention, and that intention is fed through formations. When there is contact with one or more of the senses, there is a reaction through that, but that reaction is not personal. It's a reaction in the sense that that contact activates formations. Those formations have been triggered by that contact and they, in turn, are conditioned by that choice.

Let's say you are listening to someone speak, or you're having a conversation, and somebody decides to say something that is displeasing, that is unwholesome. If your formations have been strengthened, where you decide to react in a way that is also unwholesome, then the contact with that sound – which will then trigger through the auditory nerve what that interpretation of that sound is, which is language used, the tonality and so on –, triggers a perception of what that is, and that is rooted in the formations. That formation will then activate a certain type of consciousness, which will then activate a certain reaction. Now, that reaction, if one has continually been unwholesome, will be an unwholesome reaction.

But in that process of choice, if somebody pauses and waits and sees *hold on, I don't need to act in this way, what this person says is theirs. It has nothing to do with me, it is something to do with them. What I have listened to is just a series of causes and conditions.* Then you don't react but try to de-escalate the situation, try to defuse the situation. Then, you have let go of, or at the very least weakened that formation that will cause you to react in a way that would be unwholesome. And rather, you would begin to strengthen formations, which will cause you to act, or make the choice, of trying to defuse the situation, be more loving and kinder, be more in a state of equanimity and act from that.

If you look at this continuous cycle of choices, formations, action, and rebirth – which is really embedded within in the larger scheme of dependent origination -, you will see the links of dependent origination not just in choices on a microlevel in every moment, in one lifetime, but also on a basis of countless lifetimes. And you'll realize that this choice led to this choice. It's like a network of light, where you're seeing different pathways, or different possibilities of pathways. If one were to make this choice, then it closes off this pathway, opens up another pathway, and then this is the kammic stream that runs through.

Principally, everything is from formations. When you want to do something like this, the threefold knowledge, and you go back into your past lives; you always access formations. They are the carrier of kamma. They are the carriers of the seeds of consciousness from previous lifetimes, which will activate certain types of consciousnesses.

One example is: there are underlying tendencies in an infant. An infant, somehow, when it starts to grow up, has a tendency for certain toys, certain colors, certain smells and sights. This is obviously rooted in having the conditioning in that one life, where the infant is looking at things that make it feel good. But there is still an underlying tendency that is rooted in past or previous lifetimes. The formations of previous lifetimes. Because, if that's what makes this infant feel good, it is because it is activating a certain type of formation, that had taken root from a previous lifetime. This is the causal chain from one lifetime to another. The formations are always something to be looked at if you want to go into your past lives. The whole purpose for doing this, really, is to understand the mechanics of kamma. More importantly, to understand the mechanics of cognition through the scheme of dependent origination.

More than the cessation, it's about the understanding of dependent origination, so this threefold knowledge is also one of the ways to understand dependent origination.

[Interviewer]

These almost limitless causes and conditions, when going back into lifetimes and seeing the causes and conditions and the different pathways, does the mind encompasses this in a single moment or does it arise as wisdom? And a related question to the example of the infant:

It seems like a hard drive which, in terms of formations, is being transferred from one life to the other. This is a massive amount of information and potential Formations in one being's lifetime.

Answer:

Yes, the analogy of the hard drive is a very good one to visualize. Once that hard drive is irreversibly damaged, it's copying those data, those formations, which are the seeds for kamma, in the next hard drive, depending upon what happens.

The understanding of past lifetimes goes beyond contemplating and understanding things. It can arise as insights, where you start to make the connections.

Kamma is cyclical in the process of dependent origination. It's not like: if this happens in this lifetime, then the effect of that will be in the next lifetime. It might take time for that kamma to come to fruition, to take effect. You might see the cause of this kamma a thousand lifetimes before, or one lifetime before.

But when you see a particular formation rooted to this kamma, you might be able to trace it back, depending on the lifetime.

[Interviewer]

There are so many formations that, in one's human life, they may not be triggered in this lifetime, because the causes and conditions were not present. Are they then 'moved' to some next lifetime, when they *can* be triggered, fifty or a thousand lifetimes later?

Answer:

Yes, that's a good way of putting it. Formations only arise because of external or mental contact. So, I'm talking in terms of the processes of the six sense bases. If there is some sort of input from the senses, it could trigger the activation of that formation. Let's say that in one lifetime you, the being, drowned. In another lifetime, when you get in contact with water - the skin touches the water, or just the sight of the ocean, or going into the swimming pool - will suddenly create a sense of panic or fear. So, it is activating that formation that is rooted in the experience of drowning. It is triggered by memories, but those memories are triggered in turn by the senses, and the experience of the senses.

[Interviewer]

So, certain formations may be dormant for countless lifetimes?

Answer:

Yes, and they may be never activated at all, they might just be let go of. That is why it's important to understand this in the perspective of an arahant. It's not that the arahant is extinguished, so to speak, meaning the five aggregates are extinguished because all the kammic effects have taken place. It could just be that certain kammic repercussions never happened and so, it is just completely let go of. Because there is no grasping consciousness that holds onto that formation, it just withers away, there is no nutriment to it.

This idea that one exhausts all kamma at the end of one's life, for a fully enlightened being, is more of a Hindu perspective. It's a yogic Vedantic perspective. But within the context of the dhamma, that is not the case. It's not always that *all* kamma must be brought to fruition in order for one to be extinguished, it's not necessary.

Because there is no holding on, there is no grasping consciousness towards those formations; those formations are extinguished. They are part of the aggregate of formations, so, to that extent you can say that all the kamma is exhausted. But it's not because the kamma is exhausted that one is extinguished. It is because there is extinguishment, that all the kammas are exhausted. It's a subtle difference.

[Interviewer]

In the first of the threefold knowledge, if there is for instance the merit of a lifetime, will one see an abundance of pleasurable experiences in a next lifetime?

Answer:

In one who has developed very good merit in one lifetime by wholesome actions, it's not always necessary that the fruition of that merit comes to be in the very next lifetime. In the same way, as I mentioned, where certain things are activated after countless lifetimes.

When someone is continually wholesome in one lifetime, it is the strength of those formations, rooted from those wholesome actions, that come into one's frame of mind, so to speak, at the point of death. The formations that are there, are more wholesome. There is then a greater tendency for that consciousness to grasp onto that formation. That formation, through intention, then drives forward that consciousness to then take rebirth in the next life. And in that next life - in which this consciousness dissipates, and a new consciousness arises, carrying forward those formations - it will then activate the kamma of that merit. That new being is then born in good circumstances, dependent upon that good kamma.

The formations at the end of one's life are more important. That is why there is an emphasis on making wholesome kamma, on making merit; the more one does so, the greater the tendency for those formations to arise at the end of one's life. And so, if one has not broken through to stream-entry etcetera, if one is just a person of the world, so to speak, their mindsets - because they have developed wholesome qualities of mind, even if it's not rooted in the dhamma - because they're continuously positive, beings that are continuously loving and kind, the tendency of the consciousness there will grasp onto the more dominant formations. And these are the formations that have been built up because of those wholesome actions. Even such beings have the capacity then to have a life in deva realms, or in better circumstances in the human realm.

The flipside is also true; if somebody has been unwholesome for most of their lives, there is a tendency for them to experience unwholesome qualities of mind towards the end of that life, towards termination of that life. For that reason, it is possible that it will trigger for them the activation of formations that will take root in the next rebirth, which is not so wholesome. That might be in lower circumstances or in the hell realms.

[Interviewer]

Could one say that people's minds, at the end of their lives, have primarily wholesome qualities, in terms of love for their kids, 'sacrifice' for the sake of their family, or wishing other people well?

Answer:

One could not say that as a blanket statement for everyone. It's more about the way a person's inclinations have been throughout that life. It always starts in intentions. A person can outwardly seem to be happy and calm, but it is all rooted in one's internal state of mind. If the internal state of mind, even when circumstances were not necessarily good, is rooted in the brahmavihāras, if one is still loving and kind, compassionate despite the circumstances, that is what really matters. So, of course it is dependent upon each individual's inclination, or one's collective inclinations within one lifetime. But if one continuously practices – whether one is conscious of it, or not – kindness and compassion that is rooted in that intention, then one is bound for a better rebirth.

[Interviewer]

As part of the first knowledge, would one also see the more worldly aspect of a life, for example ten lifetimes ago, where one lived and what one was doing?

Answer:

Yes. And it might also be that some people have the capacity, that visiting some places could trigger latent memories that are stored in the formations.

[Interviewer]

Is the point of the first knowledge that one sees the causes, conditions, choices and intentions, which resulted in the situation one is currently in?

Answer:

The whole point of the first and second knowledge both, is the understanding of kamma and rebirth, for the purposes of eradicating rebirth. In just this lifetime, there is constantly rebirth happening in every moment, in relation to arising and passing away of consciousness.

Another way to understand it is, that there are certain habit patterns, certain patterns of behavior, that continuously arise and cause one to get into certain circumstances, into states of existence in one lifetime. So, by extension, when one sees that these inclinations in this present lifetime are due to certain habit patterns from previous lifetimes, one can see it, reflect on it, let go of it, and no longer be conditioned by those habit patterns.

These habit patterns are really *bhava* – being or becoming – and so, when one lets go of this, there is no more becoming, there is the cessation of being, becoming. Which means, the formations are completely let go of, and the mind is freed from the impulses from that kamma. The mind is free from those patterns of thought and behavior.

[Interviewer]

What one puts energy in, that grows, and if you let go, you can respond in a wholesome, impersonal way?

Answer:

Yes, exactly.

[Interviewer]

So, if one finds themselves repeatedly in certain types of situations, you should reflect and understand that mind is inclined to find those circumstances and triggers, which generates this bhava, this being?

Answer:

Yes, and it's almost on an automatic level, until one has the insight, the mindfulness to be able to say: *Hold on, let's take a pause and see what's going on, I don't want this to happen anymore.*

Of course, *I don't want to* can be considered to be craving, but it can also be understood as a cultivated intention of saying; *I want the suffering to stop.* That can be the launchpad from where one begins a spiritual journey and realizes that these habit patterns don't serve this mind anymore. It no longer has any power. Through the process of letting go, through the process of wisdom. Then, when one comes across similar circumstances, similar people, or situations, one no longer behaves from those same habitual patterns, but rather is free of that. In some sense acts unconditional, because the mind is no longer conditioned by those habit patterns and so, one acts from mindfulness, from clarity of mind.

The Second Knowledge

The second knowledge is really understanding dependent origination and its universality. In the first knowledge, you see the thread of kamma that has led you to this moment, to this lifetime, on a macro level.

In the second knowledge you can see how it affects the rebirth, the arising and passing away of countless beings. You start to get a sense of the universality of this law of kamma, this law of dependent origination. And the fact that there is no being who can remain unconditioned, because there is always this intention in beings to have a better state of existence.

Sometimes, in that process of wanting a better state of existence, beings become heedless and act in ways that could lead them to not so wholesome states of being. These beings can be human beings, beings from lower realms, beings from higher realms, deva realms, etcetera. The universality of choice and consequence lies in the understanding of how the choices of a being, when they were in the human plane of existence, will lead them either to better circumstances in the human plane, or to better circumstances in the deva realm. In the deva realms there is still an opportunity to learn and practice the dhamma.

But there is the inclination of beings who are born in the deva realms, to run out the course of their good merit. If they were in the sensual spheres, gratifying the senses, they don't really learn anything and then they come back down, whether it's in a lower human birth, or even lower than that.

Conversely, there are beings in the human plane, that make choices that are not good for themselves, because not only are they harming themselves through certain unwholesome choices, but they make choices that inflict pain and suffering on other people. Then, there is the potential for them to get reborn in the lower realms. At that point, they are essentially paying their dues. They are paying off the debt of these unwholesome actions. Once that has been clarified, they then have the potential to be reborn again in the human realm.

It's in the human realm that choices matter the most, because it is here that will determine whether one builds up one's merit and then goes into a higher realm or whether one creates a lot of negative kamma and then has to pay one's dues.

But how many times is one going to do this? Well, beings have been doing it for countless eons[1]... They haven't learned their lessons. There is a lot of suffering on earth, but there is a lot of suffering in the other realms as well, in the sense that now they must come back to the human realm [when they were in a higher realm], or they must start over again from a lower realm. When you understand this, you understand the preciousness of the human birth, the rarity of the human birth.

And, more importantly, the blessedness of being able to be at a timespan where there are the teachings of the Buddha, so that one can get off the wheel of saṃsāra, this wheel of going about again and again and again. And then enter the stream and take a one-way ticket to nibbāna.

[Interviewer]

Does the second knowledge mean that one sees all different beings in different realms, and their choices?

Answer:

One can access certain realms while one is in deep meditation. And these realms are actually different wavelengths of existence. They are not necessarily on different planets. They are another octave of reality, so to

---

[1] **Description of an eon:**

At Sāvatthī. Then a certain bhikkhu approached the Blessed One, paid homage to him, sat down to one side, and said to him:

"Venerable sir, how long is an aeon?"

"An eon is long, bhikkhu. It is not easy to count it and say it is so many years, or so many hundreds of years, or so many thousands of years, or so many hundreds of thousands of years."

"Then is it possible to give a simile, venerable sir?"

"It is possible, bhikkhu," the Blessed One said. "Suppose, bhikkhu, there was a great stone mountain a yojana long, a yojana wide, and a yojana high, without holes or crevices, one solid mass of rock. At the end of every hundred years a man would stroke it once with a piece of Kasian cloth. That great stone mountain might by this effort be worn away and eliminated but the aeon would still not have come to an end. So long is an eon, bhikkhu. And of eons of such length, we have wandered through so many eons, so many hundreds of eons, so many thousands of eons, so many hundreds of thousands of eons. For what reason? Because bhikkhu, this samsara is without discoverable beginning... It is enough to be liberated from them."

Samyutta Nikāya 15.5 **The Mountain**, translated by bhikkhu Bodhi

(A yojana was a measure of distance that was used in ancient India. A yojana is about 12–15 km)

speak. One might be able to access certain realms, converse with these beings and get a sense of where they're at, and what caused their birth in that realm.

When you converse with them, you might get a sense of where they have been or what caused their rebirth, so it should not be just a conversation for the sake of having a conversation. It's more about getting a sense of where this being has been, so to speak, in a previous lifetime. Or even within that lifetime, what actions they did.

It's like, for example, when you spend some time with a person, you might get a sense of their inclinations, their habits, their likes and dislikes, and the way they might react or respond to certain situations. When you've been with someone long enough, you get a sense of their moods and mindsets.

When you are with these beings, whether in higher, lower, or human realms, you might get a sense of - this is their inclination and therefore this arose, because of a previous action. And therefore, that happened because of another choice they made in another lifetime.

It's just another way of seeing how dependent origination works for all beings, and that it is the blueprint for saṃsāra.

[Interviewer]

Does the total number of beings in saṃsāra stay the same, except for the beings that exit saṃsāra?

Answer:

Kamma is immeasurable and it's not random, which means that the possibilities of what can arise are (or can seem to be) random. There is a certain number of choices that have been made, that caused that kamma. So, there is a causal chain to that kamma. It's not always the case that an equal number of beings check out of saṃsāra, and certain beings remain in saṃsāra and so it's equalized, it's the same number of beings. There can be a larger number of beings checking out of saṃsāra than there are beings present in it.

Indeed, one of the ways to understand the creation of a world is because of the creation of kamma. If there is creation of kamma, there is the potential to even create worlds within worlds. It has the potential to create worlds within new universes.

The different variations and variables of kamma and how it can produce even more beings, or the potential for beings to come off the wheel of saṃsāra are incalculable.

[Interviewer]

After the second knowledge, mind understands there is nothing else outside of kamma, intention and rebirths, and they result from causes and consequences?

Answer:

Yes, exactly. And one sees the danger – and I use that word very aptly -, of believing that there is a sense of self. This is particularly seen in the brahma realms, where there are beings or deities who believe themselves to be the all-knowing, all-pervading creator. [See Majjhima Nikāya 49 **The Invitation of a Brahma**] There are beings who believe they are so and so, and this and that, that causes further suffering. When one sees this, one realizes that there is nothing, there is no inherent sense of self that continuously progresses through this chain of kamma. It's all a series of processes, causes, and conditions. To take any of this personally, or to take any of this as 'self', is very dangerous. Because it will only chain you back down into saṃsāra for that reason.

[Interviewer]

This might be potentially a very dangerous statement, but some religions look at the world in a partial way; there is a heaven, there is a Creator, but is that just looking at a fraction of what's going on, in terms of cause and consequence?

Answer:

Even within the dhamma, when one is developing right view, the mundane right view is this: that there is mother and father, there are people that one owns a debt of gratitude to, there is meaning in generosity, in giving, there is action and consequences, there are sages or beings who have fully seen through the mechanics of kamma and who are familiar with, or aware of, worlds beyond.

Now this idea of 'worlds beyond' can be interpretated in one way as, there is a heaven and there is an earth etc. and by no means is it saying that there is not, or that this should be disputed. But even that sense of heaven, which are the deva realms and the brahma realms, are limited because kamma has the potential to create new realms. [see for instance Digha Nikāya 1, **Brahmajāla Sutta**, 2.3 and 2.4] The idea that deva realms are there, is because of good kamma, because of merit. There is a populating of these heavenly realms. There is a creation of these heavenly realms, for such beings to enjoy it. However, it is conditioned by kamma.

There can come a time when – this is hypothetical, only so you will understand this point, – all beings of the heavenly realms could have exhausted all their kamma. To that extent there is no heavenly realm because there is nobody left in heaven. Likewise in hell. So, these belief systems of heaven and hell are valid to the extent that there are multiple heavens and hells, but they are not permanent.

[Interviewer]

In the second knowledge, in the human realm, does one also have interactions with other beings?

Answer:

Yes, in essence when one is in meditation, it is coming from a mind-made body, so that mind would traverse, so to speak, these different wavelengths of existence. And then there would be interactions with these beings on a mentality level.

The Third Knowledge

This is very important to know: the first two knowledges are the cherry on top. The third knowledge is really the crucial aspect. The third knowledge can arise through cessation experiences, or it can arise just by insight and the awareness and letting go of all things that could be grasped onto, or the things that have the potential to be grasped onto.

Having said that, the importance of the first two knowledges is the understanding of kamma, which you get when you understand dependent origination. The first two knowledges of dependent origination then activate the third knowledge. But this knowledge is not always dependent upon the first two knowledges; it can still arise if one understands dependent origination through a cessation experience, for example. Or through reflecting quite deeply and letting go of the links of dependent origination.

The third knowledge is in essence the knowledge of the destruction of the conditioners, the taints, the āsavas. The āsavas are essentially three:

- The potential for sensual craving
- The potential for craving for being or non-being
- The potential for ignorance

When dependent origination is seen through and through - whether it is through the first two knowledges of the threefold knowledges, or through another experience which can provide the understanding of dependent origination - then one no longer has any inclinations toward gratifying the senses. One sees the senses as a series of causes and conditions, through the process of dependent origination. There will no longer be any sensual craving. One understands that this sense of being is because of certain habitual patterns, certain tendencies that continue to be ignited and further fueled, through actions that are based in ignorance.

And because of this, there is no more tendency toward wanting to have a state of existence in this realm, or *not* wanting to get reborn in a certain realm.

Finally, ignorance – which is the complete non-knowledge of the four noble truths. In other words, the destruction of ignorance is to see that the four noble truths are there in every single moment. The understanding of the four noble truths should be seen in this way:

1. You **understand that there is suffering**, there is *dukkha*,

2. The **cause of this *dukkha*, the craving**, but it's more than that; it's more about the links of dependent origination, starting from ignorance. Ignorance, conceit, being, craving and so on, are **abandoned**. Which means that the fetters are abandoned. The fetters are the ones that are created, they are the chains that are created through the process of continually cycling through dependent origination. When one lets go of all the fetters, one lets go of all the links of dependent origination that cause those fetters as well. One abandons in the second noble truth all those factors and experiences,

3. **Nibbāna**, experiencing true knowledge and true wisdom. This is the complete relief and release from *dukkha*. That is *nirodha*, the cessation of *dukkha*. One has experienced it and **realized it** for oneself, but more importantly, one has seen, through that, the fourth noble truth.

4. The way to experience this is by **developing** the eightfold path. The only way one can get to the third knowledge, whether it is through the first two knowledges or through the experience of dependent origination, is by having **developed** the eightfold path. One has understood, to some extent, that the right view is the middle way. One should not, after having reflected and seen, indulge the senses, because it gets you nowhere. Getting indulged in the senses only leads to further rebirth. Likewise, self-mortification will not get you anywhere. So, the middle path is the balanced path; it's the understanding that one takes care of this body and its needs to the extent that it remains alive. But one develops the mind for the purpose of freedom from saṃsāra and no longer gets bound by it.

So, that is the initial understanding of right view, the middle path. And then, of course, one further develops this through right intention, which is completely having the perspective of letting go. And, more importantly, seeing that any sense of ill will or cruelty will get you into a further state of existence that is unwholesome. In the beginning, one has the intention of not harming other beings, but then it becomes automatic.

In the same way one has developed right speech, right action, right livelihood. One has perfected right effort so that one has completely abandoned all unwholesome states. The seven awakening factors are completely perfected. And one has understood what right mindfulness is, which is to see and be present in the four foundations of mindfulness for the purposes of rooting out craving, ignorance, identification, and personalizing.

And then, of course, one develops jhāna practice, however one might do it: whether it is brahmavihāra practice, through Ānāpānasati, or whatever it might be. That leads to the knowledge of the destruction of the fetters, and the taints. This ignorance is destroyed when one had the review and seen that it was through following the eightfold path, that one has understood suffering, one has let go of the factors of suffering and one has experienced the cessation of suffering. That is the third knowledge of the threefold knowledge.

[Interviewer]

By seeing this, the mind is liberated and will never believe in the illusion again.

Answer:

Yes, there are no more factors present for that delusion to arise, and that harks back to the verse of the Dhammapada [Dhp 154], where the Buddha says; *I have seen you, house builder, you can build no more.*

[Interviewer]

This is really something that one can only see for themselves. You cannot make somebody else see this, you can only show the path, explain the dhamma and give the path. One needs to walk the path by themselves. And it all comes down to intention.

Answer:

Yes, absolutely. And the whole point of this is to really come back to the four noble truths, because everything is contained in them. All the ideas and concepts that we understand through the suttas, can all be linked back to one or more of the four noble truths. If you just have the clarity of understanding and realizing the four noble truths, that is all that is required for one to attain Arahantship.

So, continually developing the path, continually having the right view, the right intention, right mindfulness so that one can have right speech in every moment, right action, right livelihood in one's life. And then constantly having right effort through that right mindfulness. It all culminates in right collectedness, which is to say that one then meditates, comes upon these levels of jhānas – the meditation levels – so that mind is malleable enough, since we're talking about the threefold knowledge, to look back through the process of the first two knowledges, see the mechanics of kamma and come to the realization of the four noble truths in that way.

The purpose of jhāna as well, all the way from the first to the fourth jhāna, is all about activating certain elements of the mind, like joy, bliss, equanimity, presence of mind, so that it is like the tilling of the soil; it's a way of bringing in the fresh manure so that you can seed the ground and give the factors of the jhāna as the water, the sunshine and nutrition. Then the insights bud when you make the right effort. And you will have the harvest of wisdom, which are the four noble truths.

[Interviewer]

That is a beautiful simile. There is nothing to hold onto, it is really something to practice, allowing wisdom to arise naturally.

Answer:

Yes, you don't have to worry about wisdom. Wisdom will naturally arise, the more you practice the eightfold path.

Sharing Merit

May suffering ones be suffering free,
and the fear-struck fearless be.
May the grieving shed all grief
and may all beings find relief.
May all beings share this merit
that we have thus acquired
for the acquisition of all kinds of Happiness.

May beings inhabiting Space and Earth,
Devas and Nagas of mighty power,
Share this merit of ours.
May they long protect the Buddha's dispensation.
Sadhu, sadhu, sadhu!

Glossary of Pāli Terms

Abhiññā Six higher knowledges that come from the practice of the rūpa jhānas: the ability to display psychic powers; the divine eye which can see other realms and other beings without being physically present; the divine ear; the ability to know the thoughts of others; recollection of past lifetimes, and the most important one of supramundane knowledge of the *arahant* who has destroyed the taints (see *āsava*)

Ācariya teacher, guide

Ajiva livelihood, living

Akusala unwholesome, harmful, demerit. Opposite *Kusala*

Anāgāmi one who has attained the third stage of *Nibbāna* and has fully destroyed the two fetters of craving and aversion. An anāgāmi will not return to the human realm and will attain Arahantship in one of a number of higher realms called the Pure Abodes. See *sotāpanna, sakadāgāmī, arahant*

Ānāpāna in-and-outbreathing.

Ānāpānasati mindfulness of breathing

Anattā non-self, impersonal, no unchanging, permanent self or essence can be found in any phenomenon. One of the three characteristics of existence

Aniccā impermanence, change. One of the three characteristics of existence

Arahant liberated being; someone who has destroyed the taints. See *buddha* and *āsavas*

Ariya a noble one, saint. Someone who has purified his or her mind to the extent of having experienced one of the eight stages of *Nibbāna*. There are eight levels, starting with *sotāpanna* path and fruit (stream-entry) - who will be reborn a maximum of seven lifetimes -- up to *arahant* path and fruit, who will undergo no further rebirth after his or her present existence. See *anāgāmi, arahant, sakadāgāmi, sotāpanna*

Ariya aṭṭhaṅgika magga noble eightfold path. See *magga*

Ariya saccā noble truth. See *saccā*

Arūpa formless. It can refer to the four formless *jhānas* and to formless realms of existence

Āsavas taints, defilements. These are sensual craving; being, or craving for existence or non-existence; ignorance

Asubha foul, repulsive. There are two meditations that the Buddha mentioned to contemplate on the foulness of the body, which help to eradicate lust and understand the impermanence of the body

Avijjā ignorance. Ignoring, not knowing, or not understanding the four noble truths. The first link in the chain of dependent origination (*paṭicca-samuppāda*). Together with *rāga* and *dosa* one of the three unwholesome roots which cause all other mental defilements and hence lead to suffering. Synonym of *moha*

Āyatana sphere, region, especially the six sense bases, namely – internally - the five physical senses and the mind as the sixth, and their – external - corresponding objects: eye and visual object; ear and sound; nose and odor; tongue and taste; body and touch; mind and mental objects, i.e., thought. It can also mean the *arūpa jhānas*, which are four formless realms that follow the fourth **rūpa** jhāna. These are the bases of infinite space; infinite consciousness; nothingness; and neither-perception-nor-non-perception

Bala strength, power. There are five powers, which are faith or conviction (*saddhā*); effort (*vīriya*); awareness (*sati*); collectedness (*samādhi*); wisdom (*paññā*). In less developed form, these are called the five faculties

Bhava (the process of) becoming, being

Bhāvanā mental development, meditation. It consists of the three eightfold path factors of right effort, right mindfulness, and right collectedness. See *jhāna, paññā, samādhi, vipassana*

Bhikkhu fully ordained (Buddhist) monk who has left the homelife. When the Buddha started a dhamma talk with '*bhikkave*', he addressed not only monastics, but anyone who was there, whether monks, nuns, female, or male lay people. This is frequently misinterpreted as meaning only monks. Bhikkhus adhere to (227) rules and etiquette as laid out in the **Pāṭimokkha**

Bhikkhunī; fully ordained (Buddhist) nun who has left the homelife. Bhikkhunīs adhere to (311) rules and etiquette as laid out in the **Pāṭimokkha**

Bodhi awakening, enlightenment

Bodhisatta literally, "awakening-being". Unawakened being who is working to become a *buddha* for countless lifetimes. Used to designate the Buddha in the time before he attained full awakening

Bojjhaṅgā factors of enlightenment, seven qualities that are needed to attain awakening. The seven factors are mindfulness (*sati*); investigation of states (*dhamma vicaya*); effort/energy (*vīrya*); joy/rapture (*pīti*); tranquility (*passaddhi*); collectedness (*samādhi*); equanimity (*upekkhā*). They are developed within the meditation

Brahmā inhabitant of one of the higher realms. Described by the Buddha as subject, like all beings, to impermanence. The Buddha explained that Brahmā's lifespan is so long that he doesn't remember that he was once born in that realm and assumes his life is eternal

Brahmavihārā the nature of a brahma, hence sublime or divine dwelling, states of mind in which any of four pure, selfless qualities can be present: loving-kindness (*mettā*); compassion (*karuṇā*); empathetic joy (*muditā*), which means to be happy of others' successes, provided they are not acquired through unwholesome actions like stealing; equanimity (*upekkhā*), balance of mind toward all that one encounters, pleasant or unpleasant. The systematic cultivation of these four qualities is practiced as a base, using the 6R's.

Buddha Being who discover the four noble truths and the eightfold path and reaches the goal of full awakening by his own efforts, without the help of a teacher. There have been countless Buddhas in the past, as there will be in the future. However, the timespan between them is hard to fathom. A Buddha only appears when the teachings from the previous

Buddha have completely disappeared. No two Buddhas will teach simultaneously

Cattāri ariyasaccāni the four noble truths

Chanda cultivated intention, wholesome desire to commit oneself to the practice and progress on the path

Citta mindset. A collection of similar themed thoughts that make up a mindset

Dāna giving, generosity, donation

Dhamma phenomenon; object of mind; natural law; the teachings of the Buddha; law of the way to liberation because one sees and accepts reality as it truly is -without adding conceit or craving to it - which leads to awakening.

Diṭṭhi view, understanding, position

Dosa aversion. Together with *rāga* and *moha* one of the three unwholesome roots.

Dukkha suffering, unsatisfactoriness, stress, displeasure. One of the three characteristics of existence (see *lakkhana*). The first noble truth (see *saccā*)

Jāti birth, existence

Jhāna wholesome mental state of mind where mindfulness and collectedness go hand in hand. There are eight such states which can be attained by the practice. The understanding of the nature of reality deepens in each subsequent jhāna. Cultivation of them brings insights into the true nature of reality, develops the seven factors of enlightenment, and the gradual abandoning of craving and conceit. (See *arūpa*)

Kalyāṇamitta literally, "friend to one's welfare", a wise person who guides someone towards liberation, a 'dhamma friend'

Kamma every action by a not yet fully awakened being, formed through thought, speech, or bodily action, that will come to fruition in one's future, either almost immediately, or in the near or distant future. Good intentions lead to pleasant results, bad intentions lead to unpleasant results. See *saṅkhārā*

Kammanta bodily action

Karuṇā Selfless compassion (see *brahmavihārā*)

Kāya physical body

Khandha mass, group, aggregate. A human being is composed of five aggregates: form or matter (*rūpa*), feeling/sensation (*vedanā*), perception(*saññā*), formation (*saṅkhārā*), and consciousness (*viññāṇa*). In an unawakened being these are affected by clinging. An arahant still consists of these five aggregates, but without any residue of clinging left

Kilesa mental defilement, unwholesome mind state

Kusala wholesome, skillful, good. Opposite *Akusala*

Lakkhaṇa sign, distinguishing mark, characteristic. The three characteristics (*tilakkhaṇa*) of existence are *aniccā*, *dukkha*, *anattā*. All conditioned phenomena are impermanent and lead to suffering, all phenomena – including the unconditioned – are impersonal.

Lobha greed. Synonym of *rāga*

Magga path

Moha ignorance. See *avijjā*

Muditā empathetic joy. See *brahmavihārā*

Sīla, morality, ethics. Training to act in wholesome, harmless ways toward oneself and other beings in body, speech, and mind

Mara certain deva that personifies temptation

Mettā selfless good will, benevolence toward oneself and all living beings. One of the qualities of a pure mind (see *brahmavihārā*)

Moha ignorance, delusion. Together with *rāga* and *dosa* one of the three principal mental defilements. Synonym of **avijjā**

Muditā empathetic, sympathetic, or altruistic joy. A selfless joy for the wholesome successes of other beings. (See *brahmavihārā*)

Nāma mind, specifically the mental qualities of feeling, perception, intention, contact, and attention

Nāma-rūpa, mind and matter, mentality-materiality

Ñāṇa knowledge

Nibbāna the end of all craving; freedom from suffering; the ultimate reality; the unconditioned

Nikāya volume, collection. The Buddha's discourses have been collected into five volumes, each according to length or a certain theme

Nirodha cessation of feeling, perception, and consciousness. Often incorrectly used as a synonym of *Nibbāna,* but it is a state that can precede Nibbāna. *Nirodha saccā*, the truth of the cessation of suffering, third of the four noble truths. (See *saccā*)

Nīvaraṇa: obstacle, hindrance to wisdom. The five hindrances are greed; hatred; mental or physical sluggishness, also called sloth & torpor; restlessness and remorse; doubt in the *buddha, dhamma, saṅgha*, and not knowing the difference between what is wholesome and unwholesome

Pali The language in which the texts of the teachings of the Buddha were written down

Paññā wisdom. The practice of the noble eightfold path is divided into wisdom *(paññā)*, ethics or morality *(sīla)*, and meditation *(samādhi)*. (See *magga*)

Parinibbāna final dissolution of the five aggregates of a *buddha* or an *arahant*, the end of the cycle of rebirth

Passaddhi restfulness, tranquility. Synonym for *samatha*

Paṭicca-samuppāda the chain of dependent origination, consisting of twelve links in an unawakened being. The process starts at ignorance, by which suffering keeps getting created

Pāṭimokkha basic code of monastic discipline, which is contained in the suttavibhaṅga, a division of the vinaya piṭaka in the Pali Canon

Pīti Joy, a factor present in the first two jhānas, as well as one of the seven factors of awakening. See *bojjhaṅgā, jhāna*

Rāga craving. Together with *dosa* and *moha* one of the three unwholesome roots which cause all other mental defilements. Synonym of *lobha*

Ratana jewel, gem

Ti-ratana: the Triple Gem of the *Buddha, Dhamma,* and *Saṅgha,* which Buddhists take as their refuge

Rūpa matter, form. See *āyatana, khandha*

Saccā real, true. The four noble truths are the *ariya saccā*

Saddhā conviction or faith in the *Buddha, dhamma* and *saṅgha*

Sādhu good, well said. An expression of approval of what has been said from the perspective of the noble eightfold path

Sakadāgāmī one who has attained the second stage of *Nibbāna* and has weakened the two fetters of craving and aversion. A sakadāgāmī will return once to the human realm and will then attain Arahantship. See *anāgāmi, arahant, sotāpanna*

Samādhi collectedness, the unification of the mind around the object of meditation, without suppressing or ignoring awareness of other things that happen, like the arising of a hindrance

Samatha restfulness, tranquility. Synonym for *passaddhi. Samatha Bhāvanā,* the development of tranquility. See *Bhāvanā*

Samma right

Sampajañña clear comprehension, understanding feeling, thought and perception as they arise, as they remain present, as they pass away

Saṃsāra cycle of rebirth, which can only be escaped by attaining Nibbāna

Saṅgha the community of the noble ones who attained a stage of *Nibbāna*. Also, the monastic community

Saṅkappa intention, choice

Saṅkhāra formation, volitional activity. One of the five aggregates (*khandha*), as well as the second link in Dependent Origination (*paṭicca samuppāda*). Saṅkhāra is the carrier of kamma, the action that gives future results and thus is responsible for shaping one's future life. There are three types of formations; bodily, verbal, and mental

Saññā Perception, one of the five aggregates (*khandha*). It is conditioned by one's past *saṅkhāra*, and therefore conveys a misperception of reality

Sati awareness. Observing the body in the body, feeling in feeling, thought in thought, mind state in mind state, while understanding their arising, their presence, and their passing away. A constituent of the meditation part of the eightfold path (see *magga*), as well as one of the five mental strengths (see *bala*) and the seven factors of enlightenment (see *bojjhaṅgā*)

Satipaṭṭhāna the establishing of awareness in the four aspects of body, feeling, thought, and mind states

Sīla morality; ethics. Abstaining from unwholesome physical, verbal, and mental actions that cause harm to oneself and others. For a layperson, it is practiced in daily life by following the five precepts

Sotāpanna one who has reached the first stage of Nibbāna. One who attained path, is called a minor sotāpanna. Three of the ten fetters get eradicated; the fetter of personality view; the belief that rites and rituals can lead to Nibbāna in and of themselves; doubt in the *buddha, dhamma, saṅgha*, and not understanding the difference between what is wholesome and unwholesome. See *ariya*

Sukha happiness, bodily ease and comfort

Sutta discourse of the Buddha or of one of his leading disciples. Initially they were passed on orally, later they were written down

Taṇhā literally, "thirst". Includes both craving and aversion. The Buddha identified it as the cause of suffering, which is the second noble truth. In dependent origination (**paṭicca samuppāda**), **taṇhā** originates as an unwholesome reaction depending on the previous link of feeling (*vedanā*)

Tathāgata literally, "thus gone" or "thus come". One who, by walking on the path of reality has reached ultimate reality, i.e., an enlightened person who did not have a teacher. The term by which the Buddha commonly referred to himself

Ti-lakkhaṇa see *lakkhana*

Tipitaka literally, "three baskets". The three collections of the teachings of the Buddha, namely:

Vinaya-pitaka, the collection of monastic discipline

Sutta-piṭaka, the collection of discourses

Abhidhamma piṭaka, the collection of the higher teaching, i.e., systematic philosophical exegesis of the Dhamma. It was added as a 'third basket' centuries after the Buddha's *parinibbāna*. The study of this in and of itself does not lead to *nibbāna*

Upekkhā equanimity; a state of mind that is balanced, stable, not involved in emotional turmoil. One of the four pure states of mind (see *brahmavihārā*) and the final one of the seven factors of enlightenment

Vācā speech

Vāyāma effort

Vedanā feeling/sensation. One of the five aggregates (*khandha*). It is the experiencing of a sense contact

Vicāra Examining thought needed to keep the attention on the *mettā* or another meditation object. See *vitakka*

Vicaya investigation of *dhammas*

Vīmaṁsā analysis, reflection

Vimutti freedom, release. Synonym for *Nibbāna*

Viññāṇa consciousness, cognition. One of the five aggregates. See *khandha*

Vipassanā insight as a result from *manasikāra*. Synonym: *dhamma vicaya* (see *bojjhaṅgā*)

Vīriya effort

Vitakka Applied thought. The attention turning toward *mettā* or another meditation object. **See** *vicāra*

Yatha-bhuta literally, "as it is". The existing reality

Yathā bhūta ñāna dassana knowing and seeing reality as it is.

Yoniso manasikāra attention rooted in reality; wise attention taking to heart how reality is arising as it arises

Bibliography

Maurice Walshe (2012) *The Long Discourses of the Buddha, A Translation of the Dīgha Nikāya*, Wisdom Publications.

Bhīkkhu Bodhī, (2000) *The Connected Discourses of the Buddha, A Translation of the Saṃyutta Nikāya*, Wisdom Publications.

Bhīkkhu Bodhī, (2012) *The Numerical Discourses of the Buddha, A Translation of the Aṅguttara Nikāya*, Wisdom Publications.

Bhīkkhu Ñānamoli *and* Bhīkkhu Bodhī, (2000) *The Middle Length Discourses of the Buddha, A Translation of the Majjhīma Nikāya*, Wisdom Publications.

Thānissaro Bhikkhu, (rev. edition, 2013) *Itivuttaka, This Was Said by the Buddha*, printed for free distribution.

Bhīkkhu Bodhī, (2017) *The Suttanīpāta, An Ancient Collection of the Buddha's Discourses together with its commentaries*, Wisdom Publications.

Gil Fronsdal (2006) *Dhammapada, A New Translation of the Buddhist Classic with Annotations*, Shambhala Publications.

Bhante Vimalaraṁsi, (2017) A Guide to Tranquil Wisdom Insight Meditation (T.W.I.M.)

David Johnson, (2021) The Path to Nibbāna, DSMC Publishing

Bhante Vimalaraṁsi, (2014) Life is Meditation, Meditation is Life

Appendix A Meditation

Brahmavihārās

The four Brahmavihārās are

Loving-kindness or mettā

Compassion or karuṇā

Empathetic joy or muditā

Equanimity or upekkhā

The Buddha describes them as divine dwellings or sublime abodes, which will lead to a rebirth in the brahma realm. These states are not jhānas in and of themselves, but they are the layer on top of certain jhānas, as it were:

Loving-kindness with the fourth form (rūpa) jhāna

Compassion with the first formless (arūpa) jhāna of infinite space

Empathetic Joy with the second arūpa jhāna of infinite consciousness

Equanimity with the third arūpa jhāna of nothingness

This is as far as the brahmavihārās can take you. Equanimity is the final one and stops at a certain point. The mind will then withdraw from external reality and shift to the fourth arūpa jhāna of neither-perception-nor-non-perception, where it starts to impersonally observe itself, mental states arising and passing away. This is called observing the quiet or tranquil mind. This final jhāna can then lead to the cessation of perception and feeling.

Loving-kindness is the antidote to ill will. Practicing this will let go of all ill will. The Buddha said that if there is still some ill will left, one has not yet fulfilled the development of loving-kindness. Loving-kindness is the feeling and sincere intention for all beings to be happy and free from suffering.

Compassion is the antidote to cruelty. Practicing this will let go of all inclination of wanting to harm oneself or other beings. The Buddha said that if there is still some thought of harming left, one has not yet fulfilled the development of compassion. Compassion is the feeling and sincere intention for all beings to be free from suffering, understanding their distress and wanting to help them if one can. But it is also understanding that they need to gain their own insights to be able to lift themselves out of this suffering.

Empathetic or appreciative joy is the antidote to jealousy. Practicing this will let go of all inclination of jealousy and judgements. The Buddha said that, if there is still some jealousy left, one has not yet fulfilled the development of empathetic joy. This is the feeling and sincere intention to share in the happiness that beings feel when they have successes or good fortune in live, which is attained through wholesome endeavors.

Equanimity is the antidote to lust and irritation. Practicing this will let go of all inclination of desiring things and easily having some aversion towards things. The Buddha said that, if there is still some lust or irritation left, one has not yet fulfilled the development of equanimity. Equanimity is a strong balance and calm in the mind, which is not carried away by emotions around the vicissitudes of life, good or bad. It is not indifference, but a sublime, mindful steadiness of mind.

6R's/Right Effort

The four right efforts are

- Recognizing unwholesome states of mind arising
- Abandoning those unwholesome states
- Bringing up a wholesome state of mind
- Maintaining that wholesome state of mind

The 6 R's are:

1. **Recognize** there is a distraction. Don't analyze or label it. The more you do this, the more habitual it will become to notice when you get distracted. This stops the arisen unwholesome state (first right effort)
2. **Release** the distraction, let it go, allow without fighting against it. You don't keep your attention on it because that will make it bigger, giving it even more energy. It might disappear, it might stay. Just shift the attention to the Relax step (second right effort).
3. **Relax** the tension, caused by that distraction, in the body and mind.
4. **Re-smile**, going back to a wholesome state (third right effort)
5. **Return** to the meditation object (wholesome object) (fourth right effort, together with the next step)
6. **Repeat** = continue what you're doing. maintaining that loving-kindness until you get completely distracted again.

These 6 steps are always practiced in this order, without skipping any of them. They are not practiced so much as separate steps but will become a flow, a 'rolling of the R's' as it is sometimes described.

Jhānas

There are four jhānas, also called the form or Rupa jhānas. They are fine material realms and often described as pleasant abidings. The Buddha describes them as followed:

First jhāna - Secluded from sensual pleasures, secluded from unwholesome states, one enters and dwells in the first jhāna, which consists of joy and happiness born of seclusion, accompanied by thought and examination.

Second jhāna - With the subsiding of thought and examination, one enters and dwells in the second jhāna, which has internal confidence and unification of mind and consists of joy and happiness born of collectedness, without thought and examination. It is often called the jhāna of Noble Silence.

Third jhāna - With the fading away as well of rapture, one dwells equanimous and, mindful and clearly comprehending, one experiences pleasure with the body; one enters and dwells in the third jhāna of which the noble ones declare: 'One is equanimous, mindful, one who dwells happily.'

Fourth jhāna - With the abandoning of pleasure and pain, and with the previous passing away of joy and dejection, one enters and dwells in the fourth jhāna, neither painful nor pleasant, which has purification of mindfulness by equanimity. It is described as the imperturbable, or the beautiful.

Arūpa jhānas

There are four formless states, the arūpa jhānas. They are described as peaceful abidings. These are forms of the fourth jhāna:

Infinite space – "Here, with the complete transcendence of perceptions of forms, with the passing away of perceptions of sensory impingement, with nonattention to perceptions of diversity, aware that "space is infinite," one enters and dwells in the base of the infinity of space. This is called the base of the infinity of space."

Infinite consciousness – "Here, by completely transcending the base of the infinity of space, aware that "consciousness is infinite," one enters and dwells in the base of the infinity of consciousness. This is called the base of the infinity of consciousness."

Nothingness – "Here, by completely transcending the base of the infinity of consciousness, aware that "there is nothing," one enters and dwells in the base of nothingness. This is called the base of nothingness."

Neither-perception-nor-non-perception – "Here, by completely transcending the base of nothingness, one enters and dwells in the base of neither-perception-nor-nonperception. This is called the base of neither-perception-nor-non-perception."

Each of these eight meditative states can lead to nibbāna. While they can be attained one after the other, each of them can lead to an attainment with the insight necessary.

Hindrances

There are five hindrances, but basically any state that is not wholesome can be considered a hindrance, a distraction.

Hindrances block the way to developing wisdom and need to be recognized and let go of.

They are:

1. Desire, lust. The mind suddenly moves toward wanting pleasant things to happen, or to remember pleasant experiences
2. Aversion, ill will. One wants to get away from unpleasant things. This can be remembering an argument, or feeling boredom, annoyance towards hindrances, etcetera
3. Sloth & torpor. Sloth is physical tiredness and torpor is a dullness of the mind. One feels sleepy, dreamy, or is in a state where the mind is not mindful and does not really observe anything. It's also sometimes called 'sinking mind'. It can be pleasant, but it is useless for the meditation.
4. Restlessness & anxiety or remorse. This can be restlessness of the body, having an urge to move. Or it can be mental, where one gets assailed by streams of thoughts and imagery.
5. Doubt. One is unsure how to practice. One is doubtful whether this is the practice one should be doing to attain the end of suffering. Or one does not know the difference between wholesome and unwholesome states of mind.

The seven factors of awakening or enlightenment factors

These seven factors are: mindfulness; investigation/discrimination of states; effort or it's also called energy or enthusiasm; rapture or joy; tranquility; collectedness; and equanimity.

The seven factors of enlightenment are developed within the jhānas, whether in daily life or in meditation. They will balance themselves within the practice, but you can also use them in the higher jhānas when the mind starts to lean towards dullness or restlessness, by lightly intending a certain factor to become a bit more prominent. That's all you need to do, it requires a very subtle intention, not forcefully trying to bring it up, or personalizing it by thinking; I need to use this factor. Also, it's not that you need to juggle all these states, trying to balance them yourself. For the most part, this will happen by itself, the deeper the mind gets, and you will probably only need to nudge a factor to help let go of restlessness or dullness of mind.

These factors all start with mindfulness. It is the basis that activates the factor of discrimination of states/investigation, which then activates the factor of energy/effort, and so forth. The deeper one gets in the meditation, the more they start to get balanced. And when they are perfectly balanced, one can experience nibbāna. The seven factors are not only linear – going from mindfulness to equanimity– but they are also interdependent and cyclical. So, you can't always really isolate one factor, without other factors getting developed as well.

The Three Symptoms of Reality

After cultivating some level of insight and knowledge, you will be able to understand that all experiences, objects, causes and conditions are not worth holding on to, because all conditioned phenomena are **impermanent**.

And they can cause **suffering** by identifying with it. They are all unsatisfactory by nature.

Therefore, they are all impersonal and cannot be considered a sense of self that is satisfying, unchanging, permanent, and independent of causes and conditions.

Appendix B Noble Eightfold Path and Precepts

Noble Eightfold Path

1. Right view. There are two types of right view. The mundane right view is understanding that *"There is that which is given and what is offered and what is sacrificed; there is fruit and result of good and bad actions; there is this world and the other world; there is mother and father; there are beings who are reborn spontaneously; there are good and virtuous recluses and brahmins in the world who have themselves realized by direct knowledge and declare this world and the other world."* The supramundane or transcendent right view is attained by the arahant and is the complete comprehension of the four noble truths

2. Right intention– threefold, namely renunciation, letting go of sense desires; non-harming or compassion; non-ill will or mettā.

3. Right speech – *"It is spoken at the right time. It is spoken in truth. It is spoken affectionately. It is spoken beneficially. It is spoken with a mind of good-will."*

4. Right action– abstaining from killing, stealing and sexual misconduct

5. Right livelihood/living – not engaging in the trade of meat, poisons, weapons, human beings, or intoxicants

6. Right effort– see appendix A on Right Effort and the 6R's

7. Right mindfulness– the four foundations of mindfulness

8. Right concentration or Right collectedness – the practice of the four rūpa jhānas - see appendix A

Precepts

Buddhist monks keep 227 precepts and Buddhist nuns keep 311 precepts. Lay followers keep at least 5. Some lay followers practice 8 precepts, which is beyond the scope of this book. Taking the precepts, adhering to them, is essential. It is a minimum requisite of engagement that the meditator should commit to on retreat. They are part of the eightfold path.

1. I undertake to keep the precept to abstain from killing or harming living beings on purpose
2. I undertake to keep the precept to abstain from taking what is not given
3. I undertake to keep the precept to abstain from sexual misconduct
4. I undertake to keep the precept to abstain from telling lies, using malicious, divisive, or harsh speech, or idle chatter
5. I undertake to keep the precept to abstain from taking drugs or alcohol

Often, suttas clearly state that these precepts include not inciting other people to break the precepts for you, or to approve of them doing so.

Appendix C Attainments

There are eight attainments of nibbāna. All eight of them result in becoming a noble one, worthy of gifts, a field of merit for the world.

Path of stream-entry, minor sotāpanna

Fruition of stream-entry, sotāpanna

The results are:

one will never be reborn anywhere lower than a human realm

one will take rebirth for seven lifetimes at most

one has fully destroyed the first three (of the ten) fetters of

- personality view – thinking there is something like a permanent soul or entity
- doubt – doubt in what is wholesome and unwholesome, doubt in the correct practice and doubt in the Buddha
- rites and rituals – believing that rites or rituals can lead to nibbāna

Path of once-return, sakadāgāmī

Fruition of once-return, sakadāgāmī

The results are:

Weakening the two fetters of lust and aversion. Strong desire changes more to preferences and strong aversion becomes slight dislike. One will be reborn one more time in a human or deva realm.

Path of non-return, anāgāmi

Fruition of non-return, anāgāmi

The results are:

Complete destruction of any form of lust and aversion. One cannot have lust or desire anymore, including sexual lust. One does not experience aversive states like anger, depression, anxiety. With this attainment the five so called lower fetters are fully destroyed. Five higher fetters remain.

One will be reborn in the Pure Abodes and attain Arahantship there. There are still five higher fetters that need to be destroyed. This means there are still subtle attachments left, including taking experience as pertaining to a *me, myself, I.*

Path of full awakening, arahant

Fruition of full awakening, arahant

The results are:

The five higher fetters are destroyed.

They are

1. Subtle desire to exist in fine material form, a rūpa realm
2. Subtle desire to exist in immaterial form, an arūpa realm
3. Conceit, the underlying perception of self-identity. Everything is clearly seen as impersonal processes, caused by previous causes and conditions, including the arahant's body and mind
4. Restlessness and worry
5. Ignorance. This is the most important one. The arahant has attained supramundane right view and fully understands the four noble truths and how the laws of the dhamma work.

The arahant attains the two extra factors of the eightfold path (number 9 and 10, so to speak). They are:

- Right Knowledge
- Right Liberation

The arahant has forever cut off the links of dependent origination from craving onwards. Or put differently, they are still made of the five aggregates, but they are no longer affected by clinging.

The arahant will not be able to get reborn, nor would they wish for it. There is no nibbāna element in the sense of a realm for arahants and Buddhas, nor is there something like a universal or eternal consciousness. At death, the five aggregates fall apart for the final time and the final arisen consciousness cannot latch onto a new existence.

Appendix D Dependent origination

This is a simplification of the links which arise and pass away thousands of times every second.

The most basic understanding of dependent origination is the law of cause and effect;

- When this exists, that comes to be.
- With the arising of this, that arises.
- When this does not exist, that does not come to be.
- With the cessation of this, that ceases.

The origin of this whole mass of suffering:

With (the link of) ignorance as condition, formations (come to be), and so on for the rest of the links.

The cessation of this whole mass of suffering:

With the remainderless fading away and cessation of ignorance comes cessation of formations, and so on for the rest of the links.

(SN 12.61 Uninstructed)

The twelve links are:

1. Ignorance – not understanding, knowing, or ignoring the four noble truths (understanding suffering; abandoning the cause of suffering which is craving; attaining cessation of suffering; developing of the eightfold path that leads to the cessation of suffering)
2. Formations – bodily, verbal, and mental formations, the carriers of kamma
3. Consciousness – the cognizing element, the knowing, the awareness of things
4. Mentality-Materiality – this mind and body
5. Six Sense Bases – the internal and external senses, where the internal are the sense organs, and the external are the events that trigger a sense

400

activation. Eye and form; ear and sounds; nose and odors; tongue and tastes; body and tactile sensations; mind and thoughts

6. Contact – the coming together or the internal and external sense base and consciousness; for instance, the eye, photons, and eye-consciousness
7. Feeling – the experience of the sense contact; pleasant, unpleasant, or neutral. It is conjoined with perception.
8. Craving – I like something, and I want to have or keep it; I don't like something, and I don't want it; I am, taking things personal, belonging to a sense of an eternal self
9. Clinging – the stories and ideas, proliferation of why you like or dislike something
10. Being/Becoming – these ideas accumulate into an existence, a personality, a library of how you usually respond to situations
11. Birth – the result of the previous links, where one reacts in unwholesome ways; rebirth
12. Suffering, Aging and Death – the end of that action, the end of one's existence

Appendix E Resources

Links to these Dhamma talks

Day 0: Introduction and Instructions

https://youtu.be/PM-MkPaSRLU

Day 1: Right Intention and Right Effort

https://youtu.be/DrGfHc62qQE

Day 2: Right Mindfulness

https://youtu.be/oO-eEY4AtxM

Day 3: Right Collectedness

https://youtu.be/sFLLkExGStk

Day 4: Right View

https://youtu.be/OXjhDZwGFMQ

Day 5: The Five aggregates

https://youtu.be/7NRC2CifACU

Day 6: Consciousness and Rebirth

https://youtu.be/HB8n9AT4N4U

Day 7: Kamma and Cessation

https://youtu.be/n-tLuIRTEJ0

Day 8: Eightfold Path of the Noble Ones

https://youtu.be/t9H64jfl0Ws

Day 9: The Arahant

https://youtu.be/sWJanEntOqs

YouTube Channels

Bhante Vimalaraṁsi

Collection of hundreds of Dhamma talks that Bhante has given during physical retreats

https://www.youtube.com/channel/UClyJoOstQCuCdIyQU080g2w

Suttavāda Foundation

Delson has given many Dhamma talks that are live streamed here

https://www.youtube.com/channel/UCzz4BAb8RZN8Weq2I9NGJ2w

TWIM Meditators Support Group

Dhamma talks given by Delson and other teachers

https://www.youtube.com/channel/UCn8hmMn9y87RUR3ecYk9I8A

Other resources and QR codes

<u>**Dhammasukha.org**</u> - the website from Bhante Vimalaraṁsi, where the TWIM meditation originated. Here, you can find many books, articles, videos and the newest information on physical and online retreats.

If you are in interested in forgiveness meditation, you can also find information on how to practice it, and how to join an online forgiveness retreat.

<u>**Suttavāda Foundation**</u> – here you can find up-to-date information on physical and online retreats, FAQ about the Dhamma, the practice, Dhamma talks, and much more.

<u>**Dhamma Sukha group on the web**</u> - A group where monastics, teachers and practitioners discuss TWIM and the Dhamma. It was created by Sāsana Dipika Venerable Khanti Khema. David Johnson, personal attendant to Bhante Vimalaraṁsi, participates here as well. Groups.io/Dhammasukha.

Useful links and QR codes

https://suttavada.foundation

10-day online retreat playlist on YouTube

https://www.youtube.com/playlist?list=PL7nOoZpeUEOrWtPO1eK_ftD
m1rphjOYbj

Please find below readable links and QR codes under the Suttavāda Foundation domain name, as alias to the YouTube videos for the Online Retreat.

The dana link points to the Dana page on the Suttavāda web site. These links can be used in the Mind without Craving book.

The subdomains are retreat_intro, day1, day2, day3, day4, day5, day6, day7, day8, day9 and dana.

As an example:

http://retreat_intro.suttavada.foundation leads a browser to
https://www.youtube.com/watch?v=PM-
MkPaSRLU&list=PL7nOoZpeUEOrWtPO1eK_ftDm1rphjOYbj&index=1

retreat_intro.suttavada.foundation

day1.suttavada.foundation

day2.suttavada.foundation

day3.suttavada.foundation

day4.suttavada.foundation

day5.suttavada.foundation

day6.suttavada.foundation

day7.suttavada.foundation

day8.suttavada.foundation

day9.suttavada.foundation

dana.suttavada.foundation

Made in the USA
Las Vegas, NV
06 December 2022

61336577R00233